Musical Nationalism, Despotism and Scholarly Interventions in Greek Popular Music

Musical Nationalism, Despotism and Scholarly Interventions in Greek Popular Music

Nikos Ordoulidis

BLOOMSBURY ACADEMIC
NEW YORK • LONDON • OXFORD • NEW DELHI • SYDNEY

BLOOMSBURY ACADEMIC
Bloomsbury Publishing Inc
1385 Broadway, New York, NY 10018, USA
50 Bedford Square, London, WC1B 3DP, UK
29 Earlsfort Terrace, Dublin 2, Ireland

BLOOMSBURY, BLOOMSBURY ACADEMIC and the Diana logo
are trademarks of Bloomsbury Publishing Plc

First published in the United States of America 2021
This paperback edition published 2022

Copyright © Nikos Ordoulidis, 2021

Cover design: Louise Dugdale
Cover image: Yannis Tsarouchis, *Angel with Greek Maritime Flag*, 1948. Watercolor on paper, 62 x 50 cm. Private collection © Yannis Tsarouchis Foundation.

A first approach to one part of the present issue was published in Greek by Fagottobooks (2017): *Synnefiasmeni Kyriaki kai Ti Ypermacho–Kathreftisma i antikatoptrismos?*

All rights reserved. No part of this publication may be reproduced or transmitted in any form or by any means, electronic or mechanical, including photocopying, recording, or any information storage or retrieval system, without prior permission in writing from the publishers.

Bloomsbury Publishing Inc does not have any control over, or responsibility for, any third-party websites referred to or in this book. All internet addresses given in this book were correct at the time of going to press. The author and publisher regret any inconvenience caused if addresses have changed or sites have ceased to exist, but can accept no responsibility for any such changes.

Whilst every effort has been made to locate copyright holders the publishers would be grateful to hear from any person(s) not here acknowledged.

Library of Congress Cataloging-in-Publication Data

Names: Ordoulidis, Nikos, author.
Title: Musical nationalism, despotism and scholarly interventions in Greek popular music / Nikos Ordoulidis.
Description: New York City : Bloomsbury Academic, 2021. | Includes bibliographical references and index. | Summary: "Discusses the changing relationship between Greek Byzantine music and Greek popular music in the contemporary Greek state"– Provided by publisher.
Identifiers: LCCN 2020034850 | ISBN 9781501369445 (hardback) | ISBN 9781501369469 (pdf) | ISBN 9781501369452 (epub)
Subjects: LCSH: Popular music–Greece–History and criticism. | Popular music–Greece–Byzantine influences. | Popular music–Political aspects–Greece–History. | Nationalism in music.
Classification: LCC ML3499.G8 O74 2021 | DDC 781.6309495–dc23
LC record available at https://lccn.loc.gov/2020034850

ISBN: HB: 978-1-5013-6944-5
        PB: 978-1-5013-6948-3
        ePDF: 978-1-5013-6946-9
        eBook: 978-1-5013-6945-2

Typeset by Deanta Global Publishing Services, Chennai, India

To find out more about our authors and books visit www.bloomsbury.com and sign up for our newsletters.

to my cosmopolitan grandfather

Contents

Glossary and transliteration ... ix
Further clarifications ... x
List of illustrations ... xii
Preface ... xv
Prelude ... xx

Part one A story of origin

1   A laiko (popular) song by Tsitsanis (1948) ... 3
2   A hymn from the Orthodox musical tradition ... 10
3   Comparison of the two pieces by Ilias Petropoulos (1968) ... 14
4   Comparison by Mikis Theodorakis (1970) ... 22
5   The stance of the laiko musician ... 34
6   Manos Hadjidakis and laiki music ... 39
7   The music critic Sophia Spanoudi ... 42
8   Two key personas of laiki music: Perpiniadis and Keromytis ... 47
9   Postlude ... 54

Part two The two musical worlds: The Byzantine and the laiko

10 The Greek nation state and ecclesiastical music ... 63
11 Systemizing chanting and the protagonists ... 72
12 The 'musical issue' at the forefront once again ... 82
13 Urban music: Examination of a remarkable network ... 88
14 Reaffirming the laiko ... 101

Part three Factual highlights regarding ecclesiastical music

15 The reference text and the musical act ... 109
16 'Notes not noted in the text': Constantinople as a reference point ... 111
17 Style, scores and the teacher ... 117
18 Modernists and conservatives ... 122

Part four Analyzing the two musical pieces

19	Starting with the sound	133
20	Starting with the sheet music	139
21	A historical recording of the hymn	148
22	Postlude	170
23	Epilogue	173

| Works cited | 179 |
| Index | 195 |

Glossary and transliteration

The text and the examination of the relationship between the popular and ecclesiastical music unfold by initially placing two monumental musical pieces at the epicentre. Because the two musical pieces are so frequently mentioned in the book, their English versions ('Cloudy Sunday' and 'The Akathist Hymn') shall be used in order to facilitate an unencumbered reading of the text. In addition, it should be noted that the ecclesiastical musical pieces are referred to, mainly, by the first words of their text. Referring to the piece throughout the whole book as 'The Akathist Hymn' was deemed preferable to the direct translation of the first words of the text, that is, 'Τη Υπερμάχω Στρατηγώ' (ti ypermácho stratigó) as 'To Thee, the Champion Leader'. When the whole service of *The Akathist Hymn* is referred to, then it shall be clarified as a service and not as a particular hymn.

The titles of musical pieces appear in inverted commas, while collective musical works (for example, an LP/CD album) are rendered in italics. The first time that a musical piece is mentioned it is written in all of its forms, that is, in its original Greek language, noting both the transliterated form and its English translation in brackets or in a footnote, depending on the current text in which it appears. Subsequent mentioning of the piece shall be in its English translation form. This model is based on the recommendations of the Modern Greek Studies Association (MGSA) (www.mgsa.org/pdfs/JMGSAuthorGuidelinesOct2015.pdf).

Regarding transliteration, again the recommended MGSA model is followed, apart from the following cases: (a) the letter 'η' is always the Latin 'i'; (b) the letter 'ω' is always 'o'; (c) the first appearance of a transliterated form of a Greek word is rendered with an accent (except from bibliography list), and names are not accented; (d) the letter 'φ' is 'ph', apart from names where it is 'f', and this is because the overwhelming majority of Greeks use 'f' when writing their name in Latin script; (e) certain cases are excluded where a particular person chooses a particular rendition themselves (for example, Hadjidakis, and not Hatzidakis, as it would be rendered adhering to the MGSA system); (f) the term 'ήχος' (echos, mode in Byzantine music) is written without an accent and with an 'e' instead of an 'i', and this is because it was ascertained that this is its usual form in Byzantine musicological discourse.

Further clarifications

Discography documentation abides by the following model, based on the relevant scientific literature: song title; label of release; matrix code; catalogue code; date or year of recording (depending on what is available from sources); link on the internet for audio reproduction of the piece. The discography validation throughout the book comes either from the Ordoulidis database (2014) with regard to recordings by Tsitsanis or from the Maniatis database (2006) with regard to recordings by other Greek composers. For issues concerning documentation of historical discography of Greek-speaking urban laiko song, see Smith (1989 and 1991), Pennanen (1995 and 2005) and Ordoulidis (2017a).

Often in Greece, 'rebetiko' is divided into two categories, the Smyrna style and the Piraeus style, even though many times the term is used exclusively for the Piraeus style and in particular for the marginalized repertoire, a part of which entered discography.

Λαϊκός δρόμος (laïkós drómos, popular mode) refers to a modal music entity, a term used by Greek musicians of popular genres to describe a mode, δρόμος (drómos, road), as it is named in Greek. The term λαϊκό (laïkó) generally means popular, even though as a translation it is not quite accurate, mainly concerning aesthetic. The term is used throughout the book in its transliterated form (mainly as laiko and laiki and without the accents) denoting the significance referring to both the Greek-speaking and alla greca repertoire, as regards its performance practices. With regard to the laïkoí drómoi (plural of laïkós and drómos), which as entities participate in a large network, conferring with the rest of the 'residents' of this singular musical 'ecumene', see, for example, Beaton (1980), Manuel (1990), Pennanen (1997, 1999 and 2004), Ordoulidis (2011 and 2014), Mystakidis (2013) and Andrikos (2018). The term in the three genders is as follows: laïkós (masculine), laïkí (feminine), laïkó (neuter). In the plural: laïkoí, laïkés, laïká.

The term 'modeness' is used purposefully in order to include definitions usually consigned to the words 'popular', 'East' and 'modality'. The problems regarding the first two are patently clear: the in-between 'places' between the poles of the high-status and the popular and that of the East and the West are innumerable, and hardly distinguishable. The third word, modality, presents two problematic points: on the one hand, it has been wrongfully connected to Eastern musics, even though it does not constitute their exclusivity; on the other hand, it describes a simple systematic analysis, of melodic movement and (rarely) its harmonization. The alternative term 'modeness' renders, in its totality, the behaviour of a musical entity with its specific characteristics, rhythm, melody, harmony and so on as the epicentre, not, however, as a theoretical substance with self-contained rules, but as an implemented case. In other words, how it functions in the artistic act is examined: its creation context and utilization, the implementation of its protagonists (musicians, intermediaries, audience), performance practice and technique, technological issues and so forth. This approach incorporates those elements described by the terms 'East' and 'modality', simultaneously expanding their scope. At the same time, though, it highlights a fundamental characteristic of popular music expression, which is none other than the orality and ensuing fluidity during realization.

For European scales, the model called Major–Minor was chosen (initial letter a capital when talking about scale, drómos, echos – Byzantine mode – or makam); for laikoi dromoi Minore–Matzore; for chords in laiki music minor–major was chosen (initial letter small, since we are talking about a type of chord). Additionally, notes are written in the form of degrees (I, II, IV, etc.), but also by name (C, D, F, etc.). Notes/degrees are written with an initial capital. When talking about analysis which concerns Byzantine music as well, then, for comparison purposes, the respective names are used (Ni, Pa, Ga, etc.); when makam is used as well, its own names are also used (Rast, Dügah, Çargah, etc.).

It should be noted that problems exist concerning the significance of the terms used to describe music manifestations which are not high-status music in Greece. Usually, the laiko is equal to urban popular. The rural repertoire is often referred to as δημοτικό (dimotikó, folk), while in recent years this has been replaced with the term παραδοσιακό (paradosiakó, traditional). This issue is examined analytically in the following chapters (see also Kallimopoulou, 2009, and Kokkonis, 2017). In the present book, 'δημοτικό' (dimotikó) is translated as 'folk' while 'παραδοσιακό' (paradosiakó) is translated as 'traditional', in order to illustrate the definitions of each author. Concerning other cases, the author chooses to use the term 'laiko', meaning both forms (which evidently cannot be so simplistically classified, as the idioms are multifarious and complex), or the term 'rural laiko', meaning the rural forms.

Illustrations

Music transcriptions

3.1	Transcriptions of both pieces by Petropoulos (1996: 40)	15
3.2	Petropoulos transcription of the word 'Kyriaki', translated in staff notation from Byzantine notation	16
3.3	Petropoulos transcription of the word 'Kyriaki' in staff notation	16
3.4	A classic behaviour at the end of the melody, also described in theoretical books	17
3.5	'Στρατηγώ' phrase written in Byzantine notation by Petropoulos	18
3.6	Translation in staff notation of Music transcription 3.5	18
3.7	'Στρατηγώ' phrase written in staff notation by Petropoulos	18
4.1	Transcription of 'The Akathist Hymn' by Theodorakis (2011: 1148)	28
4.2	Possible final cadences for 'The Akathist Hymn'	29
4.3	'Speechless be the lips of the impious ones' by Theodorakis (2011: 1151)	30
4.4	Translation in staff notation of the opening of 'Speechless be the lips' by Georgiadis (1916: 59)	30
4.5	Transcription of 'Cloudy Sunday' by Theodorakis	31
4.6	Cadence of 'Cloudy Sunday' in Theodorakis transcription (2011: 1151–3)	32
8.1	Musical example by Perpiniadis on the origin of the Minore, as performed during the interview	48
8.2	Gospel by Keromytis	51
8.3	Keromytis song from Gospel	52
10.1	Opening of the first transcription in Sigalas's book (1880)	69
10.2	Translation in staff notation of the opening phrase of the first transcription of Sigalas's book (1880)	69
16.1	The 'common melody', as shown in Progakis (1909: 188)	114
19.1	Old zeibekiko rhythmic pattern	134
19.2	Transcription of 'Cloudy Sunday' in staff notation	135
19.3	Transcription of 'Cloudy Sunday' in Byzantine notation	136

20.1	Manuscript of 'The Akathist Hymn' by Ioannis Lambadarios and Stefanos Domestichos (1850: 392)	140
20.2	Simple translation in staff notation of 'The Akathist Hymn' of Ioannis and Stefanos	141
20.3	Advanced translation in staff notation of 'The Akathist Hymn' of Ioannis and Stefanos	142
20.4	Manuscript of 'The Akathist Hymn' by Georgios Progakis (1909: 188)	143
20.5	Comparison of manuscript by Ioannis and Stefanos with that of Progakis's	144
20.6	Simple translation in staff notation of 'The Akathist Hymn' of Georgios Progakis	145
20.7	Advanced translation in staff notation of 'The Akathist Hymn' of Progakis	146
20.8	Comparison of the transcription of 'The Akathist Hymn' of Ioannis and Stefanos with that of Progakis's	147
21.1	Transcription in Byzantine notation of 'The Akathist Hymn' from the performance of Iakovos Naupliotis	149
21.2	Transcription of a performance by Naupliotis by Angelos Voudouris (Voudouris, 1997: A: 257)	150
21.3	Translation in staff notation of 'The Akathist Hymn' of Voudouris	151
21.4	Analytical transcription in staff notation of Naupliotis's performance in the Orfeon recording	152
21.5	Transcription of 'The Akathist Hymn' in Byzantine and staff notation by Psachos (*New Formiga*, A', 1 March 1921 – Thanasis Trikoupis archive)	154
21.6	Transcription in Byzantine notation of 'The Akathist Hymn', by Psachos (1909: 42–4 – Aristotle University Library)	156
21.7	Translation of Music transcription 21.6 ('Akathist Hymn' by Psachos) in staff notation	159
21.8	Transcription of 'The Akathist Hymn' by monk Nektarios, utilizing the formula of Naupliotis (1935: 385–6)	161
21.9	Translation in staff notation of Music transcription 21.8 ('Akathist Hymn' by monk Nektarios)	163
21.10	Transcription of 'The Akathist Hymn' in staff notation, by Sakellaridis, utilizing the formula of Naupliotis (1909: 127)	164

21.11	Transcription in staff notation by Pachtikos, utilizing the formula of Naupliotis (1910: 81–3 – Aristotle University Library)	165
21.12	Citation of transcriptions by Ioannis and Stefanos, Progakis and Naupliotis	168
21.13	Citation of the three texts and part of 'Cloudy Sunday'	169
22.1	Common holding of the ison in the transcription by Ioannis and Stefanos (Byzantine notation)	171
22.2	Common holding of the ison in the transcription by Ioannis and Stefanos (staff notation)	171
22.3	Common holding of the ison in the transcription by Iakovos Naupliotis (Byzantine notation)	172
22.4	Common holding of the ison in the transcription by Iakovos Naupliotis (staff notation)	172
23.1	Melody activity in 'Devil Pray'	175

Figures

1.1	The record label of the original recording of 'Cloudy Sunday' (Panagiotis Kounadis archive)	3
1.2	Royalties payment receipt which includes 'Cloudy Sunday', 1960 (Tsitsanis family archive)	6
1.3	Royalties payment receipt which includes 'Cloudy Sunday', 1963 (Tsitsanis family archive)	7
1.4	Royalties payment receipt which includes 'Cloudy Sunday', 1971 (Tsitsanis family archive)	8
1.5	Royalties payment receipt which includes 'Cloudy Sunday', 1978 (Tsitsanis family archive)	8
13.1	The birth certificate of Aristeidis Peristeris (22 March 1855), found in the General Archives of the State in Corfu	92
14.1	Thoughts on the creation puzzle of the work	103

Preface

The similarity between Vasilis Tsitsanis's 'Συννεφιασμένη Κυριακή' (synnefiasméni Kyriakí, cloudy Sunday) and the hymn of the Orthodox tradition 'Τη Υπερμάχω' (ti ypermácho, the akathist hymn) is today a popular subject of discussion on the internet. Not only in the forums of rebetiko fans but also in those of ψάλτες (psáltes, chanters [plural] – ψάλτης, psáltis [singular]. For example, www.rembetiko.gr and www.analogion.com). These two potential communities concern me personally, since their focal point has defined me from a very young age.

My father, George Ordoulidis, who today is Ἄρχων Μαΐστωρ (Árchon Maïstor, Master Maistor)[1] of the Great Church of Christ, introduced me to the chanting lectern when I was still a child. Apart from the systematic study of Byzantine music,[2] I took on the responsibility of my first music role as a γιουσουφάκι (giousoufáki),[3] which is an expression used in the world of the chanters to describe a young assistant. Many years later, as a student at the Department of Music Science and Art at the University of Macedonia in Thessaloniki, it was natural and inevitable that I choose the Byzantine discipline. In fact, my undergraduate engagement in this particular subject led to the development of a proposal for the undertaking of a doctoral dissertation at the University of Macedonia, which was accepted. This, however, did not come to pass, due to the fact that I had already gone abroad to further my studies. Parallel to Byzantine music, another world was revealing itself to me, as I was in the process of discovering the so-called European classical music. From the age of six I received

---

[1] This is a title granted by the Ecumenical Patriarchate of Constantinople to chanting personas who boast a rich corpus and activity concerning issues which relate to either ecclesiastical music or generally ecclesiastical issues.
[2] The term 'Byzantine music' is now a prevalent one for the ecclesiastical music of the Greek Orthodox Church.
[3] The term in Greek is often used with negative connotations, signifying the subjugation of a young person, usually, to a master. In addition, the term is used to describe young boys of the Ottoman Empire, who were under the protection and jurisdiction of lords. In the chanting world, however, it has a positive connotation, as it describes boys, mainly prepubescent, who participate in chanting choirs and are distinguished by their vocal skills and their musical perception (see, for example, Athanasios Karamanis chanting with young Augoustinos Andrikopoulos: https://youtu.be/-V3F3NYdKtE). I owe my thanks to Merih Erol, who pointed out what perhaps should have been self-evident, that is, the term originates from Yusuf, which is none other than the name Joseph, referred to not only in the Christian bible but also in the Quran and the Torah.

private lessons in classical piano, which in turn led me to the conservatory. Notwithstanding the sterile atmosphere which oftentimes frustrated my creative expectations, the great music of the Western world left its indelible mark on my soul. One by one, I obtained my degrees in my conservatory courses, and when the time came to choose a field for my postgraduate studies in England, I decided on classical song which, along with the piano, I had already studied in Greece.

My love for the opera was from the beginning unequivocal. However, this did not stop me from being just as interested in popular music. In the 1990s, during my teenage years, I was an avid listener to the hits of the 1970s and the 1980s. Not only did I love British rock but I also loved classical rock, progressive and power metal. I discovered, and have loved until today, Pink Floyd, Rory Gallagher, Black Sabbath, Iron Maiden and Dream Theater. During the same period, I discovered the rebetiko, Nikos Papazoglou, Sokratis Malamas and the like. I started performing on the πάλκο (pálko, music stage), an amateur still, compensated though. As the years went by, the cracks multiplied, some even developing into chasms. My European music teachers advised me to leave aside whatever did not fall into this category, especially the popular versions. On the other hand, the masters of the chanting lectern believed indubitably that it is impossible for one to serve two worlds, and that I would not be able to refuse the mysticism of the 'according to us, East'.[4]

My doctoral dissertation began with a popular Greek music concert, which was the reason for my association with my later-to-be-supervising professors, Derek Scott and Kevin Dawe. 'Was that a C minor?' asked Derek Scott while listening to a seventh minor chord (C minor) in D Hitzaz laiko mode. 'Do you play without music scores?' asked Kevin Dawe. Ethnomusicology and popular musicology suddenly opened their doors, giving me the chance to study, what up to then had been characterized as pointless, worthless, simplistic, commercial, pessimistic, inartistic and even forbidden.[5] My doctorate was dedicated to Vasilis Tsitsanis and the problems concerning research in Greek laiki music. In 2012, when my doctorate was completed, I started to examine the correlation between Byzantine and laiki music, due to the relevant literature on 'The Akathist Hymn'

---

[4] Καθ' ημάς Ανατολή (kath' imás Anatolí): this phrase constitutes one of the most powerful stereotypes in Greek rhetorics, which have the Greekness of Asia Minor and the region of Constantinople as their core. For this specific issue, see Kontaratos (2007).
[5] Unavoidably, Theodore Gracyk's book *Listening to Popular Music Or, How I Learned to Stop Worrying and Love Led Zeppelin* (2007) comes to the forefront.

and 'Cloudy Sunday.' With the passage of time I realized the special dynamic of this particular discourse and considered it purposeful to examine it more analytically. Ultimately, now every time I surf the internet and encounter all sorts of music referrals, I gaze at a world accepting of creativity, dynamic and inexhaustible. In contrast, I have great difficulty comprehending the rhetoric concerning musical descent or pedigree, which usually leads to narrow-minded intolerance. Beginning with the writing of this book, I perceive music as a uniform art, which supersedes ideologies and geographical boundaries. My manifold endeavours have led me to regard aesthetic autonomy as a περιχώρησης (perichoresis, co-existence),[6] as I will try to explain in the following pages.

The first part of the book examines certain viewpoints that have been expressed on occasion concerning the correlation between these two music genres in general, but also the descent of 'Cloudy Sunday' from 'The Akathist Hymn.' More specifically, the epicentre of these analyses is addressed by Ilias Petropoulos and Mikis Theodorakis, by whom these two pieces of music have been compared.[7] The examination of these analyses bore the need to extend the search into the world of journalism, which, in its majority, from the start embraced and supported the pattern framed by Petropoulos and Theodorakis. In addition, the viewpoint of the protagonists themselves of laiki music of the past century could not be omitted. Not only what they have to say but also the reasons that led them to produce this particular rhetoric are examined and analysed. Regarding Tsitsanis himself, a large part of his interviews were catalogued, in which his own personal views are testified on the issue of the origins of his song.

In the second part of the book, the historical correlation between the two musical genres is examined, composing a singular musical historiography which often revolves around the issue of Greekness. It was considered particularly crucial that certain historic key events be mentioned and addressed as a

---

[6] The word 'perichoresis' comes from the vocabulary of the Orthodox Fathers, mainly as expressed by Maximus the Confessor. Often in theological texts, it is translated as perichoresis, circumincession, co-existence and co-habitation.

[7] Ilias Petropoulos was one of the most 'revolutionary' personas in different aspects of his life. He was one of the first, if not the first, who took an interest in the rebetiko. His essay Ρεμπέτικα τραγούδια (rebétika tragoúdia, rebetika songs) (1968) constitutes the 'Bible' for the rebetiko enthusiasts and contains a diversity of texts, written mainly by him, but also a plethora of photographs. Mikis Theodorakis constitutes a major representative of the Greek state abroad. His music as well as his political life preoccupy people from diverse scientific fields, not only in Greece but also abroad. His corpus is immense both in size and in diversity and for many constitutes the bridge between post-war urban laiko song and the so-called artistic laiko song, which according to some he himself first created with another ambassador of Greek music abroad, Manos Hadjidakis.

foundation, given that the particular relationship shared between laiki and Byzantine music is not the product of recent years, but stems from that first period of the Greek state. What is more, the various stereotypes which developed, and in good part became established, are examined, not only in Byzantine music but also in laiki music. The historical background of any musical genre assists in the emergence of its multifaceted nature, not only in theory but also in practice.

The third part of the book concentrates on the relationship between teacher and pupil, which is the core of what is usually called ύφος (ýphos, style).[8] The examination of certain chanter schools and the discussion between tradition and innovation in a musical practice make for particularly interesting topics. Negotiating how a musical text and its content is reformed with every new performance raises questions of authenticity, supplementation to the performance and interpretation in chanting, that is, what happens every time the optical dimension of a piece is rendered vocal.

Finally, in the fourth part of the book, a purely music analysis, a new comparison is conducted of the two pieces, 'Cloudy Sunday' and 'The Akathist Hymn'. For both musical pieces, transcriptions were used using not only the Byzantine notation but also the European and the Turkish makam. The *modeness* which regulates each creation is addressed as the epicentre, with the aim of comparing and discovering similarities and differences. The examination of this modeness reveals the way with which musical genres belong to a common musical 'ecumene', on the one hand each maintaining their autonomy and, on the other, constantly conversing among one another but also with other 'residents'.

Apart from the preconditioned and unconscious moulding that has been taking place esoterically, many are those who assisted in its formation, each from a different position and manner. I owe my heartfelt thanks to my friends Harris Sarris, Spilios Kounas, Olga Siapati and Stelios Berber, for our conversations and their advice. To dear Vasilis Mauraganos, Christos Kanteritskos, Thanasis Trikoupis, Panagiota Anagnostou, Nikos Dionysopoulos and the Aristotle

---

[8] Even though it shall be examined and analysed in various parts of the book, it was deemed necessary to copy an excerpt from the third part at this point, in order for one to have an initial idea concerning the term 'yphos', as it is used in the chanting world. 'The focal point of this discussion is what is usually called "yphos" by the circles of the chanting world, which constitutes an element acquired after years of practice beside a teacher, who imparts his yphos to his students. Yphos is intrinsically connected to the practice of performance and entails vocal timbre, articulation, pronunciation, breathing, vocal placement, rhythmic conduct, intervals, kinesiology of the performer, facial expressions, variegation, dynamics, intonations and much more. In essence, all the qualitative characteristics concerning the manner of interpretation, rendition and performance of an artistic creation, which will ultimately identify not only a whole school but also a unique performance.'

University Library for the documented material, their proposals, suggestions and ideas, with which they were so generous for the whole duration of the book. To Dimitris Papanikolaou and Polina Tambakaki for their comments, constructive discussions and support in the present enterprise. To Charles Howard, Tony Klein, Panagiotis Kounadis, Martin Schwartz and Thanasis Gioglou, for their valuable contribution concerning discographical documentation and for the provision of sound documentation. To Dimitra Papaioannou for an impeccable and extremely pleasant collaboration regarding the finer points. To my teacher, Periklis Mauroudis, for the years of imparting knowledge and care. To my dearest friend Kostas Vlisidis for the magnanimity with which he offered his knowledge and wisdom to my every effort at research. To another of my teachers, Derek Scott, to whom I owe my gratitude, for the elimination of guilt with which I was burdened concerning popular music, and for the scientific tools he introduced me to. Last but not least, Georges Kokkonis and Maria Zoubouli, for all that was given to me unsparingly and which will accompany me forever.

Nikos Ordoulidis

Prelude

It is Sunday, 23 October 1949, nine months after Manos Hadjidakis's celebrated discourse on the rebetiko,[1] with which, it is claimed, it was exonerated.[2] Mikis Theodorakis writes in the newspaper *Σημερινή Εποχή* (simerini epochí, present times):

> The songs that show us the way in which ecclesiastical hymns are assimilated are 'Merakia' and 'Synefiasmeni Kyriaki' (Theodorakis, 1949: 159).

This publication seems to have served as a springboard for a common ground that has not stopped being called upon regarding a wide range of aspects, every time that a correlation between laika songs and Byzantine music needs to be proven. This common ground has been expressed in two studies, which musicologically compared two emblematic pieces, 'Cloudy Sunday' and 'The Akathist Hymn'. The first study is Ilias Petropoulos's monumental *Rebetika Songs*, which was published in 1968: 84–5. The second study comes from the pen of Mikis Theodorakis and is a part of the texts written by him after 1970. A part of this analysis is found in the first volume of the first edition of the book *Το χρέος* (to chréos, the debt) (1974: 379). In 2011, Crete University Press reissued this historical collection, adding the texts written in the period 1974–96.

---

[1] As it was stated before, often in Greece, 'rebetiko' is divided into two categories. Here we encounter an issue of great contention. Firstly, this separation is the product of the moulding between the vernacular and invalidated research on the rebetiko. A lacuna remains regarding the examination of the recording corpus with aesthetical rules, in order for the periodization of the rebetiko to be actualized on musicological terms as well. The literature on periodization of the rebetiko has already been commented on adequately (Smith, 1991; Pennanen, 1999; Gauntlett, 2001; Kokkonis, 2005). The term 'Smyrna-style' itself is quite problematic, as a good part of the repertoire does not come from Smyrna. Even what was recorded or flourished there is more a product of the cosmopolitism of the area and cultural convergence, rather than Smyrna-style, at least in geographical terms. Additionally, in stereotypical periodization and genre classification of the rebetiko, the term 'Smyrna-style' is usually identified with santurs and violins, something else which is problematic. Σαντουροβιόλια (santuroviólia, santuroviolins), as it is often called in Greece, constitute only one part of this repertoire. Furthermore, during the peak of the Piraeus style (based on the bouzouki as it is now separated in bibliography: Manuel, 1990; Pennanen, 1999; Gauntlett, 2001), the other styles, techniques, performance practices and so on do not instantly cease to exist; in fact, they conform and co-exist, even though the repertoire obviously leans towards the form that has the bouzouki and the guitar as its focal point. If we take into account other places of recording, such as America, we will see that genre classification is much more complex than it seems.

[2] For Hadjidakis's relationship with the rebetiko and its supposed exoneration, see Michael (2014), Tambakaki (2015), and Kokkonis, Ordoulidis, Anagnostou, Rombou-Levidi, Zoubouli and Tambakaki (2019).

These analyses have forged the connection of these two pieces in the modern Greek conscience. The undeniable fact of their correlation was established on the most important foundations of the construction of a national identity, dominating a cultural entirety with a multifaceted composition of historical reality. The acceptance of the correlation between the medieval prayer, which kept the residents of Constantinople up all night during the siege of the Avars, and the popular song which enciphers the resistance during the German invasion is tantamount to the recognition of the timeless spirit of combat that dominates Hellenism, the type of tangibility that the modern Greek needs in order to believe.

If, however, we go to the trouble of repeating the gesture and pour over the two texts and research not only the physiology but also the genealogy, will we persist with the same arguments expressed by the relevant literature? Is Tsitsanis's song the mirror of notes of the emblematic Byzantine hymn, the projection of a musical genetic code that dominates Hellenism throughout the ages? Or is it perhaps just a mirage, one of those that quench the thirst of only the eyes, abandoning the travellers of the desert and depriving them of the vital resources that their course demands?

Part one

A story of origin

1

A laiko (popular) song by Tsitsanis (1948)

Vasilis Tsitsanis's 'Cloudy Sunday' was recorded for the first time on 11 August 1948.[1] The label on the seventy-eight rpm record states (see Figure 1.1):

Vasilis Tsitsanis
His Master's Voice, OGA 1396-1, AO 2834
License number 316-14800 (see Censorship Committee)
Prodromos Tsaousakis and Sotiria Bellou
Accompanied by laiki orchestra
V.TS.-AL.G.

Figure 1.1 The record label of the original recording of 'Cloudy Sunday' (Panagiotis Kounadis archive).

---

[1] 'Cloudy Sunday' original recording: https://youtu.be/8QroGi1vRuU. By using internet links for a major part of the audiovisual material, the article by Phillip Tagg 'Why Are Popular Music Studies Excluded from Italian Universities?' comes to the forefront (2014: footnote 2).

The recording consisted of two bouzoukis, a laiki guitar,[2] and two singers. This type of orchestra is rather common for the time, even though the mood for reform of the laiko aesthetic from within is tangible:

- The command of the vocal lines shared by Tsaousakis and Bellou is more complex in relation to the existing bouzouki-based repertoire.
- The tonality choice initially takes us by surprise. One would expect for a C or a D to be chosen, tonalities used mainly in this type of melodically structured song, due to the fact that they comprise eminently male tones. In addition, the tonalities from B to D constitute the overwhelming majority of Tsitsanis's song sung by Tsaousakis. What is more, the song was established later in the tonality of D (something that still holds true today). Even so, with the desire for orchestration of the voices on the one hand and the singularity regarding the range of Bellou's voice on the other, G was chosen,[3] in this way dividing the piece in two, the first half being performed by Tsaousakis. In the second half, Bellou takes over and is now in command of the melody.
- The characteristic ornamentation of the instrument constitutes a new proposal that Tsitsanis puts forward, in essence setting up the first bouzouki school in laiki music. The erratic appoggiaturas, his aggressive and crystal-clear pick, and the shifting of melodic time constitute his most characteristic innovations, compared to the up to then tradition.
- The arrangement innovations with the second bouzouki, even though it goes without saying that we see them in previous recordings, mainly by Spyros Peristeris,[4] constitute now an established new circumstance that Tsitsanis structures, using oftentimes a third bouzouki in his orchestrations. However, the roles of the instruments are no longer restricted to the trite first-second voice in parallel thirds, but introduce counterpoint dynamics.

There is a great response from the audience towards the song, and its popularity is legendary. A plethora of recordings follow, some by the composer himself

---

[2] The term 'laiki guitar' is used by the world of the rebetiko (protagonists and audience) to denote the difference not only in performance practice of the instrument but also in its manufacture.
[3] As we shall see further down, the recording teeters between F sharp and G. This concerns issues with the revolution speed of the record. It may be due to the initial etching of the seventy-eight rpm record, but it could also be the result of subsequent conversion into digital form and the by-chance deviations in the rotation of the seventy-eight-rpm record during reproduction. Lastly, it could also be the result of deviations in the reference tone during tuning.
[4] Regarding the work and the role of Spyros Peristeris in Greek laiki music, see Ordoulidis (2017b).

and others without his involvement. There is diversity in aesthetics approach, changing, in many cases, a lot of its basic characteristics. This is what happens generally with popular music; the fluidity of its nature is ascertained by its evolution through time, as it is reborn every time through a new rendition, ageing albeit continually refreshed.

The three official recordings of 'Cloudy Sunday' by Tsitsanis took place in 1948 and 1959. In the first two recordings, which were both recorded in 1948, Prodromos Tsaousakis and Sotiria Bellou, and Marika Ninou,[5] Vasilis Tsitsanis and Ioannis Salasidis sing, respectively. In the first reading, perhaps due to the short time period, these two performances present quite a few similarities. A more thorough study, however, proves the diversity which dominates the spirit of each, which is obviously due to the malleability which characterizes the musical genres that have as their core the orality of a performance. And so, we observe differences in performance tempo, something that has a direct impact on the qualitative characteristics (phrasing, basslines in the accompaniment, bouzouki ornamentation as well as others). Also, the distribution of the sung phrases differs significantly, seeing as three voices participate in the second recording, instead of two as in the first. The third recording, with singers Stelios Kazantzidis, Giota Lydia and Marinela,[6] generates even more interest as regards diversity.

At this point, we must stress the importance of the issue of identifying the songs with the performers, a phenomenon directly linked to popularity which does not concern only the song but a certain performance of the song. In other words, the interpretation of a musical text (which redefines the content, the meaning and the message of the song) will guarantee either popularity or rejection by the audience. In the case of the third performance, Kazantzidis's rendition overshadows the other voices; thus, they are rarely mentioned. In this particular recording, Kazantzidis presents a sample of his own singing style, which already plays a vital part in the course and development of the urban laiko genre (for Kazantzidis, see Oikonomou, 2015), a style that did not take long to reach the dimensions of a school. Although quite a few of the characteristics of the next period, regarding vocal practice, are perhaps obvious in Ninou's performance, Kazantzidis emphasizes the leading role that the voice is to now adopt, abandoning the aesthetics of collectivism which we see in the previous

---

[5] 'Cloudy Sunday': Philips, PE 402036, 1948: https://youtu.be/8nXpxuHVZqs.
[6] 'Cloudy Sunday': HMV, OGA 2851–AO 5546, 31 March 1959: https://youtu.be/ZG8AiQQrrTc.

stages of urban laiko song.[7] For example, he does not adhere to the rhythmic flow that the orchestra constructs, projecting his vocal phrases and preferring, often extremely accented, embellishments on notes of medium and long duration. All the aforementioned are characteristics which prove the versatility of urban laiki music, let alone a song hailed as incredibly popular, something which equals innumerable performances in the per se places of performance of laiki music, that is, the music halls (for a sample of the popularity see the royalties payments in Figures 1.2 to 1.5).

Not only for symbolic but also for practical reasons, Tsitsanis's first recording shall be used here as a basis, which could be considered as a major point in

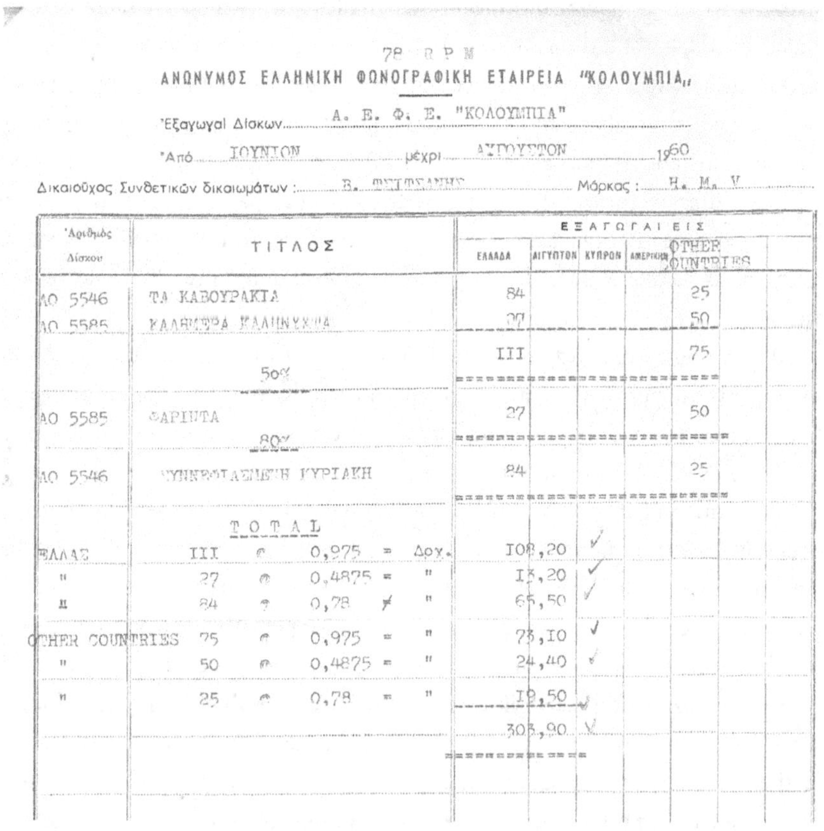

Figure 1.2 Royalties payment receipt which includes 'Cloudy Sunday', 1960 (Tsitsanis family archive).

---

[7] Regarding the collectivism in rebetiko and laiko, see Ordoulidis (2014: 57–9).

ΑΝΩΝΥΜΟΣ ΕΛΛΗΝΙΚΗ ΦΩΝΟΓΡΑΦΙΚΗ ΕΤΑΙΡΕΙΑ "ΚΟΛΟΥΜΠΙΑ"

Ἐξαγωγαί Δίσκων ἀπό ...IOYNION... μέχρι ...AYΓOYΣTON 1963... 196...

Δικαιοῦχος Συνθετικῶν δικαιωμάτων : ... Β. ΤΣΙΤΣΑΝΗΣ ... Μάρκας : ... H.M.V. ...

Ἀριθμός Δίσκου	ΤΙΤΛΟΣ	ΕΞΑΓΩΓΑΙ ΕΙΣ		
		ΕΛΛΑΔΑ	Η.Π.Α.-ΧΑΝΑΔΑ	ΛΟΙΠΑΙ ΧΩΡΑΙ
7PG 2501	Η ΓΕΡΑΚΙΝΑ	1215		
" 2530	ΑΛΑ ΤΟΥΡΚΑ ΧΟΡΕΨΕ ΜΟΥ	21		121
" 2547	ΙΣΩΣ ΑΥΡΙΟ	194		
" 2568	ΤΑ ΚΑΒΟΥΡΑΚΙΑ	1198		
" 2808	ΣΤΑ ΤΡΙΚΑΛΑ ΣΤΑ ΔΥΟ ΣΤΕΝΑ	1994		
"	Η ΑΧΑΡΙΣΤΗ	1994		
" 2859	ΚΑΤΣΕ Ν'ΑΚΟΥΣΗΣ ΜΙΑ ΠΕΝΝΙΑ	159		
" 2911	ΘΕΛΩ ΝΑ ΕΙΝΑΙ ΚΥΡΙΑΚΗ	169		
" 2917	ΣΤΡΩΣΕ ΜΟΥ ΝΑ ΚΟΙΜΗΘΩ	203		23
"	ΓΙΑ ΤΑ ΜΑΤΙΑ Π'ΑΓΑΠΩ	203		23
" 3066	ΠΑΙΞΕ ΧΡΗΣΤΟ ΤΟ ΜΠΟΥΖΟΥΚΙ	48		
"	ΤΗΣ ΤΑΒΕΡΝΑΣ ΤΟ ΡΟΛΟΙ	48		
" 3115	ΜΕΙΝΕ ΑΓΑΠΗ ΜΟΥ ΚΟΝΤΑ ΜΦΥ	1047		59
"	ΔΕΝ Σ'ΑΚΟΥΣΑ ΜΑΝΟΥΛΑ ΜΟΥ	1047		59
" 3120	ΦΤΩΧΕΙΑ ΠΟΥ ΜΕ ΚΟΥΡΕΛΙΑΣΕΣ	25		
" 3279	ΚΛΑΨΕ ΣΗΜΕΡΑ ΚΑΡΔΙΑ ΜΟΥ	12538		661
" 3307	ΥΠΑΡΧΕΙ ΜΙΑ ΦΛΟΓΑ	4028	10	335
		26131	10	1281

50%

7PG 2561	Ο ΤΣΟΛΙΑΣ	48		

80%

457PG 2568	ΣΥΝΝΕΦΙΑΣΜΕΝΗ ΚΥΡΙΑΚΗ	1198		

75%

7PG 2530	ΤΟ ΚΟΚΚΙΝΟ ΜΑΝΤΗΛΙ	21		121
" 2911	ΧΧΧΧΧΧΧΧΧΧΧΧΧΧΧ ΤΟ ΧΑΣΤΟΥΚΙ	169		
" 3120	ΓΙΑ ΝΑ ΣΕ ΚΑΝΩ ΑΝΘΡΩΠΟ	25		
		215		121

Figure 1.3 Royalties payment receipt which includes 'Cloudy Sunday', 1963 (Tsitsanis family archive).

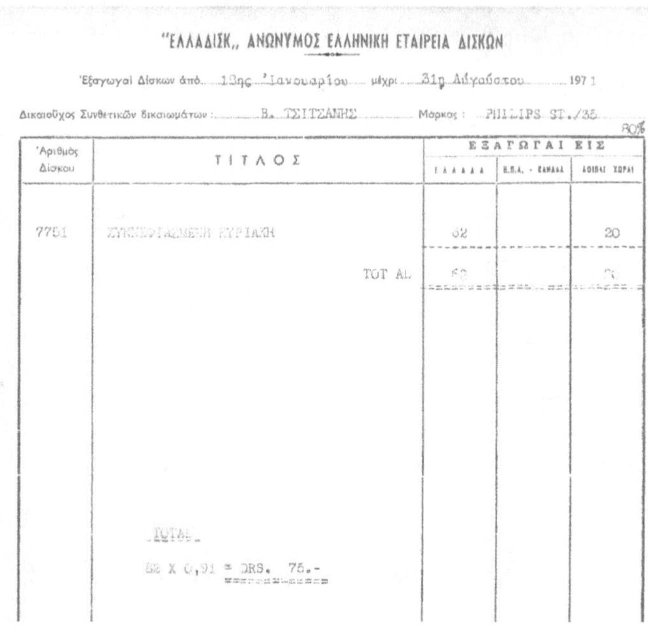

"ΕΛΛΑΔΙΣΚ„ ΑΝΩΝΥΜΟΣ ΕΛΛΗΝΙΚΗ ΕΤΑΙΡΕΙΑ ΔΙΣΚΩΝ

Ἐξαγωγαί Δίσκων ἀπό 1ης Ἰανουαρίου μέχρι 31η Αὐγούστου 1971

Δικαιοῦχος Συνθετικῶν δικαιωμάτων: Β. ΤΣΙΤΣΑΝΗΣ Μάρκος: PHILIPS ST./35 80%

Ἀριθμός Δίσκου	ΤΙΤΛΟΣ	ΕΞΑΓΩΓΑΙ ΕΙΣ ΕΛΛΑΔΑ	Η.Π.Α. - ΚΑΝΑΔΑ	ΛΟΙΠΑΙ ΧΩΡΑΙ
7751	ΣΥΝΝΕΦΙΑΣΜΕΝΗ ΚΥΡΙΑΚΗ	62		20
	TOTAL	62		20

TOTAL

82 X 0,91 = DRS. 75.-

Figure 1.4 Royalties payment receipt which includes 'Cloudy Sunday', 1971 (Tsitsanis family archive).

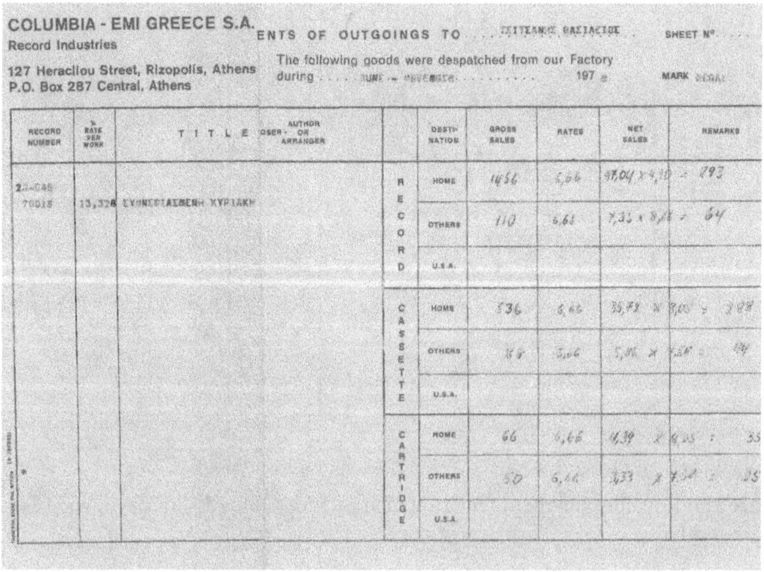

COLUMBIA - EMI GREECE S.A.
Record Industries
127 Heracliou Street, Rizopolis, Athens
P.O. Box 287 Central, Athens

ENTS OF OUTGOINGS TO ... ΤΣΙΤΣΑΝΗΣ ΒΑΣΙΛΕΙΟΣ ... SHEET N°

The following goods were despatched from our Factory during ... 197 ... MARK

RECORD NUMBER	% RATE PER WORK	TITLE	AUTHOR USER OR ARRANGER		DESTINATION	GROSS SALES	RATES	NET SALES	REMARKS
70015	13,328	ΣΥΝΝΕΦΙΑΣΜΕΝΗ ΚΥΡΙΑΚΗ		RECORD	HOME	1456	6,66		293
					OTHERS	110	6,66		64
					U.S.A.				
				CASSETTE	HOME	536	6,66		
					OTHERS				
					U.S.A.				
				CARTRIDGE	HOME	66	6,66		
					OTHERS	50	6,66		
					U.S.A.				

Figure 1.5 Royalties payment receipt which includes 'Cloudy Sunday', 1978 (Tsitsanis family archive).

Greek laiki aesthetic. As a necessity for the present study, this particular first performance was rendered on staff notation, where the recording of the vocal part is accompanied by the rhythmic pattern of the chordal sequence (see Part Four). This musical text was translated[8] subsequently into Byzantine notation (παρασημαντική, parasimantikí), so as to facilitate the comparison to the Byzantine hymn.

---

[8] In many parts of the book, the term 'translation' was preferred instead of the term 'transcription', when dealing with the transfer of Byzantine notation to staff notation. This practice was preferred in order to highlight the singularity of the description of a music phenomenon with two so very different writing systems. Since each writing system carries its own idiomatic tendencies, during the transfer of one text to the other, the latter is compelled to imply the idioms of the former, without the ability to describe them accurately. In other words, each writing system, often, also applies specific practices and habits to a musical act which has as its starting point a musical transcription.

2

A hymn from the Orthodox musical tradition

'The Akathist Hymn'[1] is an original[2] kontákio[3] and belongs to the hirmologic[4] type of Plagal of the Fourth echos.[5] Even though 'Cloudy Sunday' is associated with 'The Akathist Hymn's' version in the brief type,[6] it must be noted that it

---

[1] Due to the many terms in Byzantine terminology, in this chapter, the direct use of the terms in their English translation, or their transliterated form, was considered preferable, in order to facilitate the cohesion of the text. Definitions of the terms are given in the footnotes.

[2] The αυτόμελα (autómela, model melodies), the original/model melodies are a distinct category of unique melodies which loan their music to other hymns which are called προσόμοια (prosómoia).

[3] 'The Kontakion (κοντάκιον or κονδάκιον) consists of from eighteen to thirty, or even more, stanzas all structurally alike. The single stanza is called Troparion; its length varies from three to thirteen lines. All the Troparia are composed on the pattern of a model stanza, the Hirmus (ειρμός). A Kontakion is built either on the pattern of a Hirmus specially composed for it, or follows the metre of a Hirmus already used for another Kontakion, or group of Kontakia. At the beginning of the Kontakion stands a short Troparion, metrically and melodically independent of it: this is the Prooemium (προοίμιον) or Kukulion (κουκούλιον), which, at a later stage, often consists of two or three stanzas. Prooemium and Kontakion are linked together by the refrain the Ephymnium (εφύμνιον), with which all the stanzas end, and by the musical mode (ήχος)' (Wellesz, 1961: 179). Today, in essence, the term *kontakio* is used as a synonym for *prooemium*.

[4] 'Hirmologion (το Ειρμολόγιον). Exclusively destined for the chanter, this book contains the model stanzas (ειρμοί) – with or without the melodies – according to which the stanzas of each of the nine Odes of the Kanons are to be sung' (Wellesz, 1961: 141). 'Sticherarion (Στιχηράριον). A bulky volume, the main part of whose contents are the Stichera (στιχηρά *sc. τροπάρια*) of the Evening and Morning Office, arranged according to the cycle of the ecclesiastical year, the Stichera of the movable feasts from Lent to Trinity, those of the Oktoëchos, and, in addition, several groups of Stichera for special occasions' (Wellesz, 1961: 143). 'The "Sticheraric style" is, as has already been said, more ornamented than the "Hirmologic". We find five or six notes combined in a group on a single syllable, which need no longer be one which is important in the text. From now on the music has the preponderance over the text' (Wellesz, 1961: 317).

[5] Ἦχος (ήχος), plural echoi (ήχοι) – Byzantine mode/s, literary meaning 'sound/s'. The echoi constitute modal music entities which refer to the theoretical system of Byzantine music. They often correspond, are parallel or compared to the Turkish makams and the drómoi of the laiko. Their names are as follows: First, Second, Third, Fourth, Plagal of the First, Plagal of the Second, Plagal of the Third or Varís, Plagal of the Fourth. 'The mode, we may therefore conclude, is not merely a "scale" but the sum of all the formulae which constitute the quality of an Echos. This definition is in conformity with that given by Chrysanthus of Madytos in his Great Musical Theory (1832): Echos is the scheme (ιδέα) of the melody, arranged according to the practice of the expert musician, who knows which tones should be omitted which chosen on which one should begin and on which one should end' (Wellesz, 1961: 326).

[6] Σύντομο (sýntomo, brief) can also be translated as fast, quick, short or simple. It refers to the melodic construction style.

exists as a slow and a slow-brief[7] hirmologic type too. According to the theory of Avraam Euthymiadis, in the hirmologic style 'every syllable of the words of a lyrical text lasts, usually, one and rarely two or at the most three single beats' (Euthymiadis, 1972: 345). Generally, the Byzantine pieces of the slow type are characterized by a more complex form, where the same syllable may last for several beats. But also the atmosphere, as a whole, that is cultivated by the slow melody is quite different aesthetically from that of the brief, even though they belong to the same echos.

Even though there are a multitude of manuscripts and transcriptions for 'The Akathist Hymn', for the present study those of Ioannis Lambadarios and Stefanos Domestichos (1850)[8] and those of Georgios Progakis (1909), which are considered classical by researchers, were chosen. In essence, they are transcriptions of the old form of music notation style to a newer one, as decided by the three-membered Music Committee proposed by the Ecumenical Patriarchate of Constantinople in 1814, consisting of Chrysanthos from Madytos, Grigorios Protopsáltis and Chourmouzios Chartofýlakas, the findings of which yielded the issuing of the theory book of Chrysanthos in 1832,[9] even though it seems that the new system (as well as a part of the theory of Chrysanthos) was already being used before the reformation by the Committee (see Chatzigiakoumis, 1974 and Xanthoudakis, 2007: 141). Hence, these transcriptions are 'explanations' of older transcriptions.[10]

At this point, a clarification is deemed necessary in order to emphasize that chanting, with the exception of certain particular cases, is urban music, and is by nature just as fluid as its counterparts. Given its singular notation feature, the time and place of its performance is crucial to the formation and evolution of its particular characteristics. While it confers and interacts with other musical idioms, now and again it activates its innovativeness, at times in a conventional manner and at others in an unconventional one.[11]

---

[7] Αργό and αργοσύντομο (argó, slow and argosýntomo, brief-slow).
[8] 'Lambadários' (Left Chanter) is the one who conducts the left chorus/lectern. Δομέστιχος (Doméstichos) is the assistant of one of the two main chanters (First or Right Cantor and Left Chanter). Historical figures of the chanting world, up to about the nineteenth century, were known by their titles, which function more or less as a sort of surname.
[9] Regarding the reform of 1814, see Romanou (1985).
[10] In terms of these 'explanations', see Wellesz (1961), Stathis (1978), Khalil (2009), Alexandrou (2010), Arvanitis (2010) and Chaldaeakes (2015).
[11] The invasion of technology in present-day performance practices of ecclesiastical music is a typical example. The use of an electronic holding of the ison is now widespread, a small synthesizer with a potentiometer for frequency fluctuation, which with the pressing of the keys produces pre-recorded voices. The holding of the ison is available in digital applications too, for smart phones and tablets. On

During the long duration of the ecclesiastical year, 'The Akathist Hymn' is chanted on different occasions. Certainly the most important being that which directly recalls the historical context of its creation, meaning the service of the Salutations of the Holy Virgin,[12] this takes place every Friday of Lent after Ash Monday[13] and up to the sixth week of the fast.[14] In the first four weeks of the fast, it is also chanted every Sunday during the Divine Liturgy.[15] Additionally, it must be noted that 'The Akathist Hymn' constitutes the kontákio of the celebratory service of the Annunciation,[16] which, anyway, takes place during the period of the Lent. On the aforementioned occasions, the hymn appears in different forms, which are deemed worthy of description in order to compile its main musical characteristics, its aesthetics and its relevant meaning and general significance.

The Salutations are celebrated for five successive Fridays. For the first four Fridays, the service is similar, as are the forms of the hymn, which appear as follows: after the performance of the Canon,[17] the two chanting choruses (which, according to tradition, are called Right and Left Chorus) sing the lyrics of 'The Akathist Hymn' alternately, in its slow version. In practice, this performance could be construed in many ways, according to each oral tradition depending on the place and/or the teacher of the chanter, the dexterity of the chanters, but also the degree of their musical – but not only – literacy. In the same service of the Salutations, 'The Akathist Hymn' is chanted, however, also as a kontákio, in its brief form, after the stanza[18] of the Oíkos, by the priest, that is to say one stanza every Friday and all together the fifth Friday of the fast. On this fifth Friday, after

---

11 May 1992, the Church of Greece sends a circular to churches, prohibiting the use of the electronic holding of the ison. On 14 February 2019, it once again sends a circular with the same content but this time prohibiting electronic applications as well. At the same time, it recommends restraint regarding even the use of electronic books via tablets (the circular in question: www.ecclesia.gr/greek/holysynod/egyklioi/304_14022019.pdf).

[12] Χαιρετισμοί της Θεοτόκου, chairetismoí tis Theotókou.
[13] Μεγάλη Τεσσαρακοστή, megáli tessarakostí; Καθαρά Δευτέρα, kathará Deutéra.
[14] Των νηστειών, ton nisteión.
[15] Θεία Λειτουργία, theía leitourgía.
[16] Ευαγγελισμός της Θεοτόκου, euangelismós tis Theotókou.
[17] 'The Kanon is a complex poetical form, made up of nine Odes (ωδαί), each of which originally consisted of from six to nine Troparia. At a later date, owing to the introduction of a number of additional monostrophic stanzas, only three of the Troparia of each Ode were used in the service. Structurally, therefore, the Ode is no different from a short Kontakion; the difference between the two forms lies in their content. The Kontakion is a poetical homily; the name Odes of every Kanon are modelled on the pattern of the Nine Canticles from the Scriptures and have the character of hymns of praise' (Wellesz, 1961: 198). 'In the Psaltika the Kontakia are reduced to two stanzas, to the Prooemium (or Koukoulion) which is now called Kontakion and the first stanza, which is called Oikos. There is only one Kontakion which has come down to us with the music of all its twenty-four stanzas, this is the "Akathistos" hymn, of which the Laurenziana at Florence possesses one complete copy in Codex Ashburnham' (Wellesz, 1961: 144).
[18] Στάση, stási.

the Small Compline,[19] the choruses chant the hymn 'To Prostachthén Mystikós'[20] to the melody of 'The Akathist Hymn,' twice in its slow form and once in its brief, as prescribed by the Typikó.[21] The first stanza and the Canon follow. On the last Friday, the First and the Third ode of the Canon is executed, while on the previous Fridays it is performed in its entirety outright. After the third ode of the Canon, the Typiko prescribes the performance of 'The Akathist Hymn' in its slow form, with alternate choruses. The second stanza of the Oíkos by the priest follows and, consequently, the fourth, fifth and sixth ode of the Canon, in order for 'The Akathist Hymn' to be performed again, without the Typiko prescribing if it is to be in its slow or brief form. The third stanza of the Oíkos by the priest follows and the seventh, eighth and ninth odes of the Canon, in order for 'The Akathist Hymn' to be performed once again, again without stating the type of performance. The fourth stanza of the Oíkos follows, which ends with the repetition of the first stanza. Performance of 'The Akathist Hymn' in its brief form is defined by the Typiko, and, after the Thrice Holy prayer[22] that follows, the hymn is once again rendered, this time as a recitation.[23]

As mentioned before, 'The Akathist Hymn' is also performed during the Divine Liturgy of the first four Sundays of the fast, as a kontákio following the dismissal hymns.[24] At this point, we observe another factor, which determines its aesthetic. In the case of there being a co-liturgy,[25] that is, more than one priest taking part in the liturgy, it is they who chant the kontákio inside the Holy Altar.[26] In this case, the hymn is performed as a brief hirmologic melody, usually, however, in slow tempo. In essence, it is a slower version of the allegro performance by the chanters. This difference plays a determining role in the development of the melody and the embellishments, with serious repercussions on the whole atmosphere.

The Salutations are an especially popular service, and a plethora of recordings exist. Certain recordings found on the internet come from televised broadcasts of services (such as the Ecumenical Patriarchate, the Temple of the Resurrection in Jerusalem, the Metropolitan Cathedral of Athens et al.), while others come from discography and take place away from their natural place of performance (such as those of Theodoros Vasilikos, the choir of Lykourgos Angelopoulos, the choir of Georgios Kakoulidis et al.).

---

[19] Μικρό απόδειπνο, mikró apódeipno.
[20] Το προσταχθέν μυστικώς, that which has been secretly ordered.
[21] Τυπικό, rite.
[22] Τρισάγιον, triságion.
[23] Χύμα, hýma.
[24] Απολυτίκιο, apolytíkio: hymns dedicated to specific saints and celebrations.
[25] Συλλείτουργο, sylleítourgo.
[26] Ιερό Βήμα, Ieró Víma.

3

Comparison of the two pieces by Ilias Petropoulos (1968)

The approach of Ilias Petropoulos in *Rebetika songs* (1996: 40–1) highlights two crucial issues that concern various similar instances: firstly, the effort of the collectors-enthusiasts of the rebetiko, which with great sacrifice collected their material and rendered it publicly available. One of these – if not the 'father' – is undoubtedly Ilias Petropoulos (1928–2003). The second crucial issue relates, in good part, to their zeal, by virtue of which they sailed unchartered – up to then – waters. This is a consensus that multiply signifies the general methodology of his book. The ruling concept, which has a direct impact on the results of the research of Petropoulos, is firstly folkloric.[1] It has been evaluated and commented upon in a diversity of ways by subsequent researchers.[2]

Focusing on the comparison of 'Cloudy Sunday' and 'The Akathist Hymn', Petropoulos endeavours to prove the emanation of the former from the latter, citing the initial phrases of their musical notation (see Music transcription 3.1). This is rendered twofold, not only in the European but also in the Byzantine system, whose goal is to demonstrate Tsitsanis's imitation of the Byzantine hymn, who seems to have conveyed the as is sequence of the musical notes of 'The Akathist Hymn' to the popular melody.

From a musicological standpoint, it is unheard of to compare two completely differently textured creations, which are performed in utterly discernible contexts. The compression of their musical description to a notation form is

---

[1] For a more interesting and analytical commentary on Petropoulos's singular folklore stance, see Papanikolaou (2011).
[2] See, for example: Pennanen (2004), Holst (2006) and Tragaki (2007).

Music transcription 3.1 Transcriptions of both pieces by Petropoulos (1996: 40).

by definition problematic. Even if we accept this compromise, the approach of Petropoulos is certainly subject to regard on more than one point:

1. He does not clarify which particular performances he documents. Is 'Cloudy Sunday' sung by Prodromos Tsaousakis and Sotiria Bellou, with Marika Ninou, Vasilis Tsitsanis and Ioannis Salasidis, or by Stelios Kazantzidis, Giota Lydia and Marinela? Is 'The Akathist Hymn' performed by Spyros Peristeris, Iakovos Naupliotis or the choir of the Mount Athos fathers? Obviously, all the randomly aforementioned performances as well as any other existing ones differ, not only quantitatively but also qualitatively regarding their characteristics as we shall see later in the chapter. In any case, this particular transcription of the song does not come from any of the three aforementioned recordings. The melodies of both pieces are transcriptions in an

unrealistic pitch, as it is impossible for them to be performed by either a male or a female voice.

2. The transcription of 'Cloudy Sunday' manifests small divergences from that in the European and the Byzantine version, and more specifically in the syllable '(Κυ-)ρια-κή' (Kyriakí, Sunday).[3]

Music transcription 3.2 Petropoulos transcription of the word 'Kyriaki', translated in staff notation from Byzantine notation.[4]

Music transcription 3.3 Petropoulos transcription of the word 'Kyriaki' in staff notation.

In addition, at the end of the melody we do not see the classical gravitation of the note D towards the note E, a classic behaviour of the Plagal of the Fourth echos (that is, we do not see an augmented D).

3. The chords are erroneous, as the sequencing of degrees of the particular phrase in the original recording is I–II–I, without the mediation of

---

[3] The syllables to which the text refers to are those which appear without brackets. The latter are used in order for each word to be fully rendered.

[4] The music transcriptions in staff notation but also in the makam system were actualized with the Finale 2014 software.

Music transcription 3.4 A classic behaviour at the end of the melody, also described in theoretical books.

either IV or V as Petropoulos documents. On the contrary, one could argue that the starting point of his transcription is of a live performance of 'Cloudy Sunday', and not one of the recorded ones. However, were this the case, the sequencing would include the degrees I–II–V–I, without the mediation of IV. Based on the submitted documentation, two are the possible versions of the phrase 'συννεφιασμένη Κυριακή' (synnefiasméni Kyriakí, cloudy Sunday), either I–II–V–I or I–II–I. In the phrase, 'μοιάζεις με την καρδιά μου' (moiázeis me tin kardiá mou, you look like my heart), the sequencing of degrees could be II–V–I or II–IV–V–I, where the chord of the IV degree is performed on the syllable 'την' and not on the syllable 'μοιά(-ζεις)' of Petropoulos's transcription (see the transcriptions in the fourth part). A variation exists in the third recording of the song, sung by Stelios Kazantzidis and considered the most popular: the chord sequence consists of the I–II–I degrees in the phrase 'συννεφιασμένη Κυριακή' and II–V–I in the phrase 'μοιάζεις με την καρδιά μου'. Consequently, neither in this case does the transcription of Petropoulos merit credibility.

4. Petropoulos numbers the groups of notes that comprise the contentious phrase, in order to prove the faithful mimicry of the modern melody. While in the first phrase ('συννεφιασμένη Κυριακή') the numbered notes 1 to 7 of the hymn correspond to the notes 1 to 7 of the song, in the second ('μοιάζεις με την καρδιά μου'), numbers 8, 9 and 10, this does not happen.
5. In the Byzantine transcription of 'The Akathist Hymn', in the syllable '(στρα-τη-)γώ' (stratigó, champion) the Byzantine neume kentímata is placed.[5]
In reality, at this point the neume apóstrophos is required and synechés

---

[5] Κεντήματα, literally meaning 'embroidery'.

elaphrón.⁶ It is widely known that in the Byzantine notation system every character gives an instruction that relates to the previous one. That is, the characters/neumes lead based on where the melody is on the previous character. Therefore, the apóstrophos is the descent of a note ('voice'⁷ according to chanting terminology), while the synechés elaphrón, which is a compound character comprising of one apóstrophos and one elaphrón, is equal to two apóstrophoe that are performed in one beat (every character, unless otherwise stated and apart from the yporroï,⁸ uses up one beat). In the transcription of Petropoulos, the introduction of the kentímata, which is the ascent of a note, leads the melody on another course.

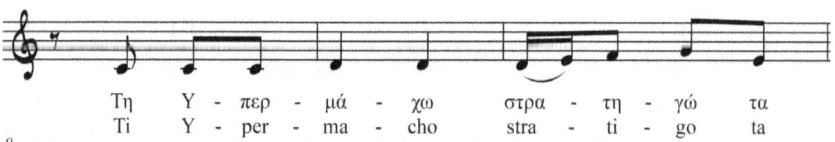

Music transcription 3.5 'Στρατηγώ' phrase written in Byzantine notation by Petropoulos.

Music transcription 3.6 Translation in staff notation of Music transcription 3.5.

Music transcription 3.7 'Στρατηγώ' phrase written in staff notation by Petropoulos.

---

⁶ Απόστροφος, apostrophe; συνεχές ελαφρόν, continuous/running light.
⁷ Φωνή, foní.
⁸ Υπορροή, literally meaning 'flow down' or 'sub stream'.

6. The fact that Petropoulos finds himself on paths that he cannot negotiate comfortably is also demonstrated by the holding of the ison, which is noted under the melodic line of the hymn. The documented alternative I–II–V–I, in the phrase 'τη Υπερμάχω στρατηγώ τα' (ti Ypermácho stratigó ta, to Thee the Champion leader), has no substance, as there are only three existing versions: with a single holding of the ison on either the note Ni[9] (C/I) during the whole duration of the phrase or Ni–Di–Ni (C–G–C/I–V–I) or Ni–Pa–Ni (C–D–C/I–II–I). In the next part of the hymn's phrase, 'νικητήρια' (nikitíria, victory), again Petropoulos uses a holding of the ison which does not correspond to reality. In this particular case, there are two versions: either a single holding of the ison on the note Ni (C/I), or moving from Ni (C) to Vou (E/III), on the syllable 'ρι'. The only time where a holding of the ison on the low Di (G) in this particular phrase ('νικητήρια') has been observed is in the case of a polyphonic performance of the hymn, credited to Ioannis Sakellaridis.[10] However, the lower Di is performed on the syllable 'νι' and not on the syllable 'ρι' as Petropoulos claims.

7. Lacking in theoretical training, as far as Byzantine music is concerned, Petropoulos is ignorant of the fact that the dominant note Vou (E) constitutes one of the imperfect cadences in the Plagal of the Fourth echos.[11] Thus, we are not dealing with a 'rest' in the melody on E, as he describes. At this particular point, 'The Akathist Hymn' moves towards a complete cadence on the note Ni (C), while 'Cloudy Sunday' descends on Vou (E). If something is to be proven with the aforementioned, it is the common atmosphere which the pieces in question share, a common aural logic, that concerns audiences and composers, which 'dictates' what is and what is not suitable, where each phrase will end and in which way it will be performed. However, to prove relations of origin and interdependence, much more is required.

8. In his analysis, Petropoulos claims that 'in the 8 [note of his numbering] the four notes of "The Akathist Hymn" are the acoustic equivalent of the

---

[9] The names of the notes in Byzantine music are Νη, Πα, Βου, Γα, Δι, Κε, Ζω and Νη. Their transliterated versions are used: Ni, Pa, Vou, Ga, Di, Ke, Zo, Ni.

[10] 'The Akathist Hymn', polyphonic by Sakellaridis: https://youtu.be/h6VoOG7BsDA.

[11] In Byzantine music theory, the καταλήξεις (katalíxeis, cadences) are divided into three main groups: the εντελείς (enteleís, complete), where the sentence is complete with the melodic line (in the hymn); the ατελείς (ateleís, incomplete), where there is a cadence or simply a pause in the music, but the lyric sentence is not yet complete (in other words, at a comma or a semi-colon); and the τελικές (telikés, final) cadences.

eight of Tsitsanis. The only difference is the mood for ornamentation of the rebetiko in contrast to the lucid rule of the Byzantine melody'. At this point, two questions arise: on the one hand, the 'acoustic equivalent' highlights the subjective acoustic criterion of Petropoulos – that is to say, the phrase in question in 'Cloudy Sunday' (according to him) 'looks like' the corresponding one in 'The Akathist Hymn'. In a more musicological language, we could be talking about common modal atmospheres, or common aural logics, but this approach requires a vaster complexity. Clearly, at this point Petropoulos abandons his fundamental reasoning, which is to prove Tsitsanis's copying of the melody note by note. In contrast, he uses expressions such as 'mood for ornamentation' and 'lucid rule', without giving them substantial content. Indeed, given that he does not compare two specific performances but the two pieces in general, then one could invoke cases that eschew his observations dramatically. Oftentimes, chanting does depict a 'mood for ornamentation', while the rebetiko moves towards a frugal and lucid style, for example, if one compares Thrasyvoulos Stanitsas on the one hand with Stelios Keromytis[12] on the other.

9. Petropoulos claims that a whole complex of notes, the 'group 9', as he characteristically names it, is 'the very harmony and the very mood' in both pieces. There is, however, no validation in this statement, as indeed the melodic part of the hymn is directed towards ending on Vou/E, which is the third degree, while the song begins its closing phrase directed at the base Ni/C. In other words, the mood and the atmosphere of both melodies are different.

10. With regard to the musicology of the laiko genre, after the fifth note of the controversial phrase, a note which Petropoulos characterizes 'of small significance' follows. Evidently, he does not comprehend that, quite the contrary, the particular note (the sixteenth C) is crucial to the aesthetic substance and the style of the piece. Even though it does not belong to the basic melodic structure, it is this note, together with other similar ones, that will determine distinctiveness in a performance, as required by the aesthetic of the laiko. For example, the singing style of Kazantzidis is characterized by exaggeration on these types of notes, to which he often imparts greater emphasis in relation to others that

---

[12] It should be noted that Stelios Keromytis is often referred to as Kyromitis.

belong to the central structure of the melody. In contrast, the style of Tsaousakis is characterized by employment of less artifice. What we mean to say is that they acquire different meaning and weight via the general formation of the melody. It is details such as these that redetermine many of the general characteristic, as the harmonious atmospheres that are constructed in every performance and the rhythmic flow of the melody.

Judging from the aforementioned, we reach an obvious conclusion that Petropoulos attempts an analysis of which he is not in full command. It is typical that he considers that the chords utilized by Tsitsanis 'are the simplest ever'. This phrase alone is enough to illustrate his lack of understanding concerning Tsitsanis's work, which brought about a revolution in laiki music, granting – among other things – chordal harmony a lead role. The irony of the matter is that, precisely for this innovation, he has been accused of 'westernizing' the rebetiko tradition.

One can find a concise copy of Petropoulos in Maria Konstantinidi's book *Κοινωνιολογική ιστορία του ρεμπέτικου* (koinoniologikí istoría tou rebétikou, sociological history of the rebetiko) (1994: 123-4). The author supports her viewpoint concerning the descent of the popular song from the ecclesiastical hymn, analysing the correlation in seventeen lines, emphasizing at the end that 'it regards a spontaneous and subconscious influence of Byzantine music, which exists in every Greek'. Particularly interesting is the photographic appendix in the book, which begins with an ancient Greek anaglyph, which, according to the author 'depicts a muse holding a trichordon or pandura' (1994: 169). Then, photographs from the Roman and Byzantine periods are presented, which depict plucked instruments, in order for a comparison to be made with the next group of photographs, now depicting the contemporary period and inhabitants of the Greek peninsula or of Asia Minor, who are also depicted playing a plucked instrument. Finally, the photographic material culminates in the rebetiko period and the bouzouki, thus presenting another aspect of the ideology of historical continuation. This mindset, using photographs, follows once again the example set by Petropoulos, who presents a great deal of photographic material in his book, beginning in antiquity and culminating in the rebetiko (1996: 283-686).

4

Comparison by Mikis Theodorakis (1970)

The claim that 'Cloudy Sunday' originates from 'The Akathist Hymn', but also the general connection between urban laiki music and Byzantine music holds a special place in Theodorakis's book *Για την ελληνική μουσική* (gia tin elinikí mousikí, about Greek music) (1986). This book is a collection of published articles by Theodorakis, among which we find the celebrated article from 1949 in the newspaper *Present Times*, with which the discourse relating to the connection of the two musical pieces begins.

In this particular publication, Theodorakis expresses a sui generis 'decalogue of good Greek music', of which the laiko appears to have the following two features:

1. It teaches us how to creatively assimilate tradition, Folk and Byzantine (mainly) music and
2. In itself it offers new ways of melodic expression which, if and when they are assimilated, in conjunction with the harmonic simplicity they present, will contribute to the creation of an authentically laiko and truly Greek Music School (Theodorakis, 1949: 169).

In order to idealize the laiko, Theodorakis downplays the importance of documentation, magnifying the particular characteristics of the laiko. Consequently, we observe a unique exoticism, which also determines the relevant vocabulary: 'authentically laiko', 'truly Greek' music. An aphoristic attitude towards anything that does not fulfil the requirements is evident, requirements which dictate the constitution of a 'mechanism creating folk, laiki music' (Theodorakis, 1949: 159).

However, what is the context of the word 'people' (λαός, laós) in this type of rhetoric? If one is to observe 'folk and laiki music' of the period, it would be difficult to come across such homogeneity and rigidity so as to excuse some form of archetypal authenticity. In contrast, the material in question, not only in an urban but also in a rural capacity, is characterized by a polymorphic syncretism. This is clearly evident in all sources of recordings, which illustrate the manner with which performers manage older melodic prototypes: common melodic formations and formulae are remoulded from place to place, from composer to composer and from performer to performer.[1] If artistic and cultural evaluations are fecund here, it is difficult for one to comprehend the whole scene on national terms.

Of course, in subsequent years, national obsession even led to the construction of 'authenticity gauges': trying to negotiate the issue of Greekness in music, based on the evaluation of Nikos Skalkottas's compositional work, Ioannis G. Papaioannou expressed thirteen relative criteria (1997: 32), and even if the benefits of the doubt were given, under no circumstances would they be considered musicologically valid. On the other hand, Theodorakis does not progress to the systemization of the national criteria for authenticity; rather, he prefers to renounce whole genres, which are credited with disdainful characterizations:

> Was the kantáda [serenade] beneficial or harmful? Undoubtedly harmful. Romantic superficiality, melodic vulgarity, morbidity. All these corrupt many generations of young people musically. (Theodorakis, 1949: 160)

At the time that the aforementioned was being written, the kantáda, in all its forms, is especially popular. However, its multitudinous audience is arbitrarily excluded from the term 'people', according to Theodorakis. If we seek the viewpoint of the musicians of the laiko, concerning the kantáda, this argument appears groundless. Tsitsanis himself, who is idealized by Theodorakis, says characteristically in an interview in the newspaper *Κυριακάτικος Ταχυδρόμος* (kyriakátikos tachydrómos, the Sunday postman), 15 April 1951:

> I did write a few kantádas then, which were successful, 'Χωρίσαμε ένα δειλινό' [chorísame éna deilinó, we broke up one twilight], 'Το φιλί δεν είναι κρίμα' [to filí den eínai kríma, to kiss is not shameful], 'Ο Ζητιάνος' [o zitiános, the beggar] et al. (Tsitsanis, 1951: 170)

Theodorakis obviously does not mean the same form of composition. Nonetheless, the kantáda is not scorned by Tsitsanis, who chooses this particular word to describe a whole category of his compositions.

---

[1] For an organized, validated/documented and digitalized sample of historical Greek-speaking material, see the Virtual Museum of the Kounadis's Archive: www.vmrebetiko.gr.

The word 'rebetiko' is charged with a respective atmosphere of ambivalence. A few months earlier, Manos Hadjidakis had appealed to Greek intellectuals in order to restore the genre. His main argument was Greekness: the Byzantium is Greek; the rebetiko uses elements of Byzantine music; thus, the rebetiko is Greek. This argument was also adopted by Theodorakis, who classifies Byzantine music education as laiki music education:

> First of all, it is widely known that the poor Greek boy at a young age often goes to church. Especially if he has a good voice, and so helps with the 'chorus', holding the 'ison' and from time to time does [sings] a 'parallel third'. (Theodorakis, 1949: 165)

While, however, it is Theodorakis's intention to integrate Byzantine music into the laiko genre, in essence he does the opposite, presenting the laiko as a result of the Byzantine.

> There is hardly any laiko song that does not form its in-between cadences in a purely ecclesiastical way. (Theodorakis, 1949: 163)

It is probably historical continuation that urges him to adopt the common origin argument that he tries to validate with sentences such as the one mentioned earlier, which is vague and general. Whatever force his argument has is self-evident, considering that the laiko and the Byzantine are both accommodated in a broader cultural construction, of which, however, they are not the exclusive tenants. The reference alone to the 'chorus' and the 'parallel third', used by Theodorakis, recalls a long history of dialogues with other musical trends (Byzantine music, supposedly, is characterized by a defining monophony, on which a variety of doctrines were founded, as we shall see further down). The chanting tradition to which these terms belong to is the school of Ioannis Sakellaridis and the schools that were developed on the islands of the Ionian, which were vehemently doubted by the defenders of the 'authentic' Byzantine yphos, very often characterized as 'Italian' or 'Western'. Let us not forget that Theodorakis was born, in 1925, on the island of Chios, which is characterized by (as other islands in the Aegean) a particular cosmopolitism. His father was from Crete, in which, for years, a singular polyphonic chanting discipline/school is prevalent. Tradition says that this school influences the Corfu chanting school, after 1669, when Venetian-occupied Crete is conquered by the Ottomans. As a family, the Theodarikises were in constant motion, as his father was a public servant and was constantly assigned to different regions. Some of these stations may in themselves served as important for the chanting stance with which Mikis came into contact. From 1933 to 1936, that is, from the age of eight to the age of eleven, he lived in the town of Argostoli, in Cephalonia, an Ionian island, which engages in the renowned Ionian tradition.[2] From 1937 to 1938, he lived in Patras, a prominent cultural centre for at least a century (travelling troupes and performances from Italy, local mandolinatas, polyphonic choirs, etc.).

But the rebetiko itself is comprehended by Theodorakis in a narrow genre perspective:

> The 'rebetiko' is played exclusively with the bouzouki and this instrument determines the melodic datíles: plucking, the main and characteristic feature, but also 100% a creation of the new form. (Theodorakis, 1949: 162)

By identifying the rebetiko with the bouzouki, Theodorakis skillfully excludes all other music that is included in the broader use of the term and which is characterized by a completely different instrumentation. However, this kind of stylized approach does not seem to concern him. On the contrary, he focuses on the points which could function symbolically in the double construction of Greekness and 'laikoness'. A typical characteristic of this approach is an incident which took place during Theodorakis's concert in Nikaia (Athens) in 1983, a few months before the death of Tsitsanis.[3]

Taking the stand, the composer clearly places Tsitsanis in the leading role among the rest of the creators of the laiko, to whom he even refers to eponymously: Vamvakaris, Papaioannou, Mitsakis, Kaldaras, Chiotis and Bithikotsis. Every previous inclination in this capacity, Peristeris, Tountas, Skarvelis, Semsis, Karipis, Dalgas, Roukounas, Eskenazi and so on, is missing, in order for Theodorakis to sanctify the world of the bouzouki, with which Theodorakis lays claim to the laiko, adopting it as his prime instrument. As Papanikolaou so aptly comments on Theodorakis's intervention in all its totality: 'That is, the stance is ethno-populist and sweeps across the whole cultural board. Clean up the bouzouki from the dens and make it a national symbol with a political façade' (Papanikolaou, 2011: 60). On the microphone, Theodorakis lauds Tsitsanis, stressing the points which conform to his own personal ideas, politically and aesthetically:[4]

---

[2] For ecclesiastical four-part harmony in Crete and the Ionian, see Filopoulos (1990: 73–7).
[3] The concert in Nikaia: https://youtu.be/B11n6uctHD4; https://youtu.be/h-BEeXn9TqA [visit on 20/10/2010 and 10/5/2015].
[4] '... in the underground life that the ruling class had condemned him to' (Theodorakis's speech). This notion brings what Papanikolaou describes as the 'cultural politics of music' within the Greek post-war period to the forefront (Papanikolaou, 2007: 61).

> How did this miracle come to pass and this young man from Trikala [a city in central Greece],[5] who moved to Thessaloniki as a teenager, is able to incarnate in his soul and mind the quintessence of our musical tradition and to give it back to us in new simple and perfect musical forms?

In this phrase a considerable theory about Greekness is summarized, constructed by the first years of the Neo-Greek state, in complementary contexts such as those of the National Music School, ecclesiastical music and folklore: every authentic Greek piece sums up, with simplicity and perfection, the quintessence of a tradition, which is the very soul of the Greek people.

Theodorakis expresses his relevant views more analytically and vividly in his book titled *Μουσική για τις μάζες* (mousikí gia tis mázes, music for the masses), which was published in 1972, in which he explains what the right music for the people is and how it is to be created, which is by evangelizing the reincarnation of the old, which he considers entirely perfect, into the new, of which he is the bearer with his work. While speaking in front of Tsitsanis in Nikaia, he places 'Cloudy Sunday' on the prototype pedestal of such a reincarnation, disdainfully condemning all the other categories of song:

> Light [songs], light-laiko, Turkish, Indian, about infatuation, and vlach [with negative connotations concerning vlach descent],[6] pretentious highbrow and mixolydian; so much has been written after Cloudy Sunday, who can recall?

In this phrase all the intertemporal marginalized idioms are condensed, concluding with an indirect allusion to Plato's Republic, who excludes the mixolydian from the accepted modes. Along the lines of the ancient philosopher, Theodorakis takes it upon himself to separate the wheat from the chaff. His evaluation results in a lyrical address:

> Singer of romiosýni,[7] celebrator of the soul of our people. ... We, a whole generation, musicians and poets, acknowledged and acknowledge you as our teacher.

---

[5] The location of the city of Trikala: https://goo.gl/maps/cQukuRHXrvq.
[6] In contemporary Greece, the word 'Vláchos' does not denote origin from the region of Walachia, in the Romania-Moldavia of today. Instead, the word is used to imply the peasant, the uncultured, of low birth.
[7] The word 'romiosyni' (ρωμιοσύνη) is the focal point of this debate concerning Greekness, which is also the core of this book. Even though it shall be analysed further down, it must be noted here that the term 'romiosyni' denotes the historical continuation of the Greek nation from antiquity to the present, including the period of the Byzantine Empire as well. The word comes from the term 'Romiós' (Ρωμιός), which mainly refers to a Greek-speaking Christian resident (hence the word

The 'we' signifies here the responsible collective role that young artists should take on, always within a given historical continuation. To emphasize this continuation, Theodorakis skillfully proposes the Byzantine even though he does not clearly name it: the role of celebrator is attributed to not only the singer of the laiko, but also Greekness in the sense of 'romiosýni'.

Once his speech is completed, a scene of particular semiotic weight takes place. Tsitsanis gets up on stage and both artists perform 'Κάποια μάνα αναστενάζει' (kápoia mána anastenázei, some mother sighs) together.[8] The laikos composer plays bouzouki and sings in his characteristic nasal manner; it goes without saying that he also does his characteristic parallel third. Seated beside him, Theodorakis also sings with his own epic and staccato style, veering off occasionally into light melodic variations. In the last verse of the song, while Tsitsanis performs the lyrics 'ο λεβέντης να γυρίσει απ' τη μαύρη ξενιτιά' (o levéntis na gyrísei ap' ti maúri xenitiá, may her young lad return from the dismal foreign lands), Theodorakis dubs 'ξενιτιά' (foreign lands) to 'Ικαριά' (Ikariá – a Greek island, place of exile for the communists during the Civil War, 1946–9). The delivery with which he transforms the sorrow of the person in dismal foreign lands to the sorrow of the leftist exile is so emphatic, whereupon repetition of the lyrics Tsitsanis falls into line with him, albeit without enthusiasm. Despite the opposing rhetoric, in this particular instance it is not he who is the 'teacher'.

Indeed, Theodorakis often uses his pen to refer to the heritage of Greek music and to design its future. He feels bound to this cause, as is evident by the publication in 1974 of a series of texts, with the characteristic title *Το χρέος* (to chréos, the debt).

The negotiation of the renowned comparison between 'The Akathist Hymn' and 'Cloudy Sunday' is also found among these texts. Before proceeding to a more analytical approach, it is deemed necessary to pay attention to one of the 'regulating' principles, which after his favourite fashion he expresses in a categorical manner:

> Greek music heritage is fundamentally melodic. The elements of rhythm and harmony play a frugal secondary role in traditional music. (2011: 1147)

This phrase is once again dangerously generic. What is 'Greek music heritage'? What are its factual and aesthetic boundaries? Which are the criteria with which

---

'Rûm' in Turkish), which in turn comes from the word Rome, evidently from the transfer of the capital of the Roman Empire to Constantinople, which is referred to as the 'New Rome'.

[8] Parlophone, GO 3796-B. 74100-I, 31 May 1947: https://youtu.be/cn7b5ozshlg; https://youtu.be/B11n6uctHD4?t=214.

rhythm and harmony are granted a secondary role in relation to melody? The following is not dedicated to some relevant clarifications, but to the expression of his own Greek contributions:

> In my music there are elements of the Byzantine and folk. Besides, this is something that not only have I never hidden, but on the contrary have confessed it at every opportunity and, indeed, with pride. (2011: 1148)

To illustrate the integration of Byzantine melodic formations into folk and laiko, he invokes once again the relationship of 'Cloudy Sunday' and 'The Akathist Hymn,' citing his own transcriptions (see Music transcriptions 4.1, 4.3 and 4.5).

Music transcriptions 4.1 Transcription of 'The Akathist Hymn' by Theodorakis (2011: 1148).

In contrast to Petropoulos, Theodorakis uses the whole hymn, obviously aiming for a systematic and holistic analysis. However, also in his transcription, serious errors are found, since gravitations and idiomatic behaviours of the melodic lines are omitted. As a result, a D sharp on 'B' is missing, an F sharp on 'Γ' and a B flat on '7'. This is a serious omission for an approach that supposedly recognizes the historical role of Byzantine music, and where one would expect a more meticulous treatment of its singularity. In addition, there are serious mistakes in the text which, supposedly, its dynamic and its impact on the people render it a potential national hymn: 'ανακράζω σοι οι πόλεις σου' (anakrázo soi oi póleis sou, your cities cry unto you), instead of 'αναγράφω σοι η πόλις σου' (anagráfo soi i pólis sou, your city is attributed to you). The final cadence of the hymn holds especial interest, as it deviates from its two possible versions, which are the following.

Music transcriptions 4.2 Possible final cadences for 'The Akathist Hymn'.[9]

It is indeed a puzzle why Theodorakis chose the cadence that he did, as even European harmonized versions usually use the second version of the aforementioned transcript, and rarely the first. In any case, the cadence of Theodorakis has never been heard during the conduction of a service.

Trying to explain how so strong a melody is created, he identifies 'its character', which is 'its basic-characteristically internal relations that govern its "construction"', through its sound, which he calls 'its face' (2011: 1148). Having thus discerned form from structure, he explains how the evolution of music, generally, and European music, in particular, was based 'to a great extent on the evolution of the intervals in use' (2011: 1149). He matches classicism with the prevalence of 'perfect intervals of the fourth and the fifth as well as the intervals of the third', the romanticism of the overindulgence of the 'minor and major sixth and the minor seventh'. Nearing the end of the nineteenth century, he ascertains that 'we observe, timidly at first, the utilization of the remaining intervals, that is the diminished, the augmented, and the major seventh'. This 'evolution' in the perception of musical aesthetic focuses his attention on intervals as the exclusive tool of its negotiation. Consequently, he goes to the trouble of separately documenting small structural units of the melody of 'The Akathist Hymn', noting the degrees above it. This allows him to comment on the relative relationships, setting up a relative graph. The resulting interval relationships are to be used later, when he tries to detect them in 'Cloudy Sunday' as well.

In order to support his theory, Theodorakis extends his observations to another hymnological example, the 'Άλαλα τα χείλη των ασεβών' (Álala ta cheíli ton asevón, speechless be the lips of the impious ones), which he documents in the staff notation system, as seen in music transcription 4.3.

---

[9] Even though it shall be analysed in the rest of the book, it must be noted at this point that staff notation is used in the examples instead of the Byzantine in order to facilitate a less complex flow in the text and an easier understanding of melody motion for readers who are not familiar with Byzantine notation. In any case, it is relatively well known that there is a difference in the intervals in tonal well-tempered theory from that of Byzantine ecclesiastical music.

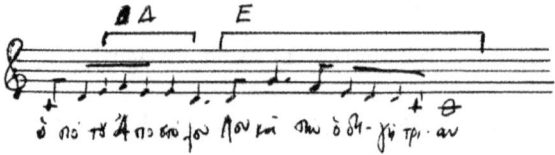

Music transcriptions 4.3 'Speechless be the lips of the impious ones' by Theodorakis (2011: 1151).

Here, too, the transcription has shortcomings. On the one hand, the word 'ιερωτάτου' (ierotátou, sacrosanct) from the phrase 'υπό του αποστόλου Λουκά ιερωτάτου την οδηγήτριαν' (ypó tou apostólou Louká ierotátou tin odigítrian, by sacrosanct apostle Luke the Directress) has been omitted. In addition, the descent on V (G/Di) under the tonic (C/Ni) pertains to a more Europeanized, choir version of the hymn. The hymn is chanted in the Plagal Fourth of note Ga: on the note Ga the modulation token, called pthorá (φθορά), of the note Ni of the Plagal Fourth is placed and, thus, note Ga is now called a Ni note. In the two instances where Theodorakis documents a descent on V, the traditional version of the hymn contains one of its most characteristic idioms: firstly, the melody reaches up to the lower Ke (A) and not Di (G), followed by an ascent again on the base (Ke-Zo-Ni/A-B-C). This case constitutes one of the primary singularities of the Plagal Fourth, as initially Ke (A) and subsequently Zo (B) are performed augmented, attracted by the forceful centre of the base Ni (C) (see Music transcription 4.4).[10]

Music transcriptions 4.4 Translation in staff notation of the opening of 'Speechless be the lips' by Georgiadis (1916: 59).

---

[10] Both Ioannis Protopsaltis (1905: 581–2) and Triantafyllos Georgiadis (1916: 59) use this particular way to document the hymn in their Paraclete (παρακλητικός, paraklitikós) rule.

A similar aesthetic is exuded by the immediate next phrase, 'των μη προσκυνούντων' (ton mi proskynoúnton, those who do not reverence). During a traditional performance, however, an intense confabulation between the Plagal Fourth and the Third echos is manifested, as at this particular point a cadence on Ke (A) takes place under the tonic (Ni/C), as a reflection of a common phenomenon that takes place in the Third echos. This descent is not included in the transcription of Theodorakis. The relationships of the degrees, as documented by him, are depicted in a graph for the second hymn as well, in order to be used subsequently for the deconstruction of 'Cloudy Sunday'.

Having thus interpreted the form and structure of both Byzantine hymns, it is easy for Theodorakis to suggest two ways with which he believes one can create if one wishes to, found on the premise of tradition: according to the first, 'we take any unaltered traditional melody, changing possibly its rhythm and placing our own harmonies below. In other words, we remove its face' (2011: 1152). As an example for this type of practice, he uses the work of the composer, believed by many to be the father of the second phase of the National Music School, Manolis Kalomoiris (1883–1962), titled *Symphony of Valour*, composed between 1918 and 1920,[11] in which 'The Akathist Hymn' is harmonized for a symphony orchestra and choir. According to the second way, the mimicry focuses on the structure. Here, too, the most conducive example he invokes is Vasilis Tsitsanis's 'Cloudy Sunday', where 'we discern assimilation of the deeper relation of Byzantine music, and in particular the two melodies we analysed before' (ibid).

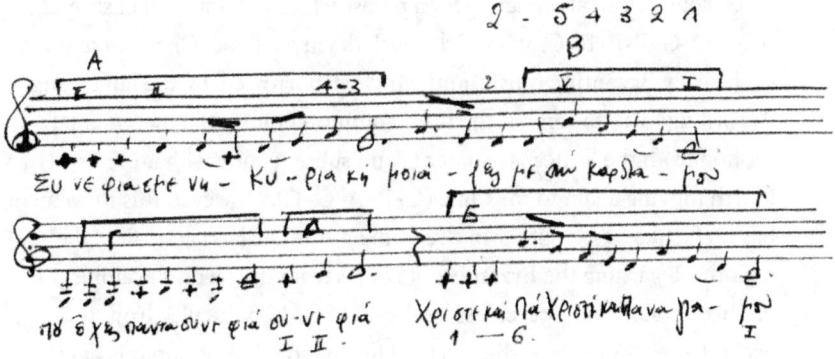

Music transcriptions 4.5 Transcription of 'Cloudy Sunday' by Theodorakis.

---

[11] Συμφωνία της λεβεντιάς, symfonía tis leventiás.

The assimilation of which Theodorakis talks about is detected, in his opinion, in five points:

1. The beginning of the melody 'is identical (three C notes before D) ... with the difference being that Tsitsanis, leaping, leads to a new descent (4–3), characteristics of the Neo-Greek laiki music' (2011: 1153). However, whether the opening musical phrase of 'Cloudy Sunday' is identical to that of 'The Akathist Hymn' depends on the version of 'The Akathist Hymn' which is chosen. For example, in the patriarchal performance, as illustrated in the recording of Iakovos Naupliotis, which shall be examined extensively further on, the sequencing of the notes does not support the argument of similarity. What is more, both Petropoulos and Theodorakis do not comprehend the dominant note Vou (E), which constitutes a common tool in both pieces and to which Tsitsanis 'leaps', as Theodorakis so characteristically writes.
2. The cadence in the phrase 'με την καρδιά μου' (me tin kardiá mou, with my heart) is evaluated by Theodorakis as typically Byzantine, as illustrated not in 'The Akathist Hymn', but in 'Speechless be the lips'.

Music transcriptions 4.6 Cadence of 'Cloudy Sunday' in Theodorakis transcription (2011: 1151–3).

Of course, it is rather daring for a phrase which is comprised of six quarter notes, D–G–F–E–D–C, and which concludes in the tonic (C), to be considered exclusively Byzantine music, and which is 'borrowed' by the laiko song.
3. According to Theodorakis, the third common point is the incremental motion from the tonic C to under G and subsequently with an interval of a fourth moving again to the tonic (C–B–A–G–C). However, this movement has no factual base, neither in Byzantine nor in the laiki version of the melody. Regarding the Byzantine, it comes from the second example of Theodorakis, the 'Speechless be the lips', and in particular from the excerpt '(χεί-)-λη των ασεβών' (cheíli ton asevón, lips of impious ones), which, as pointed out earlier, does not follow the traditional performance of the hymn. The same happens with Tsitsanis's song, as the phrase 'που έχεις πάντα συννεφιά' (pou écheis pánta synnefiá, which is cloudy all the time), which supposedly represents this incremental motion, is not correctly documented. In three major performances (Tsaousakis,

Ninou, Kazantzidis), this particular phrase begins on the II degree and leads upwards to the I of the next octave. Only in the performances of Tsaousakis and Ninou do the melodies 'meet' on the lyric 'πάντα συννεφιά' (pánta synnefiá, cloudy all the time). However, even in this case, in the performance of Tsaousakis there is an appoggiatura by the two singers (Tsaousakis and Bellou) on the syllable 'συ-(-vvε-φιά)', which is not documented; in Kazantzidis's performance, the performer makes a 'stop' on the word 'πάντα', embellishing the performance with his usual vocalese.

At this point, Theodorakis cites the transcription of the introduction of his own work, 'Το όνειρο' (to óneiro, the dream), from the long play vinyl titled *Το τραγούδι του νεκρού αδελφού* (to tragoúdi tou nekroú aderfoú, the song of the dead brother), we assume in order to underline its similarities to the Byzantine examples, as a creative integration of the ecclesiastical music into the laiki. He does not comment, however, clearly and above all Theodorakis depicts this particular melody in an elementary and monophonic way. The particular transcription is quite different from the recording of the piece, where Kostas Papadopoulos and Lakis Karnezis are first-second voice for the bouzoukis, and in fact with an interesting delay effect which doubles each note of the phrase, placing the new technological possibilities at the service of the laiki aesthetic.[12]

4. Theodorakis detects similarity in the point of repetition of the word 'συννεφιά', which takes place in the initial sequencing of the I–II degrees. We seem to find this particular sequencing in the opening phrase of 'Speechless be the lips', where three C notes lead to one D. In the case of one referring to traditional performances (or to the transcription of Georgiadis), one will ascertain that this opening phrase has the sequence: four C notes, E, D, C, B, A sharp, B, C. In other words, the interchange I–II does not exist (see Music transcription 4.4 mentioned earlier).

5. According to Theodorakis, the only significant difference between Tsitsanis and the Byzantine contributions is that he 'introduces a more modern element, the interval of the major sixth'. Here, again, the lack of familiarity with chanting repertoire becomes apparent. In reality, a plethora of documented Byzantine pieces exist which use the in question sequencing C–A (Ni–Ke), for example the brief (hirmologic) and the slow-brief (sticheraric) 'Κύριε εκέκραξα' (Kýrie ekékraxa, Lord I have cried) in the transcriptions of Petros Lambadarios.

---

[12] 'The dream', by Theodorakis. In *Το τραγούδι του νεκρού αδελφού*, LP (To tragoúdi tou nekroú adelfoú, the song of the dead brother): HMV, 2XGA 511–GCLP 5, 1962: https://youtu.be/ELljhj9Nklc.

5

The stance of the laiko musician

As a deduction of Tsitsanis's public record, that is, the release of his interviews to the press, radio/television appearances, his biography and the statements by his family and people close to him, he himself never admitted to any relation between 'Cloudy Sunday' and that of 'The Akathist Hymn'. This, however, did not prevent the permeation of the concept of the supposed relation in chanting, journalistic and the so-called 'artistic'[1] communities, especially in the world of the rebetiko enthusiasts.[2] The popularity of the argument is compounded by the fact that 'Cloudy Sunday' becomes a huge success immediately after its release and remains one of the timeless favourite songs of the modern Greek. This renders it a 'vessel of choice' for the correlation between Byzantine and laiki music, which seems to preoccupy Greek intellectuals intensely. The case of Sophia Spanoudi is widely known; starting off as an avid opponent of the rebetiko, she eventually, however, lauded Tsitsanis and converted to a staunch proponent of the new laiko character, in which she sees the 'transubstantiation' of many elements of the Byzantine melody (Spanoudi, 1951).

Nestoras Matsas, in his article published in 1952, admits that he initially resisted Spanoudi's ascertainment, but in the end he recognizes the justification: 'The authentic laiko song, the one that springs from the soul spontaneously, has prevailed and the more time goes by, the more its value emerges' (Matsas, 1952). Georgios Giannakopoulos's attitude is similar in his article published in 1960: 'This singular music [by Tsitsanis] is richly endowed with the influence of the Byzantine element.'

Well worth noting is the fact that the whole negotiation of the issue is spent on phrases that are in no way musicologically validated. It seems that the 'consent' which concerns an issue of 'national' character does not need proof from the

---

[1] Έντεχνοι, éntechnoi.
[2] Kostas Vlisidis calls the relative rhetoric 'rebeto-philological journalism'. See preface in Gauntlett (2001: 11).

aspect of music itself.³ Even the heretic poet Dinos Christianopoulos succumbs to this appealing argument: on 13 February 1961, in the newspaper Δράσις (drásis, action) his interview with Tsitsanis is published. Christianopoulos's closing comment is as follows:

> My mind travels way back, to our Byzantine roots. To the 'melodists' of our ecclesiastical music, to Romanos, Damaskinos and the others; poetry, music and performance was all theirs. And to the unknown singers and lyre players, who at dances and festivals improvised music and verse simultaneously. This is the place from which Tsitsanis comes, Genuine Greek, for whom music and poetry is one and the same.

The pretty picture painted here is profoundly poetical. For musicological science, however, it is extremely difficult to integrate into the same uniform frame musical creations that come from pre-capitalistic rural societies, the melodists of a long-standing ecclesiastical phonetic tradition and the all-inclusive urban locations of Neo-Greek entertainment. The very concept of 'composer' finds no common ground on the three levels: it is debased in the first case, where improvisation and re-creation play a vital role. It is important in the second, where the poet-composer is prevalent for many centuries, before handing over the reins to the composer-chanter.⁴ In the third case, the laikos creator unfurls in a completely different realm, where discography outranks all previous networks of performance and aesthetic influence.

In spite of this, the cliché is alive and well. In 1972, Leuteris Papadopoulos interviews Tsitsanis. In this conversation, which was first published in 1998, he asks him how he justifies the existence of Byzantine elements in his music. Tsitsanis's answer is disarming: 'I don't! My music is mine! Virginal!'. Even more disarming is his reaction in 1972 when asked by Giorgos Lianis: 'Is it true that Cloudy Sunday and The Akathist Hymn have a common metre and rhythm?' 'I am not a church-goer,' he answers (Tsitsanis, 1972).

In other words, not only does Tsitsanis not admit his 'interaction' with Byzantine music, but he also categorically states that he has no connection to it, even when pressured to support the opposite. This carries even more weight if we take into account his derisive diction as supportive of 'national' music and

---

³ At this point, Dafni Tragaki's chapter in *Rebetiko Worlds* (2007: 270–1) comes to the forefront, where a significant bulk of trite expressions concerning the descent of laiki music (occasionally Ottoman, too) from the Byzantine is presented.
⁴ See, for example, before the fall of Constantinople, Ioannis Koukouzelis; after the fall, Georgios Raidestinos, Petros Peloponisios and Petros Byzantios.

'Greekness', however, though, never mentioning ecclesiastical music. Indeed, he often speaks about the authentic Greek laiko song, of which he does, in fact, consider himself its representative.[5] When, however, Stathis Gauntlett asks him in September 1972 with which other musical idioms he has come into contact, he answers: 'I didn't know what Byzantine music was, nor eastern' (2001: 174–5).

In 1973, Giorgos Papastefanou, in a tribute to Tsitsanis, during the television programme 'Music writes history',[6] which he presents at the Station of the Armed Forces (ΥΕΝΕΔ, YENED), converses with the composer. One of the questions posed is what has influenced Tsitsanis while creating his own repertoire, so once again the popular question regarding tradition and Byzantine music has to be addressed:

> [GP] Have you been influenced by Byzantine music, let's say, or by folk or by any other kind of music?
>
> [VT] I have neither been influenced by folk nor by Byzantine music. I had a music world of my own, a special one. I have not been influenced by any other foreign music.[7]

On 2 June 1973, one of the most interesting interviews granted to Giorgos Pilichos is published in the newspaper *Τα Νέα* (ta néa, the news):

> [GP] I asked you the previous question, because some people, for example Ilias Petropoulos in his book 'Rebetika Songs', claim that between 'Cloudy Sunday' and the Byzantine hymn 'The Akathist Hymn' there are common points.
>
> [VT] Really, hey? Well why don't you start chanting 'The Akathist Hymn' and I will sing 'Cloudy Sunday', so we can see where the common points are, that my friend Ilias sees and I don't …
>
> [GP] All right. Let's start … (We both sing …)
>
> [VT] (Smugly): You see? Where is the similarity? I sang one melody, and you sang another. I know neither Byzantine music, nor do I go to church. I am not a 'church-goer'! Because of the work I do, the late nights, there is no time for church.
>
> [GP] I don't think that the correlation between 'The Akathist Hymn' and 'Cloudy Sunday', constitutes an implication that you consciously borrowed from this Byzantine hymn. Quite the opposite. Sophia Spanoudi herself has detected

---

[5] See, for example, Tsitsanis (1952, 1965, 1977, 1980 and 1983).
[6] Η μουσική γράφει ιστορία, i mousikí gráfei istoría.
[7] Tsitsanis-Papastefanou broadcast: https://youtu.be/imA1K9qlFgk [visited on 17/1/2016].

'Byzantine elements' which your songs undoubtedly hide – the expression is hers completely!

[VT] I don't know anything about this! This music that I write, is the music of my world! Because I am, let's say, neither a refugee, nor do I come from Constantinople, from those places which the Byzantine comes from anyway. I came from Karagounides [ethno-cultural group], I grew up in Trikala!

[GP] Yes, but the heritage, the roots of the Byzantine, are part of all of us. Besides, during the Occupation, you lived in Thessaloniki, a city with a Byzantine character, with a lot of refugees from Constantinople. Anyway, you should definitely understand that the presence of Byzantine elements in your songs does not constitute a reproach, but instead, proof that you are a gifted, a special creator.

Ten years later, in 1983, he gives an interview to the newspaper Ριζοσπάστης (rizospástis, radical) admitting a 'common starting point' for Greek music genres:

All forms of song, whether it is called folk or laiko, as I see fit to name it, have a common starting point. It is the hard times, the time when a people are deprived of freedom. Finally, the social conditions of life. (Tsitsanis, 1983)

It is expected at this stage that musicians of the laiko feel awkward to respond to the depiction that the rhetorics of Greekness in music have constituted. As we shall see in the following text, many are those who also burn with a desire for confirmation and recognition by the outside world, mainly in the subsequent years of revival and reenactment of the 1970s. It is with special interest to observe at this point that the word used by Tsitsanis when speaking about the music he serves is 'laiko' and not 'rebetiko' (Despina Michael, 1996. See also Ordoulidis, 2014: 37–41).

From the whole anthology of critique that we documented, the sole exception to the supposed 'Byzantine-descent' of Tsitsanis is the comment by Giorgos Leotsakos on 6 April 1974, in the newspaper Το Βήμα (to víma, the tribune). He relays the experience of listening to Tsitsanis sing 'Cloudy Sunday':

I will never forget how Tsitsanis himself sang 'Cloudy Sunday': with a poignant quasi-staccato at the ellipsis of every phrase, which he omitted from this wonderful song (and what a masterpiece of 'omission') the very song with which he is identified – his expressive stretching. (Parenthetically I would like to mention that this lamenting ellipsis of phrase, only more unexpected, we also see in instrumental traditional Burmese music). (Leotsakos, 1974)

Unfettered with the dogma of 'descent', Leotsakos's view, albeit emotionally charged, seeks objective references that could describe his aesthetic experience. Burmese music is the deduction made by his cosmopolitan culture. Even though this may seem too sophisticated, it is perhaps more acoustically interesting than the usual commonplace remarks regarding Byzantine music.

6

Manos Hadjidakis and laiki music

Hadjidakis is the first one who, not only as a composer but also as an intellectual, systematically and extensively engages in urban laiko song, defending it against the disdainful characterizations of which it had become the object from the 1930s.[1] The lecture he gave on 31 January 1949 at the Art Theatre[2] constitutes, in a way, the last stage of an over-a-century discussion about Greekness in music.[3] This lecture was delivered to the urban intellectuals of Athens, who were already preoccupied with a measure of the rebetiko, attributing it to vogue, as Hadjidakis himself characteristically says in his speech (see also Seiragakis, 2011). The acceptance of the rebetiko by Hadjidakis does not of course have the lofty considerations with the eclectic requirements imposed by the national school; it remains, however, an outsider approach, as he characteristically confesses some years later:

> At the time, I too, a bona fide kid on that period, first discovered, without drink or drugs, only with strong sweet coffee, Markos [Vamvakaris], Tsitsanis and Daskalakis. (Hadjidakis, 1988: 22)

While speaking in front of Athenian high society, which confronts anything laiko with great trepidation, Hadjidakis submits the rebetiko to the filter of Byzantine descent and Greekness (see Michael, 2015: 524).

> The zeibékiko[4] is the purest, contemporary Greek rhythm. On the other hand, the hasápiko[5] has assimilated a pure Greek singularity. It is on these rhythms

---

[1] For Hadjidakis's relationship with the rebetiko, see Tambakaki (2015). At this point, it is worth mentioning the first effort to direct public interest to the incriminated rebetiko, accomplished by Kostas Faltaits in his article 'Τα τραγούδια του μπαγλαμά' (ta tragoúdia tou baglamá, the baglamas songs), published in the magazine Μπουκέτο (boukéto, bouquet), edition 253, February 1929.
[2] As Polina Tambakaki notes, the 'Art Theatre' represents the name of the institution, while the name of the place/theatre was the 'Aliki Theatre' (2014: 544: footnote 28).
[3] For early influences of Hadjidakis by the rebetiko, see Seiragakis (2011). Generally, for the role played by the lecture but also the way in which Hadjidakis approached the rebetiko in it, see Gauntlett (2001: 79–81), Vlisidis (2004: 76–80) and Papanikolaou (2007: 71–5).
[4] A popular rhythm/dance, found both in urban and in rural settings. A great portion of rebetiko recordings of all periods is based on the zeibekiko rhythm/dance. For a thorough study of the people who were called 'zeibekoí', see Korovinis (2004).
[5] For the hasapiko, see Feldman (2016: 352–66) and Kokkonis (2017: 133–61).

that the rebetiko is structured, observing its melodic line, we clearly distinguish the effect, or rather, the extension of the Byzantine melody. (Hadjidakis, 1949)

What knowledge does Hadjidakis have of Byzantine melody? Theodorakis mentions in his texts that as a teenager he participated in the chanting choir; for the hetero protagonist of 'artistic' music, we have no information about initiation in the theory or practice of Byzantine music. As far as the world of chanting is concerned, both are considered 'outsiders'.

Nevertheless, Hadjidakis's lecture, in order to validate the value and the quality of the rebetiko, with which he has already started to engage in artistically, aims to prove the national cohesion which characterizes the succession of music from ancient to contemporary times, placing the rebetiko in the same context as Byzantine music and folk song.[6] Even here, though, the arguments are generic, without any musicological essence. Hadjidakis seems to support a concept, rather than laiki music itself, which he probably views rather selectively and warily.

Is then the content of the celebrated lecture overrated? Clearly, for the general acceptance of the rebetiko and its aesthetic establishment, which (in good part) Hadjidakis is credited with, not only because of his lecture but also because of his adaptations, it was Tsitsanis's role that was catalytic and the whole post-war laiki school. Through the pervasion that discography now allows, a new aesthetic of laiko song emerges even before the war, a characteristic example being 'Αρχόντισσα' (archóntissa, the mistress/lady).[7] Not only Hadjidakis but also Theodorakis uses this precise recorded material, and not the rebetiko with its marginalized verse, as, for example, 'ο Πόνος του πρεζάκια' (o pónos tou prezákia, the sorrow of the heroin-addict),[8] nor the ones that sound too Eastern, such as 'Τα λεφτά σου δεν τα θέλω εγώ' (ta leftá sou den ta thélo egó, I don't want your money).[9] Evidently, it is difficult to connect such pieces with their national musical ancestors. In other words, the rebetiko becomes acceptable via the 'benign' post-war school, and not in its entirety.

---

[6] 'Even though the triptych ancient Greece, Byzantine and contemporary Greece as an abiding unity is an ideology which Hadjidakis never really espoused to a great extent in his subsequent course, the presence of this ideology in this particular text prevails and deserves a thorough analysis' (Michael, 2014: 524). See also proceedings of the round table titled: 'Scholarly and popular intertexts in Neo-Greek music. Case study: "Six popular pictures" by Manos Hadjidakis'. Effects and Interactions; Proceedings of the annual conference of the Hellenic Musicological Society (Kokkonis, Ordoulidis, Anagnostou, Rombou-Levidi, Zoubouli and Tambakaki, 2019).

[7] Columbia, CG 1874–DG 6440, December 1938: https://youtu.be/smpBdQi4sIg.

[8] Columbia, CG 1348–DG 6185, 1936: https://youtu.be/1Ey8Egd22LI.

[9] Parlophone, 101338–B 21698, 1933: https://youtu.be/HxzkwpUQjAA.

'Artistic laiki music' (έντεχνη λαϊκή, éntechni laiki), as it is commonly referred to, is profoundly stigmatized by these aesthetic discriminations, on behalf of the 'authenticity' of the originals. In reality, the particular choices concern that which is more easily understood not only by its composers but also by its audience, remaining essentially uninformed. The 'translation' of the laiko into the artistic, whether it is done wittingly or unwittingly, as each composer self-commits to the musical language which he/she can manage with ease, was never the cause for an honourable and honest approach research-wise. Undoubtedly, Hadjidakis recognized and believed in the value of the laiko, often paying a touching homage, especially in his mature works. This does not go to show that he has a profound knowledge of it, as is seen from the way that he modifies it. The emulative bond which he forged with it is, however, so powerful that many of his popular-like pieces are incorporated into broader laiko repertoires.[10]

In the third edition of the album *Έξι λαϊκές ζωγραφιές* (éxi laikés zografiés, six popular[11] pictures) by Manos Hadjidakis, in his insert Giannis Papaioannou mentions that Hadjidakis 'sees [the laiko] as a ripe and powerful fruit of the land'. The phrase 'powerful fruit of the land' reveals the change in the recruitment of the rebetiko after its 'artistic' negotiation, with emphasis on the fact that it is of 'the land', that is, Greek.

The integration of the rebetiko into the corpus of the Greek psyche following the lecture by Hadjidakis experienced a long-standing course, with various individual ideological trends. Its 'artistic' intervention granted its place to faithful reproduction, if possible with utmost respect to the first performance.[12] Many times, it acquired folklore characteristics, accompanied by passéism and nostalgia, but also a feeling of authenticity and exclusive right concerning the genre, with a multitude of political and social extensions. Even the gesture of 'integration' itself did not stop being connected directly or indirectly nationally or even nationalistically (see Kokkonis, 2008: 43 and 83), as the issue of Greekness obfuscated rather than revealed its essence.

---

[10] For the relationship of Hadjidakis with the laiko, see Ordoulidis (2019).
[11] At this point, 'popular' is used, as it constitutes the official translation-release of the album.
[12] Outlining the custom and politics of the enka songs (a form of Japanese popular ballad), Christine Yano characterizes this form of reproduction as *ki o terasazui ni*: 'without showing off anything new' (Yano 2005: 195). This expression conveys the exact mindset which prevailed also in the mainstream revival of the rebetiko. For this issue, see Ordoulidis (2017b).

7

The music critic Sophia Spanoudi

The role of Sophia Spanoudi, pianist and music critic, is particularly crucial concerning the acceptance of the rebetiko by the Greek intellectual world, as her public statements played a determining role in the musical happenings of the country and the kind of approval these would be granted by the musical elite. Her articles and interventions in issues of music were so abundant that Manolis Kalomoiris, after her death, named her, 'the mother of Greek music' (Kalomoiris, 1952).

From the start, her attitude towards the rebetiko is negative. It is widely known the way in which the music critic congratulated the dictator Ioannis Metaxas[1] and the Censorship Committee on the banning of the song 'Βαρβάρα' (Varvára, Barbara) by Panagiotis Tountas.[2] A fanatical opponent of the rebetiko, she goes on to exaggerate and elaborate:

> It is of utmost urgency that the following songs must also be severely prohibited 'The rusk thief', 'Mean mother-in-law', 'Scratch yourself old man'[3] ... and numerous similar unspeakable ethnic Turkish-speaking and Albanian-speaking pieces [with negative connotations concerning descent], inferior, vulgar and base, which drag the art of sound through the dirtiest levels of musical squalidness. ... All these 'sorrowful remnants of slavery and loss' were transplanted and took root here, under the crystal clear Greek sky ... together with the native 'rebetiko' songs they constitute a trend of malodorous musical sewage. ... It is imperative that a responsible committee be established, comprising of leading Greek composers, the only ones who are worthy to ruthlessly throw every base

---

[1] Ioannis Metaxas was a militant and dictator, establishing his regime on 4 August 1936 and remaining in power until 1941.
[2] Columbia CG 1359–DG 6159, 1936: https://youtu.be/T7u4YWjdDps.
[3] 'Παξιμαδοκλέφτρα' (paximadokléftra), Victor Vi 58061–CG 750, 20 May 1930: https://youtu.be/7C9pX25SgP4; 'Κακούργα πεθερά' (kakoúrga petherá), HMV OW 267–AO 2011, 1931: https://youtu.be/7Z_jU2s6el8 and Columbia WG 152–DG 113, 1931: https://youtu.be/RT7GafsAYGU; 'Ξύσου γέρο' (xísou géro), HMV BG 520–AO 605, 1929–30: https://youtu.be/9GSfDe0lYIg.

and unworthy element into the fire, but also to filter the music of the laiko well. (Spanoudi, 1938: 82)

Clearly, Spanoudi's vocabulary conforms to the Metaxas dictatorship: 'unspeakable, inferior, vulgar, base, dirtiest, remnants of slavery and loss, unworthy, malodorous, sewage, squalidness', the songs of the laiko should be banned, thrown 'ruthlessly' into the fire. This censorious intervention is proposed as a 'filter' of laiki music, which would elevate it to the level of historical constitution of the 'Greek soul'. This constitution is mirrored in folk song, as directly descending from Byzantine music, as she writes in the newspaper *Τα Νέα* (ta néa, the news) in December 1946:

> The genuine soul of the Greek people is without question our folk songs ... that embrace sometimes the chromatic and sometimes the austere diatonic genus, oftentimes in harmony with the characteristic attributes of Byzantine music. (Spanoudi, 1946: 124)

This article, titled 'Denunciation of the defence', is in response to a publication supporting the rebetiko, titled 'The floor to the defence' by Paulos Palaiologou (*Ta Nea*, 23 December 1946). Content-wise, Spanoudis's article is identical to the article of 1938 cited previously; a journalistic carbon copy. The same journalistic carbon copy is also used on 17 February 1949, in her article titled 'Rebetika and bouzouki', published in *Ta Nea*. In this text, Spanoudi shows, one month after Hadjidakis's lecture on the rebetiko, that she is about to change course, something that finally happens, partially, leading to an article supporting Tsitsanis, in 1951. There is a lack of argumentation. Spanoudi repeats herself via generalizations, which do not have the validation that an adequate theoretical or practical knowledge concerning the musical genres in question would offer. Like many other so-called musicologists of the time and subsequently, she is an *outsider* who pigeonholes, evaluates and in good part censors the *insiders*.

They, who had been condemned because they 'drag the art of sound through the dirtiest levels of musical squalidness', within a span of twenty years are recognized as custodians of Greekness. Writing in 1951 in *Ta Nea*, Spanoudi distinguishes Tsitsanis and the 'genre' (author's inverted commas) which he serves thanks to its 'racial roots attributes':

> The 'rebetiko' of Tsitsanis is a musical 'genre' worthy of attention and mature in artistic essence worthy to be studied in every aspect and above all for the racial

roots attributes it presents. ... This is why this rebetiko music in its primitive on the surface form, often presents an appealing diversity with its rich scales. ... If we delve a little deeper into the study of these modes, we shall not take long to find a correspondence with the Byzantine modes. (Spanoudi, 1951)

One observes that all this talk is deprived of argumentation and validation. These have been substituted with generalizations, which are adapted to suit each direction her critique takes, even if this causes blatant inconsistencies. The 'racial' and 'roots' attributes and the dialectic concerning 'primitive' and 'complex' are flexible definitions, without carrying specific factual weight. This is why in the same text Spanoudi estimates 'that *"Cloudy Sunday"* is an evocative spiritual place, which fully transfuses the listener with its sombre atmosphere'. In order to commend, immediately afterwards, another song of Tsitsanis, 'To όνειρο της αδερφής' (to óneiro tis aderfís, the sister's dream),[4] she focuses on its narrative content:

> *'The sister's dream'* in its simplistic development narrates the tender sorrow of a young girl for her brother who is fighting for the motherland. She dreams about him and tells her mother that this is a good sign. The song ends with a fervent plea to the Holy Virgin by the two women, a most pure prayer pulsating with life-giving hope. (Spanoudi, 1951)

This 'brother who is fighting for the motherland' is one more projection of national character. The word used in the poem is 'ξενιτιά' (xenitiá, foreign land). Of course, this word is often used in Tsitsanis's lyrics in a manner that fluctuates between literal and metaphor, and there is a general admissibility that the particular song is inspired by the Civil War. It is, however, difficult to interpret the content with terms pertaining to patriotism and reverence that Spanoudi invokes. These terms are utilized, however, to lead directly to the 'Byzantine' footing:

> The 'Two boys', 'Make the bed, so I may sleep'[5] undoubtedly, hide Byzantine elements familial and modified to the intrinsic inspiration of the composer and to his fluid rhythms. (Spanoudi, 1951)

Factually, what urges Spanoudi, but also other music critics of the time, on to identify songs of the laiko with Byzantine music, is possibly the dromos Hitzaz, which always constituted the most representative sound of musical

---

[4] HMV OGA 1704–AO 2971, 14 November 1950: https://youtu.be/HwU7ZiYd-1g.
[5] Δυο παιδιά, dyo paidiá; Στρώσε μου να κοιμηθώ, stróse mou na koimithó.

orientalism, not only in Greece but also in Europe. From the particular songs that Spanoudi calls forth, the 'Two boys' is not easily identifiable. Assuming that it is 'Βίρα την άγκυρα παιδιά' (víra tin ángira paidiá, aweigh the anchors boys),[6] which she mentions earlier in the article, then it is subject to the aforementioned case. The 'Make the bed, so I may sleep'[7] is on the one hand Hitzaz, but a big part of the song (if not half) is structured within the Minore frame, transferring the tonal centre to the IV degree of the Hitzaz and generating cadences on it. The same happens with 'Aweigh the anchors boys', in the chorus where Tsitsanis presents the style which he himself has introduced, with contrapuntal activity in the voices, three in the chorus, on the IV degree and in Minore frame. How capable is Spanoudi of perceiving this type of detail? The domestic musical intellectuals receive an almost exclusively European musical education, and, on occasion, Byzantine too: their musical experiences, outside of the high-status systems are restricted, and usually directed to urban music, also of European descent (see Kokkonis, 2012). Every deviation from this well-tempered sound towards the east/orient is perceived as *alla turca*, redefined by us as *alla byzantina*.[8] As far as the intellectuals of ecclesiastical music are concerned, being in the position to comprehend more easily the stylistics of the laiko, they are hemmed in by other types of stereotypes, as we shall see further down, turning their back to the experience of the laiki performance.

Initially, not only Manos Hadjidakis's lecture but also the aforementioned article by Sophia Spanoudi was considered 'seals' of approval for urban laiko song and its re-evaluation by intellectuals and musicians themselves. To these two texts we will submit a prior third, an article by Manolis Kalomoiris in the newspaper Έθνος (éthnos, nation) 08 January 1947. With his usual belligerent rhetoric, the 'patriarch' of the National Music School states in the article that he prefers the hashish songs and the amanés (αμανές)[9] to the foxtrot and the tango.

---

[6] HMV OGA 1537–AO 2912, 15 December 1949: https://youtu.be/Rx5BtcE2njA.
[7] HMV OGA 1670–AO 2964, 12 September 1950: https://youtu.be/AKlj2BSop4k.
[8] 'The spectrum of manifestations of the relevant pursuit begins with serious efforts to detect ancient Greek (or at least Byzantine) descent in music, instruments, dances …' (Gauntlett, 2001: 63).
[9] The amanedes (plural of amanes, also called manes and manedes) could be compared to the Turkish gazel. They concern vocal improvisations, based on modal music entities, and we see them in various forms and expressions. Despite this, we understand, from historical discography that a large category of amanedes has been created, characterized by an alla greca disposition, regarding a series of characteristics, such as performance and technique practices, form, instrumentation and so on (see Kokkonis, 2017; Ordoulidis, 2018; and Kounas, 2019).

He is, however, for the education of the people, in order for them to turn to purer Greek sounds.[10] The three approaches are quite different from each other. However, a common characteristic is a selective, from the aforementioned, access to the laiko, which paves the road for its utilization, but not for its comprehension.

---

[10] 'Moreover, informed by Greek nationalist narratives of the "Turkish yoke," the view was expressed that Greek music declined and became corrupt under Ottoman rule, drawing upon the broader idea that Hellenism had suffered a cultural decline under foreign and despotic domination. In the creation of the "national school" of Greek music during the twentieth century, as prominently represented by the Greek musician Manolis Kalomoiris, the East–West problematization was very effective in the way "national" music was conceptualized' (Erol, 2015: 8).

8

Two key personas of laiki music

Perpiniadis and Keromytis

In their later life, many a laiko musician invoked Byzantine music as a keystone in their art. The more renowned of those who renounced the cloak of marginalization to adorn themselves with the robe of the Byzantine are Vamvakaris,[1] Keromytis and Perpiniadis, who from 'ruffians', who played 'drug' and 'Turkish' songs, were transformed into 'lauders' who performed 'Byzantine sounds'.[2] As Gauntlett claims about Perpiniadis, 'even the most mediocre educated performers of the rebetiko have adopted the practice of imparting prestige to the genre with reference to the Byzantium and Antiquity' (2001: 63–4: footnote 5). It is difficult to distinguish whether between the lines of the accounts lie purpose, vanity, self-censorship or honest conviction. The only certainty is that they are all absolutely groundless, and often contradictory. In order to examine them, the radio broadcasts of Sophia Michalitsi Tanga are of particular interest.

In the 1970s, Sophia Michalitsi Tanga is a radio broadcast producer and works at the National Broadcasting Foundation, subsequently at the ERT 'Second Programme', at which she seems to have been the director in 1977,[3] while in 2009 she takes on the post of director at the Radio Station of the Church of Greece.[4] During a series of broadcasts recorded at the state radio station, she interviews a series of musicians of the rebetiko.[5]

---

[1] In 1969, an LP titled *Ο Μάρκος Βαμβακάρης τραγουδά Μάρκο Βαμβακάρη* (o Markos Vamvakaris tragoudá Marko Vamvakari, Markos Vamvakaris sings Markos Vamvakaris) is released, composed of recordings conducted between 1963 and 1968. One can easily ascertain the connection to 'Byzantinism', through the font used, as obvious; see https://bit.ly/2MAvugc.

[2] See also Stathis Gauntlett (2001: 158), for the 'permutation of interest to the remote past and the search for "titles of nobility" for the rebetiko'.

[3] The information is from the personal channel of Giorgos Papastefanou on YouTube.

[4] The information is from an article in the newspaper *Ελευθεροτυπία* (eleutherotypía, free press) on 10 October 2009.

[5] These broadcasts have been publicized in the last few years on the internet, and in fact the sound is satisfactory enough to allow us to identify the speakers with certainty. The problematic point is that no further evidence is given for the validation of the broadcasts in question, and mainly their date.

Particularly interesting is the broadcast to which Stellakis Perpiniadis is a guest,[6] starting with a statement which causes Michalitsi to feel awkward; she goes on to interrupt him:

> [SP] There was relevance between Byzantine music and the rebetiko, the laiki music of that period, because of the amanedes. There were amanedes alla turca and Smyrna-style amanedes, which had no relation to Byzantine music.[7] The manedes of Smyrna originate from Balkan music: from Romanian music, from Serbian music and places like that.
>
> [SM] This is of no interest to us. We are more interested in …
>
> [SP] Yes, I just wanted to say, but it was nice! … The Minore was Minore. It is foreign, it is Romanian.

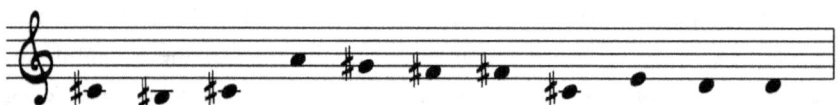

Music transcription 8.1 Musical example by Perpiniadis on the origin of the Minore, as performed during the interview.

> [SP] The Minóre, the Matzóre, tabachaniótikos, tzivaéri, galatá.[8]
>
> … Turkish music, Byzantine, has many drómoi known only to the one who plays the kanun …
>
> [SM] Would you mind giving us an example of a dromos not only in Byzantine music, known as echos, but also one in the rebetiko?

---

[6] Perpiniadis interview: https://youtu.be/W4wVlfxrOpY [visited on 26 October 2016]. Many thanks to Panagiota Anagnostou, who, while visiting the ERT archives, found the specific broadcasts. This specific pre-recorded broadcast, with Perpiniadis as a guest, was broadcast on 4 December 1975. See also the magazine *Ραδιοτηλεόραση* (radiotileórasi, radio-television), p. 303.
[7] Regarding the issues raised concerning Perpiniadis statements, see Kokkonis (2017: 97–132).
[8] 'Tabachaniotikos', 'tzivaeri' and 'galata' (ταμπαχανιώτικος, τζιβαέρι, γαλατά) are names attributed to a variety of modal music entities, whose meaning has not yet been examined in order to decode their definition. The labels of the historical records themselves constitute an extremely fertile primal source, as it is on these that we see this type of modal terminology. At times, we observe labels referring to modal music entities from which one can understand the composition of the general musical environment of specific locations and their aural reality. Such labels raise various issues concerning the utilized terminology in systematic musicology, which studies music genres from the 'East', as geographical locations are often used on the labels in order to define the characteristics of the modal music entity on which the recorded piece is based. Other times, however, they combine terminology, which reveals the *dialogical reciprocity* (see further in the following) of musical diversities. Often, via the labels the syncretism which prevails in geographically determined, but difficult to determine culturally, locations is demonstrated (see also Scott, 2015a and 2015b). The mutual appearance of terms which were subsequently connected to one of the two poles, West and East, reveal the in-between space, and it gives a sense of the aural reality of this location.

[SP] As we said before, Byzantine music is based on the taxímia,⁹ this is Byzantine music.

[SM] Yes, let's hear it. That is, acoustically, sing it, in order for our listeners to understand this difference precisely, or the relation, if not the difference.

[SP] Alright, what shall I sing, shall I sing my first song which I sang of Tountas?

[SM] Let's first start with your first hymn in Constantinople!

[SP] So you can see what it takes, what it takes from Byzantine music.

[SM] And then let's hear the Byzantine hymn, very nice!

[SP] Tountas says in his song:

[song]

[SM] Very nice!

[SP] This is alla turca, that is, it is in the eight-echos system as we said, Byzantine music.

[SM] Bravo!

[SP] And now, what shall we sing?

[SM] Its Byzantine counterpart.

[SP] Which the …

[SM] The first hymn you chanted in Constantinople …

[SP] *Την ωραιότητα* [tin oraiótita, the beauty], that one?

[SM] Bravo yes!

In the aforementioned excerpt, we initially observe that Perpiniadis offers some very interesting information regarding the modality of musical idioms of the Smyrna regions, and particularly the formulae usually called 'Minore', even naming some of its subcategories. It should, however, be noted that Perpiniadis, according to the limited biographical material available and mostly from his interviews, was born on the island of Tinos in 1899.¹⁰ His family moved to Alexandria in Egypt in 1900, where they stayed until 1906. They then moved

---

⁹ 'The taxími (plural taxímia) is a non-rhythmic improvisation based on the dhrómos of the particular song or on a combination of dhrómi. It is played at the beginning of the song. The other instruments may play the ίσο (íso), which is a single sustained note. The role of the taxími is either to show a musician's talent, imagination and skills, to emphasize the tonality and the dhrómos of the song or both. A taxími could also be played inside a song with the orchestra continuing to play the rhythm and the soloist improvising either based on the rhythm or not' (Ordoulidis, 2012: 31).

¹⁰ The location of Tinos: https://goo.gl/maps/FLB44LPAqgG2uXTp6.

to Constantinople, where they lived until 1918 when he entered the army and campaigned to Smyrna. Finally, following the end of the Greek-Turkish War, he moved to Piraeus. In other words, even though he was in a similar environment, that of Constantinople, he did not have the insider knowledge of the musical atmosphere of Smyrna, apart from the years of military service.[11]

Consequently, and during the whole of the interview, Perpiniadis identifies Turkish music with the Byzantine, implying that the terms are used as synonyms. When Michalitsi pressures him to elaborate on issues regarding modality, it seems that they have agreed beforehand to juxtapose a song by Panagiotis Tountas and a Byzantine hymn of the service of the Akathist Hymn, which Perpiniadis seems to have chanted in Constantinople. At this point, the performance of the song 'The doll of Kokkinia'[12] follows, and Perpiniadis comments, once again identifying it as 'alla turca' and the Byzantine octa-echos (οκτάηχος, or octo-echos: the theoretical system of the eight echoi). Subsequently, he performs a part of the hymn 'The Beauty of Your virginity', showing clearly that he, on the one hand, knows the melodic lines and the manner of performance, but on the other, he is not familiar with the chanting yphos, which he seems to mimic, but does not utilize it as a seasoned skill. In addition, the rhythmic conduct of the hymn, without adhering to a particular form, is closer to the style of an amanes rather than a hymn.

Can we discern from the aforementioned a relationship between Byzantine and laiki music? The producer seems determined to validate it; Perpiniadis's answers do not help. Another similar effort is again made in the interview with Stelios Keromytis,[13] which was broadcasted in two parts, on 9 and 16 October 1975:

[SM] Mr Keromytis, this tunings of the past that you know, perhaps you are the only one who knows it, does it bear any resemblance to the European tuning?

[SK] No, only the dromoi match.[14]

...

[SK] I'll try to explain in my own way: these douzénia [ντουζένια, rebetiko jargon for tunings] are tuned in another way, which the player must determine

---

[11] On details about Perpiniadis's life, see Chatzidoulis (1979).
[12] Kokkiniá: a place in Piraeus. 'Το κουκλί της Κοκκινιάς' (to kouklí tis kokkiniás); Odeon GO 1461–GA 1462, 1929: https://youtu.be/4uSYPgDWcys.
[13] Keromytis interview: https://youtu.be/_ntU8DwbUPM [visited on 2 May 2012].
[14] One can understand that Keromytis's answers are often senseless. It is precisely this that their English translation desires to reflect.

the handling too, because these douzénia should be handled differently. Because the instruments are tuned differently and the positions are changed.

[SM] And the whole sound is different.

[SK] Yes, the sound is more ecclesiastical, more Byzantine.

In this small excerpt, Keromytis tries to explain the various ways which were and are used to tune a bouzouki. Even though the terminology he uses is quite vague, assisted by Michalitsi and her interventions, the conclusion reached is that a different tuning results in a 'different' sound, which is characterized as 'more ecclesiastical, more Byzantine'. The comparison is logically what he previously names 'straight' or 'Italian' tuning, that is, D–A–D. In the second part of the broadcast, this from hearsay seems to have taken place on another day; questions are again raised concerning makams, dromoi, echoi and the consequential relationship between laiki and Byzantine music:

[SM] Mr Keromytis, are there dromoi that correspond to the ways of western European music? I mean, Minore-Matzore.

[SK] Yes, they are Minore-Matzore, they change, the ones, but not the dromoi. Because the melodies, let's say, the European ones are different.

[SM] Completely different!

[SK] Yes, while our melodies and especially the songs stem from ecclesiastical songs, from hymns.

[SM] Once you had told me that you heard a priest.

[SK] Yes, and from a priest who chanted, from his chanting, I copied and created a song.

[SM] Really?

[SK] Yes, as the priest said:

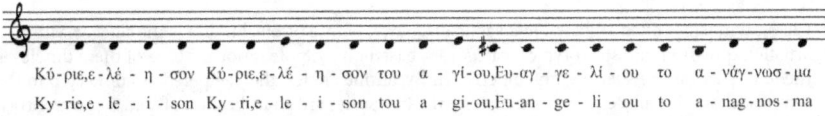

Κύ-ριε,ε-λέ - η - σον Κύ-ριε,ε-λέ - η - σον του α - γί-ου,Ευ-αγ - γε - λί - ου το α - νάγ-νωσ-μα
Ky-rie,e - le - i - son Ky-rie,e - le - i - son tou a - gi-ou,Eu-an - ge - li - ou to a - nag-nos - ma

Music transcription 8.2 Gospel by Keromytis.

[SK] And I created a zeibékiko and I say:

Music transcription 8.3 Keromytis song from Gospel.

[SK] From this melody of the priest, I copied and I created let's say a zeibekiko. That is, let me explain, our songs are ecclesiastical songs. ... They are the same. We have copied from them. And some people that condemn them, for me are completely ignorant.

[SM] Perhaps they don't understand them.

[SK] People don't know. But, those who have knowing [knowledge] of music, perceive it, that this thing stems from the church ...

In contrast to Perpiniadis, Keromytis seems to be full of confidence about the theoretical base of laiki music. Given the simplism of European music, which only uses two scales, in contrast to the diverse world of the East, it is obvious that laiki music, considering that it is richer than that of European music but also different from it, cannot stem from anywhere else but from ecclesiastical music. In order to support his argument, Keromytis assures us that he was inspired by the performance of a priest for the composition of one of his songs.[15]

If we are to be more meticulous in our observation of this example, we see an excerpt (which, apropos, cannot have come wholly from a priest, since the phrase 'Kyrie eleison' is performed by the chanter), which is performed based on the yphos of the κλιτόν (klitón, often compared with tilt – nişabur in makam), which is placed on the 'fifth or eighth degree of the natural diatonic scale of the Plagal of the Fourth echos, the well-known major mode' (Alygizakis, 2001: 98).

[15] Classical music is often affiliated to a vague discourse, whose ostensible aim is the categorization of artistic expression into stereotypical categories, based on a dipole rationale. One of these dipoles is the tempered (as prevalent) – untempered. In Byzantine circles, the 'tempered' is connected to the 'simplistic', and it replaces it out of courtesy: the two scales are an indication of 'paucity' in contrast to the rich modality of the East. Even in the meta-atonal era, for this stereotypical, oversimplified and, mainly 'from the outside' discourse, 'the tempered is related to tuning and is a technological achievement, that is, interference with nature' (Tombra-Lagopati, 2013: 178). Through a common ethnocentric perspective, it is not just the desire to prove the superiority of a culture (a type of music, in this case) compared to another, but rather compared to the whole world: 'A wholly humanistic perspective justifies the musician and scholar [Konstantinos Psachos, first teacher of the School of Byzantine Music of the Athens Conservatory] who in Greek music searches for the universal and (and why not?) genetic elements of world music mainly through the Greek tradition (Xanthoulis, 2013: 251).

In contrast, his composition, which Keromytis subsequently performs, initially vocally and then with the bouzouki, could be integrated into the modeness of the makam Muhayyer. The klitón constitutes, with the σπάθη and the ζυγός (spáthi, sabre and zygós, yoke), one of the χρόες (chróes, shades) of Byzantine music, which do not alter the scale or the genus[16] in which they are rendered, neither do they construct a new scale; they only propose 'small musical lines',[17] based mainly on the τρίχορδο formula (tríchordo, trichordal). In other words, they are transient modulations and they influence four notes; hence the acceptance of their influences on pieces which are constructed purely on scaling constitutions seems an exaggeration. Giving the narrative credibility, we could see in the association of the two melodies a moment of inspiration perhaps, but hardly a musical genealogy, as Keromytis claims. The irony is that the issue closes with the statement that those who have musical knowledge perceive the descent of the rebetiko from Byzantine music, unwittingly targeting the uneducated protagonists of the rebetiko, at the end of the day, self-censoring himself ...

---

[16] There are three genera (γένος, plural γένη, génos, plural géni): διατονικό, χρωματικό, εναρμόνιο (diatonic, chromatic, enharmonic).
[17] Panagiotopoulos (1986: 109).

9

Postlude

The discourse concerning the similarity between 'Cloudy Sunday' and 'The Akathist Hymn' brings to the forefront a more general issue, regarding the relationship of urban laiko musical idiom with that of Byzantine music. In the rhetorics examined earlier, a high-status intervention concerning the laiko is evident. The world of intellectuals, composers, music critics and journalists all seem convinced of the originating relation to the ecclesiastical tradition, which in itself, it goes without saying, is a link in the unbroken continuation of Greekness (see Kokkonis, 2008 and Tsetsos, 2011). No one is troubled by the fact that no other corresponding example in the huge discographical corpus of Tsitsanis is found, which includes no less than 554 original recordings. No one tries to listen to or understand the composer himself, who categorically states that he is not acquainted with ecclesiastical sounds. In spite of this, Theodorakis states early on his disposition to disassociate himself from the norms of the status quo:

> Because when one's argument is based on 'must', then one practises artistic morality and not scientific research. (Theodorakis, 1949: 159)

Scientific research in the particular field, seventy years later, continues to remain a substantial issue. Ideas and ideologies are deeply rooted in the unconscious, rendering them difficult to doubt. The descent of laiki music from Byzantine music is today commonly accepted and not negotiable, as witnessed with its introduction even in school manuals:[1] in the book *Μουσική-Τετράδιο εργασιών* (mousikí–tetrádio ergasión, music–workbook) in the third class of

---

[1] But even in musicological studies, which believe that 'studying, however, the chanting tradition, we shall discover the archetype of both folk and popular related songs' (Apostolopoulos, 2019: 585). Many times, in fact, for the confirmation of Byzantine descent, the following claim is enough 'in three languages, Albanian, Vlach [?] and Greek, the Ison in polyphonic song is called Ison' (Apostolopoulos, 2019: 582) or that 'we also have Kazantzidis [one of the most popular singers of the laiko] as evidence, that he would eavesdrop, as we say, behind the lectern of Sotiris Fotopoulos, a renowned chanter from Imathia' (ibid). If one listens to Fotopoulos, one realizes that his chanting practices do not follow those of the traditional and 'approved' chanting schools, as the combination of chanting together with other singing idioms is more than pronounced. In other words, if we use

junior high (2012), we see an exercise (page 35) where the initial phrases of the two pieces are cited; students are asked to circle 'the main notes of the song's melody "Cloudy Sunday" (notes, that is, where a syllable of the verse exists)'. Subsequently, they are asked to compare 'the two melodies regarding the rhythm and melodic motion. Are there common elements? Circle the correct answer: Yes or No'.

We shall ignore the arbitrary identification of 'main notes' with the syllables of the verses, which is in every aspect groundless. So, how is this particular rule defined when dealing with instrumental pieces? Or, what is valid for a melody of Byzantine music which belongs to the παπαδικό (papadikó, papadic) slow composition type, a type where a syllable lasts for many notes. It is typical that, exactly as we observed in the cases of both Petropoulos and Theodorakis, who introduce the comparison, the transcriptions of both pieces land up in school books without any reference to what performance they come from. 'National music' is not placed within historical context, pertaining to obscure and dubious 'prototypes'. Is there an aural memory which is not registered in given cultural structures and does not adhere to specific influences? The school of Sakellaridis clashes with the patriarchal yphos; 'Cloudy Sunday' is not the same to the ears of a student in junior high and to that of a mature rebetologist. Not to mention the fact that the book itself, and more specifically the main book (student's book), defines the rebetiko as exclusively directed lyrically to marginalized subjects, subsequently 'legalized' by Theodorakis, Hadjidakis, Mamangakis and other 'artistic' composers, who evolved it into the 'laiko song' (page 55). The association of the rebetiko with Byzantine music is a given in its pages, which invoke inaccuracies such as the identification of the musical dromoi with the Byzantine echoi (page 58), or the certainty that 'the musical roots of the rebetiko stem from Byzantine music and traditional songs from the Greek population of Asia Minor and the Aegean islands' (page 54). We do not know of any other gnostic subject in systematic education where scientific research that has been conducted both in Greece and abroad is bypassed to such a large extent. Certainly, regarding musical education, priority is given to ideological forms, which do not facilitate the comprehension of complex cultural phenomena such as that of music. This is a vicious circle, which begins with children and reaches

---

the logic of musical borrowing, Fotopoulos is the one drawing from the singing world of Kazantzidis rather than the opposite (see, for example, https://youtu.be/iDcnd3s3ANU).

parliament, where members of parliament are heard to use the exact same argument, comparing the two specific musical works, as in the case of Kostas Zouraris, who, while making errors in notes, tonalities, terms and so on, bases his analysis on that of Theodorakis's, in whose political movement he was a member, presenting the inseparable link of Hellenism between ancient Greece and the present (speech in parliament on 2 December 2015).[2] What is more, one can detect specific stereotypical expressions even in documentary-type programmes, such as the very popular and old 'On this day in history in the 20th century' and its sequel 'From Freud to the internet',[3] productions of National Television. The programme for 8 February, mentions Nikos Xilouris, a popular singer mainly because of his collaboration with composers of the 'artistic' laiki, such as Stauros Xarchakos and Giannis Markopoulos. The programme says verbatim: 'It was a rare voice. Authentically laiki, unpretentious, carrying the Byzantine tradition within, the folk music of Crete, the gallantry of its people, the melody of the Cretan dialect'.[4]

At this point, it is considered essential that a parenthesis be opened, concerning systematic music education in Greece and some of the innumerable murky points of the relevant legislature.[5] Academic education as well as music schools falls into the domain of the Ministry of Education, while music education in conservatories (state and private) falls into the domain of the Ministry of Culture. The study programme in music schools includes the teaching of traditional Greek music, Byzantine music and Western classical music. Both the Ministry of Education and the Ministry of Culture (that is, not only universities and music schools but also conservatories) award officially recognized degrees for both classical and Byzantine music. However, only the Ministry of Education recognizes studies concerning traditional music.

Even though the urban popular styles are widespread, Greek conservatories deny them the right to be certified through state recognition. One example of this disregard of popular music studies in Greece is the statute of the Greek State Conservatory (on which all other conservatories base their statute and

---

[2] Zouraris's speech: https://youtu.be/s90TPe7uLcs.
[3] Από τον Φρόϋντ στο διαδίκτυο, apó ton Freud sto diadíktyo.
[4] Programme 'On this day in history in the 20th century' (σαν σήμερα τον 20ό αιώνα, san símera ton 20ó aióna) – Nikos Xilouris: https://youtu.be/vARmcsUlMP4.
[5] The ideological background of the relevant legislature is connected to the period of the 1980s onwards, which is more analytically described in the second part of the book, and more specifically in the chapter '"The musical issue" at the forefront once again', where the activity of Simon Karas is examined.

teaching systems), which does not include the teaching of the popular music genre beside the other Greek popular genres (urban or rural). An excerpt from the official website of the State Conservatory of Thessaloniki mentions the following:

> The legislative decrees 1445/42, 2010/42, N. 2870/54 and the royal decree of 1957 which were published in the Government Gazette 229/11-11-1957, determine to this very day the framework of music education in our country.[6]

Another excerpt from the website of the State Conservatory begs askance: 'The purpose of its establishment was the teaching of European music and parallel support and promotion of serious Greek music' (www.odiokrat.gr). There are two obscure points here that need clarification: (1) European music must be taught, while Greek music is to be supported and promoted. Why not do both for both types of music? (2) What does 'serious' signify?

Moving on to another big part of music education, the music schools shall be mentioned. Concerning their establishment and operation in 1988, the Government Gazette states: 'The purpose of a music school is to prepare and train young people who desire to follow a professional musical direction.' This conjecture leads one to believe that there is to be no discrimination among the types of music that the music school intends to teach. Article 10 of the same Government Gazette states:

> The technical equipment of the junior high music school of the previous paragraph (that is, Pallini Junior High School) of conventional European and Greek traditional musical instruments and technical means ... is vested in the centre of contemporary music research.

In the term 'traditional music', is the urban popular included or do we mean only rural? In other words, do we indirectly determine the repertoire one is to be taught? The term 'traditional music' monopolizes all the articles published in the Government Gazette that concern music schools.[7]

---

[6] It makes one wonder about the reason why this decree, from 1957, has yet to be re-examined.

[7] For example, in the Government Gazette of 1989, Article 13, we read: 'In junior high music schools the music education subjects are the following: General Music, Traditional Music (vocal and orchestral), Choir, Contemporary Music Technology, Art of Speech Laboratory, Expression Skills, Hymnology and Individual music lessons.' Once again we need clarification concerning the term 'Traditional Music'. Is the guitar which is used in the rural music style included? If so, which guitar? The guitarist from Epirus who accompanies the dance in three is completely different from the Cretan, one who accompanies the pentozali. A different technique is used by the musician of the rebetiko, and Hadjidakis utilizes the instrument in a different way in his popularized pieces.

As regards the same article in the Government Gazette, at the end it describes the syllabus and mentions the following:

> The purpose of the Music subject is to cultivate a musical sense in the students and to generally contribute to their spiritual and mental development with the correct vocal practice, the listening to and familiarisation with good music, in particular authentic traditional and contemporary Greek music.

A spontaneous question immediately formed after having first read the aforementioned article: What, after all, is bad music? In addition, expressions such as 'in particular authentic traditional music'; is there 'fake' traditional music and, if so, which is it?

The supposed dependence of laiki music on Byzantine certainly elevates the latter, alluding to spiritual creation, not just hegemony (something that leaves no room for doubt), but exclusive. This is irrational for a historical region so rich in its diversity of timeless expressions of art, and more than anything it does no justice to Byzantine music itself, restricting the critique of evaluation to paltry 'doxology'. Justifiably, the 'crown' that Byzantine music wears grants it a singular paternalism over other musical genres. This is the reason why nobody has ever thought to comment on the reverse effects, from the laiko to ecclesiastical music, even though these are not at all negligible. For those in the know, it is evident that during the performance of the word 'Trinity' (τριάδι, triádi) of the 'Cherubic hymn' (χερουβικός ύμνος, cherouvikós ýmnos), the chanter 'converses' with other high-status and popular urban idioms, or during the 'Leitourgiká' (λειτουργικά) of the Plagal of the First echos, a clear modal Minor atmosphere is structured (the so-called 'Minore' in Greek popular music) with the holding of the ison showing an interesting and continual motion, counterpoint to the melodic lines and overstating the interchange of the I–V degree. Even in 'polychronismós' (πολυχρονισμός),[8] we observe counterpoint motions of two or even three voices. If chanting is not cut off from history, and considered a living art, its aesthetics evidently interact with the rest of urban music. The discourse among musical genres cannot only be understood as a strictly mimicking relation. With reference to theological vocabulary, we talk about 'dialogical reciprocity' (Loudovikos, 2013: 270),[9] where each genre maintains its individuality and its freedom.

---

[8] Πολυχρονισμός – many (polý) and years (chrónos): hymns chanted for the bishops but also for senior notables, wishing them many years of life.
[9] Διαλογική αμοιβαιότητα, dialogikí amoivaiótita.

During the process of performance, both the laiko and chanting manifest their ultimate syncretic core, having at the centre of their value system such a 'dialogical reciprocity'. For music, but also generally for the cultural reality which it represents, this relationship could be characterized as 'alliloperichoresis', a co-existence/reciprocal interpenetration.[10] This word was first introduced by Maximus the Confessor, and has since then taken an important place in the philology of the founding fathers,[11] which describes the fundamental Orthodox concept of the 'person' (πρόσωπο, prósopo):

> In a general supposition, the 'person' is defined as a specific human presence, found in a particular, but under no circumstances static, type of existence. Its basic foundations being; a human entity that maintains its own identity and renders its difference towards other entities as a capability not of exclusion or conflict but of mutuality and co-existence. (Kapsimalakou, 2012: 40)

In the cultural core of Orthodoxy, it is a non-sequitur to imply that a conformation such as that of Byzantine music has a sovereign role, as a genre 'father' from which any other type of worthwhile music flows.[12] When referrals are accounted for as origins, the genres that are compared to it abandon their identity, their freedom and their individuality, and they cannot be considered autonomous and self-contained entities. If, in contrast, we make an effort to comprehend the diversity of Greek music through this relationship of co-existence, certainly new paths will reveal themselves in order to facilitate the understanding of Greek musical tradition, above and beyond sterile stereotypes.

---

[10] Αλληλοπεριχώρηση.
[11] See Prestige (1928). But nowadays, younger theologians, such as Father Nikolaos Loudovikos, revisit this complex concept (see Loudovikos, 2013).
[12] In 1969, during the Junta of the Generals, a film titled 'Ο τζαναμπέτης' (o tzanabétis, the trouble maker) is released, directed by Kostas Karagiannis and produced by Karagiannis-Karatzopoulos. The same year that the aforementioned album 'Markos Vamvakaris sings Markos Vamvakaris', which used the Byzantine font on the cover, is released, two years after the acquaintance of Aggeliki Kail with Vamvakaris (see Vellou-Kail, 1978), and, generally, the same period that the interviews with the protagonists of the rebetiko take place. Approximately thirty-four minutes into the film, we see that Savvas (Dimitris Nikolaidis), one of the protagonists in the film, while being the conservative one in the family, always trying to lead the rest onto the straight and narrow, the path of the church, has returned from a nightclub, the so-called bouzoukia, having indulged in debauchery. In the scene in question, one of his brothers wants to know why he went to the bouzoukia, asking, 'At the bouzoukia, man? You! A man of ecclesiastical circles?', only to receive Savvas's disarming reply, 'Well, the bouzoukia are, after all, the evolution of Byzantine music'.

Part two

The two musical worlds: The Byzantine and the laiko

10

The Greek nation state and ecclesiastical music

The musical history of the contemporary Greek state, and in particular the relationship between Byzantine and laiki music, is cast on a multifarious and cross-curricular canvas, which historical circumstance renders even more complex.

In 1832, when the 'protocol of independence of the Greek state' is signed in London, what is 'its' music? And in subsequent years, how do musical 'annexations' follow geographical ones (the Ionian Islands in 1864, Thessaly in 1881, Macedonia in 1912, Epirus and Crete in 1913, Thrace in 1919, the Dodecanese Islands in 1947)? Does 'Greek music' include Kerkyra (Corfu), Crete and Macedonia before their political integration into Greece? The music of the refugee population of Asia Minor and Pontus, who acquired Greek citizenship after 1900? What is the relation between the high-status and that of the laiko element in this historical course? And in particular, what is the discourse between laiki and ecclesiastical music?

The questions posed are interrelated and difficult to negotiate separately. At the same time, however, it is impossible to sketch the cultural mosaic which comprises Neo-Greek music throughout the ages in a few pages. We shall try to contribute to its understanding with a new examination of the facts, getting as close as possible to the pragmatics of the examples. Following modern methodology trends, which shun forms of grand interpretation in order to focus on the musical events, using as much as possible an insider approach, with the musical sound as a starting point, priority is given to the last, without of course ignoring both its social and cultural environment. Causes and actuations, rejections and influences, movement in space and time, innovations and effects, social and aesthetic trends, official and unofficial policies, all determine the diverse aspects of the music phenomenon, which is obviously not restricted to its aural dimension; however, this last point is a safe guide in order for us to examine all the aforementioned through a coherent prism, with the hope that at the end of our route we will once again find ourselves at the junction that constituted the starting point of this book, that is, the comparison between 'The Akathist Hymn' and 'Cloudy Sunday'.

It is generally accepted that Greek music is not born with the revolution of 1821.[1] As all of the Neo-Greek culture, it is forged through evolutions of which it is rarely the direct target, while most times it concerns politics and society in general. In any case, the Neo-Greek identity is defined within an anguished political atmosphere, which constantly brings the question of 'Greekness' to the forefront, in a multitude of diverse ways. Inevitably, this influences the relation of Byzantine music with that of laiki in a determining way.

In a world of nation states, after the demise of the grand empires, issues of national self-determination are charged with a particular intensity. The geopolitical position of Greece between the stereotypical geographical boundaries of East and West, but also the restoration of the connection between past and present, which has been broken by the Ottoman era, plays a defining role in this self-determination. Often functioning as precious provisional sources, while other times functioning as a Procrustean bed, it seeks to maim complex cultural phenomena. Given that cultural boundaries do not follow the rationale of political geography, rarely converging with all sorts of nationalisms, and even nationisms. Imagined communities[2] and invented traditions[3] come forth to correct the deviations, fabricating *functioning realities*, which are supported via one of the most powerful means available to the official ruling power, the educational system. What George Dertilis calls 'mental foundations', that is, 'experiential receptions, perceptions and ideas [which] are accessible not only to scholars and the educated bourgeoisie but also to people from a wide social spectrum' (2015: 348) are capitalized on right here.

An academic, Fallmerayer, is the one who initiates the domino effect of ideologies and politics that signify the Neo-Greek identity.[4] The answer to the question of the relation between contemporary Hellenism and that of ancient, posed by the German scholar, comes from Konstantinos Paparrigopoulos, who sees the historical course of Hellenism as culturally ceaseless, albeit divided into three

---

[1] One can find a chronicle for the 'Greek song' by Lambros Liavas: *The Greek song from 1821 to the 1950s* (2009).
[2] Benedict Anderson, *Imagined Communities – Reflections on the Origin and Spread of Nationalism* (1991).
[3] Hobsbawm and Ranger (ed.), *The invention of tradition* (2000).
[4] See Fallmerayer (1827, 1830, 1984, 2002 and 2014).

main periods, ancient, medieval and contemporary.[5] His introduction shall have henceforth the role of regulator, defining the parameters of the discourse in clear and inviolable terms. Within this frame three important intellectual premises set their political course, within whose bounds the environment for the negotiation of musical issues is determined: Greek folklore studies, the Church and the National Music School. Initially, these premises act on parallel levels, without evident common signs, but with a common philosophy, which connects them on strategic levels, as, for example the publication of folk song collections. So, collectively, they created a common denominator, whatever concerns the historical continuation of Greek music, following Paparrigopoulos's charter: Greek music educes its origin and prestige from ancient Greece. In the next link of the historical chain, the Greek Byzantine is disseminated, whose leading musical vector is the Greek-speaking Eastern Church. The 'reincarnation' of this musical core in the folk song of rural Greece completes the evolutionary course of Greek music.

Given the subtractive character of musical art, tangible evidence of this continuation was impossible to demonstrate concerning the connection of the first two links. The connection, however, of the last two is crucial; it is not by chance that Chrysanthos concerns himself with this issue in the publication of his *Great Theoretical Treatise* in 1832. The content of this historical text echoes the findings of the Commission of the Patriarchate of Constantinople, formed in 1814 in order to systemize ecclesiastical music and renew its notation system.

> Our ancestral music relics, which, by general admission, connect us very closely and inextricably with that immortal antiquity, one sees them on the one hand in the sanctum of our Holy Church, whose venerated and solemn melodies are scorned with disrespect, on the other, in our folk songs, which are also abhorred by the supporters of the pernicious pseudo-culture that came from the West. (Artemidis, 1905: 4–5)

The self-evident Greek music is constantly threatened by the traditional enemy of Orthodoxy, the 'pseudo-culture' of the West. Early on, it is evident that authentic ancestral Greek music is automatically Byzantine-like and anti-European. A century later, the rapporteur of the National Music School, Manolis Kalomoiris, expresses himself in exactly the same rhetoric:[6]

---

[5] For the national view of history and the role of Paparrigopoulos, see Liakos (2001).
[6] See also Xanthoudakis (2011: 55): 'The "ideology of continuation" supports that two traditional types of music were nurtured in Greece – the music of the Eastern Orthodox Church and folk song – they maintained "genetic" characteristics of ancient Greek music, and the burgeoning trend

This tonal feeling unifies through the passage of time, creating an invisible golden musical chain, the Greek people, not only with their ecclesiastical Byzantine tradition, but also with the ancient Greek music theory. ... And we can, I think, support, without exaggerated jingoist selfishness, that the irradiation of Greek music, both in the glorious time of Alexander the Great, and later with the glory and reputation of Byzantine ecclesiastical music and from the supreme culture of the Hellenic people that the music of the Eastern and Slavic people was influenced to a much greater extent than the opposite during the years of enslavement of the Nation which could have marked the musical events of our people. (Kalomoiris, 1946)

However, the ideology of continuation is tested in musical practice, and Byzantine music is not dealt with equally by both musicians and researchers alike: George Lambelet, Pericles Aravantinos, Ioannis Sakellaridis skillfully exclude it from their theories, but the overwhelming majority of their counterparts propose it as an obvious connection to folk song.[7] Soon two musical camps are established, each expressing its own aesthetic and ideology. The first camp is the pro-European perspective, with a strategic point of reference being the Conservatory of Athens, established in 1871 and functioning in 1872. Advocated, of course, by its first director, the composer Alexandros Katakouzinos, Queen Olga and Dimitrios Koromilas's newspaper Εφημερίδα (efimerída, newspaper), in circulation from 1873 to 1922, all champion the Westernization of Greek music, including ecclesiastical, and subscribe to the musical 'world' of the *café chantants*, which had been functioning in Athens since 1871.[8]

The opposing camp is the pro-Byzantine, with the strategic point of reference being the Holy Synod and the chanting world. Advocated by the newspapers Εθνοφύλαξ (ethnofílax, guardian of nation), Αυγή (augí, dawn), Στοά (stoá), Αιών (aión, century) and Αλήθεια (alítheia, truth), it supports, as much as possible, the intact integration of the Byzantine into the modern musical customs. In

---

of antiquity-lovers which thrived approximately at the end of the 19th century petitioned these two types in an effort to revive the glorious – but lost – musical past.'

[7] For example, writings by the following have been supporting through the ages this triptych: Sigalas (1880), Artemidis (1905), Pachtikos (1905), Eutaxias (1907), Remantas and Zacharias (1917), Kalomoiris (1935 and 1957), Psachos (1978), Theodorakis (1986). Regarding the investigation of this musical historical continuation, see Beaton (1980).

[8] See Chatzipantazis (1986: 24–9). In addition, Chatzipantazis notes that from 1886 a boom of the amanes is observed which is prevalent in Athens for approximately ten years (1986: 30–1), while from 1871 a controversy between advocates of the French operetta and those of traditional customs rages (1986: 32–3). Another musical heterotopia must also be included, by the name of karagiózis (καραγκιόζης, shadow puppetry), which constitutes a reality perhaps even earlier than 1860 (see Myrsiades, 1976).

the background, it treats the musical 'world' of the *café amans*, which had been functioning in Athens since 1873 and where familial relations of traditional musical genres are confirmed, in a friendly manner.

During the last quarter of the nineteenth century, a polemic atmosphere between these two camps prevails, which Chatzipantazis (1986) describes most vividly. In this context, the 'suitably-Greek' 'national' characteristics of music easily absorb 'Western' or 'Eastern' influences, in the latter case even with the invocation of Arabic or Turkish instruments (Chatzipantazis, 1986: 37). In reality, the conflict concerns two atavisms, the anti-Turkish and the anti-Western. Primarily, the former is excused by the long-term Turkish occupation; the latter is attracted by the reaction to the foreign-imposed, royal dominion. However, the foundations and their dynamics are much more complex.

A characteristic example of the time is Isidoros Skilitsis, a scholar from Smyrna originally from the island of Chios, who leads the pro-European camp. He advocates the direct connection of the ancient world with that of the contemporary one, rejecting the 'Eastern' culture of the Byzantine and by extension its music. In one of his lectures at the Varvákeio in 1874 he, indeed, proposes replacing traditional ecclesiastical music with European polyphony. His argument is that the latter 'constitutes a genuine "daughter" of ancient Greek music, while Byzantine music is nothing but a barbaric convolution of Judean, Arabic and Turkish loans' (Chatzipantazis, 1986: 38).

Almost a decade later, Ioannis Sakellaridis supports the exact same theory, adopting an aphoristic attitude opposing the Turkish-like easternness: 'Having been purged [the melodies] of the contamination of arrhythmia and discordance; enfettered by long-time slavery ...' (1909: α'). An antiquity-lover, early on, he expresses his inclination towards the ancient authors and their theories (see 1880, 1895 and 1909), while he publishes musical texts of Byzantine hymns in European musical notation (1893, 1909, [n.d.]). These inclinations are incidental of a major controversy, which is transferred to the institutional level. In Φόρμιγγα (fórmiga, phorminx), 27 May 1902, number 16, it is announced:[9]

> The Holy Synod convened today and spoke at length about the issue of Byzantine music. Subsequently the circular was signed, which will be sent to all ecclesiastical authorities, recommending abolition of the four-part harmonization and the reinstatement of traditional Byzantine music. On the proposal of the president of

---

[9] The *Formiga* is mentioned frequently in the book. It is a periodical/newspaper of that period whose content constituted issues regarding chanting and, partially, folk song.

the Holy Synod S. Methodius, a document was drafted and sent to the Ministry of Education indicating by the Holy Synod the lack of suitably educated chanters and requesting provision by the Ministry of the necessary funding towards a Byzantine music school and the education of chanters.

This decision is instrumental for the developments, shaping not only new controversies, but also policies, with a direct impact on a wider social scale. On the one hand, they often reveal the agonizing search for identity, which leads to bizarre situations and practices, which perhaps cannot be excused even by those who inspired them. Antonios Sigalas was one such case that we shall examine further on.

Antonios Sigalas was a chanter from the island of Santorini; apprenticing at the Patriarchate he took the initiative to publish in 1880 a Συλλογή εθνικών ασμάτων (syllogí ethnikón asmáton, collection of national hymns), which he documented in Byzantine notation, intended to be used by way of a musical manual by apprentices. In the introduction, he stated his methodology:

> I did my best to preserve and not to misrepresent each authentic melody as much as possible each time, in the way it was sung then, administering a manner on the one hand vivacious and austere [clear and loud voice], on the other, simple and easy. In order for beginners, but also for more advanced musicians, and those with little experience in our ecclesiastical music to be able to sing fluently and without much preparation. (Sigalas, 1880: 5′)

The content of the collection is rather scholarly, so what does the 'genuine' melody consist of? And how is it possible to document the hymns and/or the songs without tampering, while at the same time simplifying their melodies in order for them to be performed by even an inexperienced singer or chanter? The book begins with 'Δέησι προς τον Θεόν υπέρ των Ελλήνων' (déisi pros ton Theón ypér ton Ellínon, supplication to God for the Greeks) (see music transcriptions 10.1 and 10.2).

The lyrics of this prayer are quite novel:

> Supplication to God for the Greeks
>
> Zeus, God of Gods and men, as well as king of all
> You, father of the Muses and the Graces, of Athena, of Hermes and of Apollo,
> who from your throne weighs and bestows what each deserves,
> cast your eyes, cast your eyes, and finally see us too.
>
> If you exist, Zeus, and if you truly honour virtue, most merciful,
> for how long, for how long multitudes of calamities
> let the golden age return to us.

The Greek Nation State and Ecclesiastical Music

Music transcription 10.1 Opening of the first transcription in Sigalas's book (1880).

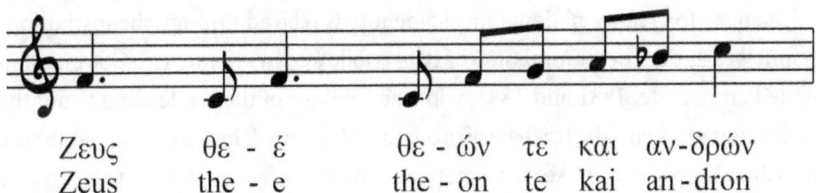

Music transcription 10.2 Translation in staff notation of the opening phrase of the first transcription of Sigalas's book (1880).

Strike, you with your lightning bolt, the enemies of the wise Greeks,
Throw with might your lightning, God of mine, on the usurpers.
Enough, wise Zeus, with the suffering of the Greeks,
Cast your eyes down from the heavens, to your glorious temples,
which have become ashes, alas, why do you delay your strike, O Zeus?

Oh wretched ones, till when, till when this night of misery?
Let the dawn of joy shine again.
Thunder from high above, you who strikes with lightning, with terrible might,
Strike the heads of the cruel barbarians, God of mine, strike them with your
  lightning,

Father and King, hear us, and blight the enemy with your thunder.
Empathize with us, O high throne, and save Greece from this suffering.

> Throw into Tartarus, O Zeus, the throne of the enemy the tyrant.
> Cast your eyes, cast your eyes, and finally see us too,
> if you exist, Zeus, and if you truly honour virtue

This first transcription contained in the book constitutes a hybrid: the lyrics invoke Ζευς (Zeus), but the musical notation is in the Byzantine system and aesthetically pertains to European marches. Indeed, one could also support a direct reference, at the beginning of the 'serenade in G major' to Mozart (K 525, known as 'Eine kleine Nachtmusik'), the modulation token of note Ni that is put on note Ga of the Varís Enarmónios echos[10] constitutes the only element not consistent with the well-tempered world.[11]

These contradictions are indicative of a series of inconsistencies between ideologies and the under-systemization of Greek music issues, which is, however, necessary for education. This is the reason for a significant number of publications with song collections (lyrics with or without musical text),[12] without, however, settling crucial inconsistencies such as the aforementioned, which as a rule are incorporated into official rhetorics and generate some remarkable critique.

The need to create a national music identity is relayed through the institutional channels early on. The Commission of 1814 is followed by another two Commissions of the Patriarchate, 1881 and 1883, with the findings of the last leading to another publication on theory in 1888. Earlier on, in 1837, Otto, King of Greece, establishes the 'Chanting School' in Athens, where attendance is free. In the same Decree (26 January), the recommendation of a national music society is announced:

> The secretariat of Ecclesiastical and Public Education is responsible for acting on the recommendation of a national music Society in order to propagate musical knowledge internally, and to improve piety in order to contribute to ecclesiastical chanting, so as to revive the zeal for the music of Greeks of the past. (Synadinos, 1919: 33)

Theodoros Synadinos, whose powerful institutional presence and substantial writings marked the first half of the twentieth century, explains that the Chanting School was not productive and did not serve the purposes for which it was recommended. This premature effort to incorporate ecclesiastical music

---

[10] This is an alternative name of the Plagal of the Third echos.
[11] A recording of the piece in commercial discography can be found on the album of Christodoulos Halaris, titled 'Pandora, Music of the Post-Byzantine high Society' (Orata, Orapan 002, 1991, track number 4).
[12] See, for example, Ennig (1883), Maltos (1885), Kosmas Madytinos (1897), Artemidis (1905), Argiropoulos (1915).

into an educational system was constructed on shaky foundations and did not come to any substantial fruition (see also Filopoulos, 1990: 87).

It should be noted that Synadinos occasionally implies that the connection of the ancient world with that of the contemporary one is feasible without the mediation of the Byzantine. It seems that his second work *Το ελληνικό τραγούδι* (to ellinikó tragoúdi, the Greek song), published in 1922,[13] is along the same lines. Already, however, before its publication, Konstantinos Psachos had arrived in Athens (1904) to take over the newly formed School of Byzantine Music, as we shall see further on.

The chanting art of the Eastern Church attracts early on the interest of academic researchers in Europe. The first names include Guillaume-Andre Villoteau (1759–1839), Louis Albert Bourgault Ducoudray (1840–1910) and Ella Adaiewsky (1846–1926). With the dawn of the twentieth century, Ediderunt Carsten Hoeg (1896–1961), Henry Julius Wetenhall Tillyard (1881–1968), Egon Wellesz (1885–1974), Hugo Riemann (1849–1919) and Hugo Gaisser (1853–1919)[14] are also added, who research and publish systematically, establishing contemporary Byzantine musicology (see Velimirović, 1968). In 1935, at the University of Copenhagen (Saxon Institute, Department of Greek and Latin Studies) Hoeg creates a historical series of publications titled 'Monumenta Musicae Byzantinae',[15] which continues up to today, to publish codes of great historical and musicological value in notation systems from different periods of hymnology. In this collection, the manuscripts constitute a base describing the Byzantine tonal atmosphere and the meaning of the ancient neumes (Khalil, 2009: 8), while chanting performance is deemed unreliable because of the influences that crept in during the period of Ottoman domination.

The Greek-speaking chanting world up to 1904 does not feature a structured organization; however, it is a living body of a long-term and robust musical tradition, which the academic world seems to treat as 'adulterated'. These external claims are dealt with almost as another Fallmerayer, activating the reflexes of proud descent and authentic identity. At the same time, internally, an additional dichotomy is rendered, the stakes being geopolitical orientation: Easternized or Westernized ecclesiastical music?

---

[13] For a fuller definition of Neo-Greek organizational bodies, institutions and foundations, see Tsetsos (2011) and Bellonis and Papageorgakopoulou (2016).
[14] For early research on Byzantine music, see, indicatively, Velimirović (1964) and Alygizakis (1985: 107–17).
[15] For the series Monumenta Musicae Byzantinae, see www.igl.ku.dk/MMB [visited on 12/03/2015].

11

Systemizing chanting and the protagonists

Reacting to the claims regarding Turkish influence, immediately after the turn of the century, the Archbishop of Athens Theoklitos requests the foundation of a Byzantine music school at the Conservatory of Athens from the director of the conservatory Georgios Nazos.[1] Reported in the *Formiga* (15 March 1905), the relevant discussions began in the summer of 1903. For Nazos, the introduction of a systematic chanting education becomes an issue of national importance. For this reason, he goes to Constantinople in September of 1903 in order to request the contribution of the Ecumenical Patriarchate and the specialists on Byzantine music, since it is there that 'through tradition everything that consists of the currently named Byzantine music is reverently maintained and it is there that an authentic style of enunciation exists rescued through succession and imitation' (*Formiga*, 15 March 1905).

While in March of 1905 he states the aforementioned, a month after his return from Constantinople, in 1903, *Formiga* publishes the following report, signed by its director Ioannis Th. Tsoklis (B΄, 11–12, 15–30 October 1903):

> Concerning the outcome of the trip to Constantinople, he told us that it had not been that encouraging, deducing from the general discussion on technique carried out between him and the local musicians, invited there for this reason by the erudite Ecumenical Patriarch Mr Ioakim III, adequate enlightenment was not forthcoming, neither was he able to acquire any information regarding what is scientifically validated concerning Byzantine music, in order to be used as a foundation for the manual which the conservatory decided to adopt. As Mr Nazos told us, he asked to be directly informed by the local musicians on the purely technical points of utilized ecclesiastical music: a) Concerning the pitch

---

[1] The Conservatory of Athens was founded in 1871 and functioned in 1872. Nazos was appointed director in 1891 (see relatively Drosinis, 1938; Kokkonis, 2008: 98–102; Charkiolakis, 2015; Barbaki, 2015: 61–2, 148; and Bellonis and Papageorgakopoulou, 2016). Georgios Leotsakos mentions that his appointment was actuated after the mediation of Andreas Sygros, a croesus from Constantinople (2000).

or the tonal base of our music. b) Concerning musical intervals. c) Concerning musical scales. d) Concerning notation, that is, musical transcription. And finally, e) Concerning the length of musical notes and rhythm.

In other words, Nazos, German bred and musically educated based on the system of Western music, has difficulty in understanding the theoretical foundation upon which a systematic education concerning Byzantine music could be structured. And because he himself is overbearing as a personality, without deviations, he discredits the chanting art as practice based and establishes four conditions for its integration into the study programme of the Athens Conservatory:

> Taking into account the all discussion, Mr Nazos reached the conclusion that ecclesiastical Byzantine music is perhaps a practice based art and not scientifically determined, however, salvaged to the present through the tradition of word to mouth; and that it is not possible at the present to be taught scientifically, as is. For this reason he suggested the following, which, primarily, were accepted. a) The potential chanters must be musically ingenious and mellifluous; in addition, apart from the presently recognized Byzantine music, that is the tradition conveyed orally, they are to be also taught European music, which is fitting to their profession, adding that it would be desirable for the clergy to start being taught Byzantine and European music according to the aforementioned terms, as with this musical education, they too would contribute to the systemization of Byzantine music under designated rules, in order for both its teaching and its performance to be conducted uniformly, something which can be accomplished only after the scientific designation of the tonal intervals in Byzantine music scales. If we achieve the uniform teaching of music in this way, the variations observed today among the different chanters in cities, who all chant in a different way, even though they have all been taught the already recognized Byzantine music, shall eclipse in the future. b) The creation of a library in which all the books concerning Byzantine music shall be collected. c) The actualization of a convention involving our and foreign musicians, six chanters, one or more physicists/mathematicians and a specialist in instrument construction for the examination and resolution of the pending issues concerning Byzantine music. And d) The manufacture of an instrument which shall facilitate the scientific study of Byzantine music.[2]

---

[2] Concerning the fourth point, it is deemed important to mention the conference titled 'The Panarmónio of K. A. Psachos', which took place on 14 October 2016 and was organized by the Faculty of Music Studies of the Philosophy School of the University of Athens (https://www.music.uoa.gr/fileadmin/depts/music.uoa.gr/www/uploads/SYNEDRIA-HMERIDES/2016oct14.pdf).

At this point in time, History manifests its sarcastic mood, as with this move Nazos obliges Byzantine music to tailor itself to the dictates of European music education, at least in the way that he perceives it. This adjustment, however, is not external or a formality, having repercussions on its very nature, since it renders one of its most fundamental elements non-negotiable, the oral tradition.

The word 'tradition' is very powerfully charged in the orthodox East. Far from being just a word, it is an institutional entity of great prestige. Not of the chanting world, it is impossible for Nazos to comprehend its singularities. The way with which he intends to impose 'systemization' leads to the formation of a study programme, which, with the subsequent mediation of the increased severity of Konstantinos Psachos, continues to exist till today in the conservatory world.[3] It makes one wonder that not one chanter uttered a word advocating the aggregation of orality in the framework of this 'systemization'. In any case, that a paradox has been established in the modern Greek conscience is impressive. While the West is deemed a pseudo-culture and enemy, not only of Orthodoxy but also of Hellenism in general, as the latter due to historical circumstances belongs to the West and is cut off from its natural environment, the East. Simultaneously, any praise for some accomplishment of Hellenism, which comes from the West, is deemed as a crown of external recognition. Following is an example of the abundant relevant literature: a chanting teacher, whose teaching often deviates from the musical and embraces the ideological, regularly mentions a possibly mythical incident, that when Camille Saint Saens, upon hearing for the first time in an Orthodox church, which he was visiting, the slow hymn in Second echos 'Lord I have cried', which is subtitled 'ancient melody', is touched, and says, 'I would exchange all my works so as to lay claim to this as my own' (see also Romanou, 1996: 66).

Returning to the historical Conservatory of Athens and the Europeanization of the School of Byzantine Music, much later, Simon Karas will express profound concerns regarding the European type of teaching of Byzantine music, referring the agreement of 1903–04. However, his concern is that this national music is alienated due to its teaching 'by Greek-European musicians, alien to its study' (Karas, 1982: vol. 1: δ), while the complete absence of oral tradition does not bother him at all.

---

[3] For example, the current operation regulations require obligatory attendance of the Byzantine music student of a course of theory lessons in European music (see Εφημερίδα της Κυβερνήσεως του Βασιλείου της Ελλάδος [Efimerída tis Kyverníseos tou Vasileíou tis Elládos, Government Gazette of the Kingdom of Greece], 11/11/1957, A´, 229 and 15 January 1966, A´, 7).

Regarding the article in the *Formiga*, we are informed that for the manning of the school under establishment Constantinople proposes Eustratios Papadopoulos, an eminent arch-chanter, theorist and teacher. However, eleven months later, in September of 1904, a student of his arrives in Athens, Konstantinos Psachos (1869–1949), who is chosen as the most suitable for the position of responsibility for which he is called upon to serve. Psachos was born in Μέγα Ρεύμα (Méga Reúma, Arnavutköy) Bosporus and received his basic (and only, based on the up to now evidence) musical education at the Seminary of the Patriarchate, by the priest Theodoros Mantzouranis. He chants in Constantinople and the surrounding areas before coming to Greece. As we are informed by the *Formiga* (2´, Article 6, 30 March 1903):

> Besides this teacher [Mantzouranis] Mr Psachos had no one else; he perfected his studies in the art of music through self-study, thus being considered a musical genius by his counterparts.

In September of 1904, the School of Byzantine Music at the Athens Conservatory begins its operations. As reported in the *Formiga* (15 March 1905), the Metropolises bear the funding:

> The Holy Synod has also accommodated the maintenance of the School, managing to collect assistance from the various State monasteries, subsequently, circulars were sent to all the High Priests of the State, managing through this to achieve the inclusion of the proportional amount in the annual budgets of the monasteries intended for this purpose.

Enterprising, with good organizational skills and by nature domineering, as soon as Psachos arrives in Athens he demarcates the new framework for the chanting art from the start. His initiative is not restricted to the School of Byzantine Music at the Athens Conservatory. He participates in the editorial commission of the *New Formiga*, together with the Archbishop Dionysios of Zakynthos (Zante) and the arch-chanter of the Metropolitan Cathedral of Athens Nikolaos Kanakakis, and the director and editor-in-chief of the *New Formiga*, Ioannis Tsoklis.

His educational activity, based on the prototype of the Music School of Constantinople, changes the face of ecclesiastical music. Many subsequent chanters consider him their teacher, and constantly refer to his work. The most emblematic case is that of Spyros Peristeris, who constitutes a separate chapter in the developments of the musical issues of the country: on the one hand, he took over the position previously held by Psachos in the Conservatory of Athens in 1937, and, on the other, he presented substantial research activity in the field of musical folkloristics, actualizing on-site recordings and publishing in both European and Byzantine notation, as editor of the Athens Academy.[4] Extremely active and prolific, he bequeaths us an important bulk of written work.

In 1919, there is a breach in relations between Psachos and the director of the Conservatory of Athens Georgios Nazos, as with Kalomoiris. It seems that his demands were not met concerning the copyright of the recordings of folk songs which he had carried out on behalf of the Conservatory (Polymerou-Kamilaki, 2013: 18). As Kalomoiris,[5] he withdraws and establishes the Conservatory of National Music, comprising of the following schools: (1) Ancient Greek Music, (2) Byzantine Music, (3) Modern Greek Music, folk songs and their related instruments, (4) Eastern Music, (5) Greek Choir, (6) Greek instruments, (7) Theory lessons (Tombra-Lagopati, 2013). The greatest challenge for Psachos seems to be the advocating of the ceaseless continuation of the chanting art through the passage of time, but also the establishment of an authentic performance yphos and a sturdy theoretical infrastructure, which could function as a prototype. To a large extent, it is his activity that renders the musical text, the notation, a firm guide in chanting performance, enforcing hereinafter its presence at the chanting lectern. His obsession with order regarding chanting renders his conduct inflexible often leading to conflict with many people, even with the Patriarchate chanters themselves, who he does not hesitate to bring to heel because they deviate from the musical texts (Psachos, 1908).

In opposition to Psachos's actions and ideology, we see another eminent person of that period; Ioannis Sakellaridis (1853–1938). Born in Litochoro, Pieria, Sakellaridis is taught chanting initially by his father, Theofanis Sakellaridis, a priest, and subsequently by the same teacher who taught Psachos, the priest Theodoros Mantzouranis in Thessaloniki, by whom he was also taught Arabic-Persian music (see Chrysostomos Bishop of Zakynthos, 1940: 9). Upon arrival in Athens, he immediately takes on a lectern in Piraeus. He serves in

---

[4] His father, Dimitrios Peristeris, a doctor by profession, originally from Rododafni near Aigio, wrote for *Formiga* and was on friendly terms with Konstantinos Psachos. It is said that his dispatch to Achaia to study and document folk songs was due to this nepotism. Peristeris undertook the reception of the research team in Mourla, organizing the residents and the school students. When the train arrives, Peristeris addresses his greeting in which it is clear how much he values Psachos (see Formiga 2, 6[8], Articles 1–2, 15–31 July 1910, pp. 3–4). In 1905, Psachos marries Euanthia Amerikanou, with Dimitrios Peristeris as his best man. In 1922, his wife dies and twelve years later, in 1934, Psachos marries, for the second time, Amalia Armao.

[5] After his withdrawal from the Athens Conservatory, Kalomoiris establishes the Greek Conservatory, to abandon this as well in 1926, establishing a new one, the National Conservatory.

various churches and the popularity of his vocal skills slowly increases, not only in the chanting circles but also externally. Apart from chanting though, there is another world into which Sakellaridis is initiated. On moving to Athens[6] to study at the School of Philosophy at the University of Athens, he apprentices for Ioulios Ennig.[7] This initiation into European music defines his aesthetic choices henceforth.[8]

Himself a hymnologist, with personal compositions from scratch and not based on the existing hymnology, he prints his numerous pieces in either Byzantine or staff notation. In fact, in 1880 he publishes his own Theoretical of Byzantine music, due to the fact that he is active as a teacher in a plethora of institutions, one of them being the National Conservatory of Kalomoiris.[9] He teaches there in 1926, having as his assistant his most popular student and continuer of his school, Spyros Kapsaskis.

On 6 June 1901, a special circular is published by the Holy Synod of the Church of Greece, with which the Synod recommends Sakellaridis's book *Holy Hymnology*, written in Byzantine notation. In the circular we read:

> The usefulness of this music book is adequately guaranteed by the name of the issuing music teacher and his well-known commitment to the music of the timeless and fruitful mother Church, and this is why the Holy Synod recommends to all in the Holy Clergy to obtain this good and useful book.

At the same time, he is also a researcher of folk tradition,[10] but more than anything he is a tireless and charismatic chanter, with an exquisite voice, which

---

[6] When Sakellaridis travelled from Litochoro in Macedonia to study and to eventually live permanently in Athens, Macedonia had yet to become a part of the Greek State.
[7] Ioulios Ennig was a music professor of the first philharmonic society of Athens 'Euterpe', established in 1870, as well as of the Conservatory of Athens, but also in public education (see Barbaki, 2015: 38, 57, 64). He also played a vital role in the systemization of school music education, writing educational books and song collections, many of which were designed to develop a national music conscience (see Zouvouli and Kokkonis, 2016: 188).
[8] According to the student register of the National University, which is available electronically (digital library 'Pergamos'), Sakellaridis seems to have graduated from the High School of Piraeus in 1876 and to immediately register in the Medical School, from which he transfers the following year to the School of Philosophy (on 13 October 1877). Among his other teachers, Konstantinos Paparrigopoulos is also there.
[9] Some of the institutions at which Sakellaridis teaches are Ριζάρειος Σχολή (Rizareios School), Μαράσλειο Διδασκαλίο (Marasleio Teaching), Αρσάκειο (Arsakeio), Εταιρεία Φίλων του Λαού (Etereía Fílon tou Laoú, society of the friends of the people), Παρθεναγωγείο Χιλλ (Parthenagogeío Hill, the hill girls school) and Hatzikyriakeio of Piraeus.
[10] He collected 175 folk songs from the regions of Olympus, Helicon and Parnassus. Based on our information, this collection is found in the folk archive of the Athens Academy, and remains unreleased. In 1882, he releases *The Muse* (folk songs collection). In 1898, the first *Tyrtaeus*, also a song collection (not only folk), and in 1907 the second *Tyrtaeus*, updated now with more songs.

makes the public rush to hear him (see Chrysostomos Bishop of Zakynthos, 1940: 10 and 12). As an active musician, active on many levels, he supports the dynamic confabulation of chanting with the world of European music and, especially, that of polyphony. Being an accomplished and popular musician, Sakellaridis is often mentioned in the Athenian press, even in the fortress of the supposedly 'authentic' Byzantine chanting yphos, *Formiga*:

> Soon a concert will take place at the Municipal Theatre dedicated entirely to our national music, by I. Th. Sakellaridis and his sons; Theophrastus[11] and Aristoxenus.
>
> The orchestra shall be comprised of seventy instruments and conducted by Mr Sakellaridis's oldest son, Theophrastus.
>
> The concert's programme shall include all the masterpieces of folk music which were collected by Mr I. Sakellaridis and harmonized by his son Theophrastus, in accordance with the requirements of the art, without destroying their initial timbre.
>
> This is the first time that a concert of this type is take place at The Athens Theatre. (*Formiga*, January 1904, 2', 17–18, p. 8)

Fundamentally, the persona of Ioannis Sakellaridis is similar to that of Konstantinos Psachos: scholars, intellectuals and knowledgeable of both musical systems, Byzantine and European.[12] However, there is one crucial difference: Sakellaridis chants incessantly, maintaining a permanent position at the chanting lectern, performing concerts of diverse repertoire (European, Byzantine and folk), not only in Greece but also abroad, whereas Psachos, from the moment he arrives in Athens, does not seem to have an especially dynamic chanting force. This 'affinity' renders the conflict between them even more acute regarding technique and the yphos of chanting performance. Sakellaridis is not conservative and is attracted to modernization. He advocates polyphony as ancient Greek aesthetic, which he validates with ancient texts, while in contrast he imputes barbarian and Turkish influences to the contemporary chanting art, which he ought to eliminate.[13] Historical continuation for him is reference to the ancient world on a different dimension, bypassing the Middle Ages, estranged due to impure heterogeneous cultural elements.

---

[11] Theophrastus Sakellaridis (1883–1950), composer and musician, was a major personage in the Athens music scene and a pioneer in Greek operetta.

[12] Analytically for Psachos, see Psachos (1978) and Karamanes (2013). For Sakellaridis, see Papadimitriou (1940) and Kalokyris (1988).

[13] See Sakellaridis (1880 and 1895). The Foreword in the two publications illustrates the change in Sakellaridis's views. See also Anastasiou (2013).

Initially he seems to subscribe to the common ecclesiastical mindset, something which of course is embraced by a large portion of the secular public. In 1880, in the preface of his book *Χρηστομάθεια εκκλησιαστικής μουσικής* (christomátheia ekklisiastikís mousikís), as a fourth-year student in the School of Philosophy, at the young age of twenty-seven, he writes:

> And while language, after our national restoration, was cultivated and fortified, tending slowly slowly to deservingly approach the ancient world, music was neglected and attacked by sciolistic copycats, and thus degenerates and perhaps with time may even cease to exist, beneath the diabolical smirk of the copycats of the West. (Sakellaridis, 1880: θ´)

In many of the prefaces of the books he publishes, as well as other types of texts, he follows this mindset, quite common for this period and specific trend, something which Psachos himself also follows later in his own texts. Twenty-eight years later, in 1908, that is, at the age of fifty-five and six to seven years after the events known as 'Ευαγγελικά' (euangeliká[14]), he writes a text, which is published in 1930, as the preface to his book *Ύμνοι και ωδαί* (ýmnoi kai odaí, hymns and odes), written wholly in staff notation. It is this preface that makes it clear that a personal internal conflict is taking place. Using a series of quotes and referrals to ancient Greek authors and texts regarding music, Sakellaridis tries to prove that since the ancient Greeks speak of consonant and dissonant intervals, resonant notes and harmony, then quite likely Western music as well has been influenced by the ancient Greek; therefore, perhaps it is not 'bad' to publish hymns written on staff notation. And while in his older texts again he follows the mindset of the period and encourages the study of Arab-Persian music because it constitutes a replica of the Ancient Greek, in this preface he says that the hymns contained in this edition are in the form which was saved by tradition 'purifying the hymns of the contamination of arrythmia and dissonance' (1930: α´).

On the contrary, for Psachos, a guarantee for historical continuation is the Byzantium, as an intrinsic link in the Greek chain, which salvages and maintains the essence of Greek civilization via Orthodoxy. Polyphonic novelties, rebuking familiar tradition, are almost the same thing as treason. The School of Sakellaridis is 'Europeanist' and 'Western', terms which mask a deeper deprecation of ecclesiastical nature.

---

[14] Strong debates regarding the issue of translating the gospels into modern Greek language.

It is known that the game was eventually won by Psachos. However, Sakellaridis was not an easy opponent. Even in 1915, eleven whole years after the triumphant arrival of Psachos, the Athenian press writes flatteringly about him and his art:

> Especially the melodic verses of the canon ... which are performed in that immortal Byzantine rhythm by the mellifluous Mr I. Sakellaridis at the Church of Chrysospiliotisa, transport the listeners mentally to the Phanarion. (Εστία [estía, epicenter], 26 December 1915)

But even posthumously, in a memorial in 1939, the speech delivered by Kalomoiris is unexpectedly eulogistic, crediting him with 'endless erudition' and 'enlightened relative progressiveness of ideas for the evolution of ecclesiastical music', having managed to pass 'the insurmountable imaginary great wall, which for most divides the Byzantine from the European musical culture' (Kalomoiris, 1940: 37).

If one is to refer to the nineteenth century, it is impressive that one will not find 'the insurmountable imaginary great wall' which has been erected between the two traditions at the time that Greek music education is being systemized. Chrysanthos from Madytos, an important scholar of the nineteenth century, whose musical writings constitute a breakthrough in Byzantine music, proves less bigoted:

> It is possible for some to like a song while others do not, especially if they are foreigners, and they are not accustomed to hearing similar melodies. Because every place has somehow its own particular music, which only the locals like. Hence, the more a musician makes the effort to get to know and study these diverse musical habits, the more he may discover a variety of thriving melodies. Because the music of every nation cultivates a certain aesthetic teleology, depending on its natural inclination. (Chrysanthos, 1832: 3: annotation 1)

Regarding the relationship between Byzantine and European music, Chrysanthos does not see it in schismatic terms. He simply draws attention to the difference of intervals:

> In order for a beginner to chant this scale correctly, he must be taught by a Greek musician; because a musician from another country performs the notes differently, according to his national custom, without managing the intervals of the tones in accordance with our way. ... Europeans represent their scale, which they call Gamma, with the following syllables, la, si, ut, re, mi, fa, sol, la; and they

begin to chant the scale from ut, performing some notes the same as us, and others differently. (Chrysanthos, 1832: 9)

It is evident that the definition of the term 'Greek' at this particular moment in time[15] does not have the 'national' context with which it will be credited later. It is important that we observe the references of Chrysanthos to European music (theory, harmony, history, instruments). In fact, in the chapter regarding harmony Chrysanthos chooses to use the staff notation, a four-part harmonization which he transcribes in Byzantine notation too (1832: 222). It seems that his rationale is that not of exclusion, but that of 'perichoresis'.

It is evident how ecumenical Chrysanthos's approach is also by the way in which he deals with the historical overview of the issue. In the chapter 'A narrative concerning the inception and progress of music', he devotes a significant part of his observation not only to ancient Greek music, as one would expect, but also to that of the Biblical-Hebrew era (see also Xanthoudakis, 2007: 146–7).

The invocation of Chrysanthos's work in subsequent years completely discounts the mindset of the author, who is interpreted via a narrow 'national' perspective (see, for example, Karas, 1982). This perspective relays bigotry to the relevant musical traditions as well.

---

[15] Besides, the first edition of this particular text seems to date back to at least 1816 (see Chatzigiakoumis, 1974 and Xanthoudakis, 2007: 141).

12

The 'musical issue' at the forefront once again

In 1921, Simon Karas leaves Ilea, a region in Peloponnesus, to come to Athens, in order to study at Law School. Soon, however, he abandons his studies, to research, on his own, Greek music, from antiquity to the present. To this aim he dedicates his life, in fact, establishing in 1929 the Society for the Propagation of National Music.[1] Through his activity in the Society, but also from his staff position which he undertakes in public radio, for the next six decades he is one of the protagonists in Greek music, which preoccupies him in all its manifestations.

> Today, through the effort of the new State regarding the spiritual elevation of the people, every musical piece, every song, shall first be listened to by a special committee which is made up of Messrs. Psaroudas, Karas, Georgiadis, Dounias, Politis and Mandanos, and then be released. The first four are to monitor the music which must not include any amanes or any Asian influence, the last two the lyrics. No repulsiveness, no immorality shall be released any more. (Alexandra Lalaouni, *Βραδινή* [vradiní, evening] 18 October 1940)[2]

Simon Karas heads a large recording and publication of Greek musical idioms campaign. His methodology follows the general gist of musical folklore, which 'shuns the "each time" in order to project the idealized "always"' (Kokkonis, 2017: 176).

Earlier, in 1924, at the young age of twenty-one, Karas manifests his radical ideas on the study of the transcription system of Byzantine music and dichotomizes the chanting world, because he proposes a new theoretical, which

---

[1] Σύλλογος προς Διάδοσιν της Εθνικής Μουσικής, Sýllogos pros Diádosin tis Ethnikís Mousikís.
[2] 'For approximately the same time period [that is, 1950s] a second book containing minutes, regarding the conventions of the Committee of assembly of Archives for gramophone records of national music (folk and laiko) on behalf of the General Directorate of the Press for the president of the government. The material comes from the Archive of the General Directorate of the Press, which includes approximately 3,100 records, years of release 1948-54. Here we see S. Karras and M. Dounias again, together with the composer Ioannis Konstantinidis and the professor of the State Conservatory of Thessaloniki D. Orpis. After 1958, the musicologist Spyridon Peristeris is added to the group, from the Folk Centre of the Athens Academy' (Kokkonis, 2018: 141).

annuls the existing rules which it had been following since 1814.³ A champion for the historical continuation of 'national' music, he excludes the urban forms, mainly the rebetiko, but also European music.

> Our ceaseless musical tradition through the ages must be evident and the work of our modern ecclesiastical musicians, a continuation of the old; and those again, ancestors and exemplars for the present ... our musical tradition and vocal and instrumental activity, which are preserved in their original form by all of us who were taught, not by Greek-European musicians alien to the study, but as defined by Chrysanthos in his Theoretical, 'by a Greek teacher, who should pay attention to the performance and the intervals of our music, as they were – always – specified'. (Karas, 1982: Α': δ'-στ')

Simon Karas uses Chrysanthos to establish an argument of exclusion, and to exercise harsh criticism concerning the educational policy on Byzantine music of the time:

> This because, for 75 years now the distortive Byzantine-European system of teaching, which is persistently applied in conservatories, results in only one thing: the so-called 'Byzantine' Schools constitute an antechamber for western music, our graduates are reduced to teachers of European music, teaching with pianos and keyboards,⁴ not Byzantine sounds and intervals, but semi-tones of the West, in state and private schools. ... It is better to have Byzantine chanters who are uneducated European-wise, rather than frauds and subversives of our musical traditions, having degrees without relevance to our national music. (Karas, 1982: Α': δ'-ε')

The danger of 'fraud' in tradition excuses the measures taken, since the existing infrastructures failed to adequately prepare their students, having 'reduced' them to teachers of European music. A shift towards the East is proposed, to the 'musical system of the Muslim people of the Near East and the Mediterranean',

---

³ For the counterargument, see, for example, Akridas (2013).
⁴ Here, Karas possibly refers to Spyros Peristeris and subsequently to the School of the Conservatory of Athens (this school shall be seen further on either as the School of the Conservatory of Athens or as the Athenian School). Many of the practices of the specific school were incriminated in the past and remain, even to the present, incriminating. The school is linked to European music, concerning not only the interval world but also voice placement. The relevant literature states the use of the piano by Peristeris during teaching and rehearsals, something which comes into conflict not only with the 'ethics' but also with the practical issues (well-tempered intervals). In oral communication with Apostolos Papadopoulos, a student of Peristeris and his successor to the right lectern of the Metropolitan Cathedral of Athens, he refers to the relevant literature emphasizing that the piano was used in order to grant a tonal point of reference for the start of rehearsal/teaching or for the supervision of its course, what is often referred to in the chanting community as 'not to lose (go higher or lower) the base' (communiqué with Papadopoulos on 10 February 2016).

which is not 'foreign', but a loan, since it is based 'on the ancient Greek music science and tradition':

> In addition, the study of and acquaintance with the musical system of the Muslim people, Arabs and Persians, of the Near East and the Mediterranean, which is also followed by the Turks ... is based on the ancient Greek music science and tradition. (Karas, 1982: Α΄: ε΄)

This theory is installed in the musical world as self-evident, without further historical or musicological research. On an ideological level, it is the extension of the mindset 'ours once more' (Herzfeld, 2002). On a factual level, it is imperative that certain aesthetic guidelines are met, indeed, exclusively and dogmatically. The true condition of music played in the Greek-speaking world, folk and urban, is not acceptable as 'national' if it does not comply with the aforementioned principles.

With regard to Byzantine music in particular, its authenticity is categorized as follows:

> The western-taught Byzantine musicologist will chant differently, the conservatory chanter of Byzantine music differently, the contemporary and novel festival-style chanter and internationally acclaimed conductor differently and in a different way the Byzantine chanter who follows the old musical tradition of our Church, here and in the province. (Karas, 1982: Α΄: στ΄)

The caustic attitude of Karas, whose patriotism is strong grounds for absolute damnation, may invoke his long-time study and research; however, he does remain an outsider with regard to the chanting act. He served the chanting lectern in a small church for a short period, from 1931 to 1934; thus, his relation to the subject is mainly theoretical.

The oral dimension of the chanting tradition, as mentioned before, is, however, very important, as recognized by Melpo Merlier:

> It is difficult nowadays to listen to good Byzantine music, not in Europe, where this scarcity is natural, but unfortunately in Greece as well. ... These records shall still be useful when the differences that exist between the printed musical texts and oral tradition are examined. It is well known how important oral tradition is in the music of the Greek Church. Even today, when everybody could be chanting 'from a parchment', and so it should be, almost all Greek chanters chant without reference to printed instructions. Thus, we see prevalence even today, beside printed ecclesiastical music, of oral tradition. Whether good or bad, this

tradition is a fact which cannot be ignored and which, one day, shall be studied. (Merlier, 1935: 16)

Melpo Merlier herself did never engage in this study. She focused her activity on recordings of Greek refugees[5] from different areas. In 1930 and 1931, she actualized 639 recordings in Athens, following a folklore methodology (see analytically Merlier, 1935). Apart from folk songs, the recordings included Byzantine hymns too; her comments on these are extremely interesting: in the debate concerning the harmonization of Byzantine music, Merlier was an advocate for the preservation of the Byzantine tradition, and against the European researchers who with their studies provoked this discourse. She considered that the solution to the problem lies in musical literacy, as proposed by Psachos, because chanting off by heart does not ensure the 'correct' interpretation, without, however, ignoring the power of oral tradition.

The faith placed by Greek researchers in the power of literacy is non-negotiable. The documentation and classification of oral tradition is an urgent priority, which concerns mainly the vast and unknown corpus of folk music. A fundamental element of Greek identity, the folk song, is at the epicentre of folklore, which thrives irrespective of academia. The School of Karas[6] is shaped through the activity of documentation and recording, both on site and in the studio. We shall not analyse, however, this significant aspect of Greek music. What we need to remember is that Byzantine music and its theoretical background was clearly considered the foundation of Greek music.

The rural repertoire collected and recorded is categorized based on the system of Byzantine echoi, which are now not eight, as Karas proposes new categorizations, making up and/or 'rediscovering' the ancient additional echoi. When in 1982 Karas published the *Method of Greek Music* (μέθοδος της ελληνικής μουσικής, méthodos tis ellinikís mousikís), he divided the chanting world: the proponents who favoured the reformation of the theoretical system with a new foundation based on antiquity, restoring 'correctness', clashed with the proponents of patriarchal tradition, using as a point of reference the findings of the Commission of 1814 and the theoretical writings of Chrysanthos. The opinion of one of the most important personas of the Patriarchate chanting style,

---

[5] The selection of music informants is based exclusively on the Greek language: 'We did not record anything from the third folklore period, that is, the Turkish-speaking Greeks from Pontus' (Merlier, 1935: 30).
[6] For the School of Karas, see Kallimopoulou (2009: 35).

who served as a Left Chanter and as a First Cantor in the Patriarchal Church, Thrasyvoulos Stanitsas, is informative regarding the conflict in question.[7]

> A: Karas, Karas … . What can one say to this man? He became arrogant, he found a certain situation here, in the land of the blind the one-eyed man is king, he is in charge of everything here, imposing himself because there is no-one else.
> … B: who are you, mister, to change nowadays, (oh, I get upset just by talking about him), to translate the old notation! Today! Today! In 1980, 87 or 75. Who are you and why was it necessary to do it? This is nonsense. Is this what you call yphos or do you have rhythm[8] conduct? Do you have anything? What is this? Who do you think you are, who gave you the right to translate the old notation as you see fit, as you like? These things have been written, have been encoded, it is over, end of the line, enough is enough.[9]

It is evident not only that this conflict is musicological, but that its historical framework needs examining, which shall interpret the positions and arguments of its protagonists.

Nowadays, this discord has reached dramatic proportions. In the standard bodies where Byzantine music is taught, mainly in the schools of the metropolises and in the conservatories, two versions exist of the theory and, consequently, of practice. The author has found himself in several such incidences in the presence of examination committees concerning certificates in Byzantine music, where the members of the committee disagree on a variety of theoretical and practical issues, even in the presence of the examinee, resulting in the creation of

---

[7] It is crucial to note that the chanting world of the Patriarchate, from the start and up to recently, was opposed to the contemporary reformations of Karas. Something which changes with the appointment of the current right chanter, in 2016, Panagiotis Neochoritis, as he is considered in chanting circles, is on the one hand low profile but, on the other, a follower of the chanting stance (theory and practice) very close to that of Karas. However, the champions of the Patriarchate yphos seem to disapprove of this appointment, as they claim that this interrupts a centuries-long continuum regarding the appointment of chanters of the Patriarchate Church. Tradition dictates that the appointment is conducted internally, and the persons must first have studied at the chanting lectern of the Patriarchate Church beside chanters, who themselves have followed the same procedure. The most crucial point is found in the chanting without the use of musical texts, but through the memorization of the musical works through the many years of experience gained beside the basic chanters.

[8] In particular, Stanitsas uses the term 'χρόνος' (chrónos, time), a term with various meanings in chanting circles. The chanting tempo conduction has its own characteristics; the Patriarchate chanters are considered ultimate experts regarding the unwritten rules of this rhythm management. For example, they use certain tendencies in breathing and in the rhythmic structure of the melody, using singular marcati, tenuti, legati and so on. These characteristics constitute a piece of the puzzle of the chanter's style.

[9] These words come from two different archives found on YouTube. Even though it is not mentioned it is evident that it is an interview. The fact that the 'A' does not exist in the second sound file is impressive, as is the parenthesis in file 'B': https://youtu.be/07qulMb_TDc; https://youtu.be/MfoOuhJr9_U.

problems concerning the issue of grading. The situation is rendered even more complicated after the explosion of interest in Eastern music traditions, in the 1980s and 1990s, introducing to the already-volatile situation the theoretical dimension of the makam as well. During this period, instruments such as the oud and the kanun were 'rediscovered', instruments which were incorporated not only in the musical act but also in systemized education (see, for example, the institution of the music schools, junior and senior high schools). These instruments offered a safer route towards familiarization with the 'indigenous', as they are usually called by the relevant circles, musical formations due to their untempered nature, utilizing once again as a foundation the mentality of 'ours, once more' (Herzfeld, 2002).[10] The theoretical duals left the practice defenceless, often causing confusion to the students and placing artistic creation on low-priority status, which should correspond to the 'correct' theory. Sokratis Sinopoulos, who describes the process and the integration practices of the makam into the teaching of traditional music as well as its systemization, has claimed that on the one hand great importance was given to the theoretical dimension, that is, the examination of intervals, scales and so on, and on the other hand two extremely interesting levels were left unexamined, which would lead to a holistic description of the musical phenomenon.

> The first concerns the particular and rather specific musical embellishments that are utilized, which determine the musical 'colour' or 'style' of every tradition, and the second as a result of all the aforementioned concerns the general sense emitted by music, both to its vector, the musician, and to its audience, that is, its style and ethos, elements which in essence determine its aesthetic context. (Sinopoulos, 2010: 111)[11]

---

[10] The oxymoron concerning the issue in question is that during the period of quite a few years ago when the educational world came into contact with these specific instruments, there was an attitude of exclusion, considering them Turkish (see relevant information in the first chapter).

[11] We must also mention a new and singular revival of folk-traditional during the 1990s and 2000s (see Kallimopoulou, 2009). For a more general view on musical revivals, see Livingston (1999).

13

Urban music

Examination of a remarkable network

The urban popular song, in Greece as elsewhere, is characterized by pluralism (Moore, 2007; Scott, 2009), and polystylism (Emmerson, 2007), something which renders standard classifications and categorizations non-conducive. For many years, in the musicological vocabulary this condition was assigned the expression 'musical hybrid'. The covert derogatory content of this term is obvious, especially when used to describe marginalized and controversial music, such as, what we consider rebetiko and amanes, and subsequently neo-folk, skyládiko and so on.[1]

Concerning music which develops in the urban laiko environment, the expression 'music syncretism' seems more suitable. The term 'syncretism', originating from religious studies, yields convergence and binding of heterogeneity during their interaction, while in contrast the significance of the term 'hybrid' is more in accordance with conflict and incongruous retraction.[2]

Respectively, 'syncretism' is also the methodology of the musicology of the music in question, which requires not only systematic analysis, but also examination of factors such as historical context and cultural osmoses or clases caused by it (i.e., by the historical context), instrument and recording technology, and above all the specific performance context with all its external references.

During the nineteenth century, in Greek-speaking urban centres, a wide instrumentation develops, with a multitude of instrument combinations, coming from miscellaneous cultural locales. The constantly evolving modeness of Smyrna and Constantinople, with its rich musical background which is

---

[1] Νεοδημοτικό, neodimotikó; σκυλάδικο, 'dog style'; 'doggish'; 'doghouse'. For neo-folk, see Kokkonis (2017: 175–93); for 'dog-style', see Oikonomou (2005), Lalioti (2013) and Sentevska (2014).
[2] Many thanks to Derek Scott, for his invaluable reflections and advice on the troublesome issue of terminology, in particular the issue of hybrid-syncretism.

offered by its ceaseless conference with the East, finds itself interacting with other cosmopolitan centres (Bucharest, Cairo, Naples), integrating distant loans, waltzes, habaneras, estudiantinas, the mandolin, the guitar and others, renewing old forms and creating new ones. It must be noted, however, that this kind of moulding does not constitute an exclusivity of the Greeks from Asia Minor and Constantinople, but also includes other ethno-cultural groups (see, for example, the Turkish 'kanto': see Pennanen, 2004: 9 and O'Connel, 2006: 276).

This intense artistic dialogue is conducted, of course, in an environment of great historical upheaval and the maelstrom of a changing world, resulting in yet another conflict of Christian and Islamic elements.[3] However, the participation in a dialogue of all those involved is characterized by a remarkable sense of 'co-existence', allowing each to project, without obstruction, their own aesthetics and dynamics (see also Samson, 2013: 133). A characteristic image of the aforementioned is granted by the history of the estudiantinas.[4]

On 7 March 1878, during the celebration of the Paris carnival, an estudiantina orchestra, comprised of sixty-four Spanish students,[5] astounded the crowds with its performance.[6] This orchestra had been formed earlier in Madrid, in order to participate, in traditional attire, in local customs, playing bandurria in the streets. An international tour commences, which takes them as far as the opposite side of the Atlantic Ocean, where this particular musical trend becomes the vogue in 1880. *The New York Times* on 26 August 1879 announces an estudiantina concert in New York on 13 October 1879, this time with twenty-two members.

Eight years after Paris, it is still in vogue, and in the Greek capital the newspaper *Acropolis*, on 21 July 1887, announces that the estudiantina orchestra had been in Athens and was preparing to go to Patras, with only six members in its orchestra.[7]

---

[3] Regarding music dialogue between Greece and Turkey nowadays, see also Erol (2015).
[4] Part of the following excerpt concerning the estudiantinas was used in the paper titled 'Cosmopolitan Music by Cosmopolitan Musicians: The Case of Spyros Peristeris, Leading Figure of the Rebetiko'. Conference: Creating music across cultures in the 21st century, The Centre for Advanced Studies in Music (25–27/5). Istanbul Technical University, 2017.
[5] The newspaper Ακρόπολις (acropolis), 21 July 1887, writes that the estudiantina consisted of thirty-two members. Despite this, the photograph in the International Museum of the Student www.museodelestudiante.com depicts more members, without clarifying, however, whether all are instrument players of the orchestra. Michael Christoforidis, in his most recent and extremely interesting article on the Spanish estudiantina, mentions that the orchestra in question comprised of sixty-four students (Christoforidis, 2017).
[6] A photograph of the Spanish estudiantina can be found here:
www.museodelestudiante.com/Fotografias/EstudiantinaEspanolaAA.htm.
[7] The estudiantina performed a concert at the Athens Conservatory on 26 and 29 April 1886 (Barbaki, 2015: 376).

The typical composition of Spanish estudiantinas consisted of various plucked string instruments, with the most popular being the guitar and the mandolin.[8] However, in engravings of that period violins, wind and percussion instruments are also depicted. In essence, they were well-organized semi-amateur music societies by Spanish university students. Their stem source seems to be the 'tuna', the street serenade (Orlandi, 2010).

As it tours all over the world, the estudiantina orchestra plants the seed of its aesthetic in the large urban centres (Sparks, 2005). An article in the Spanish newspaper *Diario de Córdoba*, on 28 February 1886, mentions that an estudiantina was in Constantinople to present their programme to the court of the Sultan Abdulhamid (Conejero, 2008: 102). It seems that the orchestra stayed for quite some time in Constantinople and Smyrna, where it was a catalytic influence on the musicians there.

The first well-known Greek-speaking estudiantina was created by Aristeidis Peristeris, father of Spyros Peristeris, and Vasileios Sideris.[9] They named their orchestra 'Τα πολιτάκια' (ta politákia, the guys from Poli, that is, Constantinople) and settled in Smyrna from 1898 to 1906. It is not clear whether they stay in Constantinople or Smyrna or when they move.[10] After 1918, Spyros Peristeris undertakes the 'Politakia', who, however, wane due to the turbulent period. Due to the death of his father, he takes over the position of first mandolin. Unconfirmed information indicates that Spyros's parents enrolled him in the Italian School of Constantinople.[11] He moves to Athens in approximately 1924 and is active as a musician. He undertakes the post of artistic director for Odeon–Parlaphone, or at the very least an important post which allows him to make decisions for the company regarding the popular repertoire, which is the segment of Gramaphone Co, under the management of Minos Matsas, with whom he cooperates discographically in the roles of composer and songwriter respectively. His stint at the company lasts approximately from 1930–4 to 1965–6, playing a key role in the essential configuration of the urban laiko song: participating as a musician, supervising, recommending, adapting, orchestrating, not only his own compositions but also those of other important musicians of the period.

---

[8] For the Spanish estudiantina, see Christoforidis (2009 and 2017) and Murray (2013).
[9] According to Kalyviotis, the estudiantina was created in 1898 (Kalyviotis, 2002: 72).
[10] Kalyviotis claims that they appeared for the first time in 1898, and according to Karakasis they settled in Smyrna in 1906 (Karakasis: 1948).
[11] At present, an effort is being made to find the history archive of the Liceo Italiano, based in Istanbul, founded in 1888 and operating up to the present. A crucial point being the familiarity that the Peristeris family, and especially Spyros, had with the Italian musical environment, that is, with the mandolin and the kantada. It is on this framework that he later bases the rebetiko of Piraeus.

Early on, research into the musical reality of Smyrna revealed two significant problematic facts: on the one hand, there is a significant time lapse between the period under examination and the time that studies concerning it began, most of which come from amateur researchers and collectors from Athens (apart from Aristomenis Kalyviotis, 2002). For many years, the official science of musicology, both in Greece and abroad, considered urban popular music manifestations the 'lesser other', resulting in it never constituting an object worthy of study. On the other hand, the fire and the mass displacement of large population groups rendered the discovery of historical material almost impossible (photographs, records, etc.). Nowadays, our knowledge concerning the music of Smyrna is much improved. To this end a multitude of contributory factors are responsible. In the field of discography, the communication between Greek collectors and those of foreigners is crucial, culminating in a dual exchange of information and, mainly, methodology.[12]

At this point, we should add a parenthesis in order to understand the identity of the protagonists of the now legendary orchestra. Aristeidis Peristeris, as shown in his birth certificate in Figure 13.1, was born in Corfu in 1855[13] and married Despina Bekou, a Greek with Italian citizenship, born in Corsica. Aristeidis's name has been detected in sources in Corfu, and efforts are being made to ascertain exact dates concerning his marriage to Bekou, whether they met in Constantinople or earlier.[14]

Vasilis Sideris was born in Urla or Naxos, whom we find still active in Athens from 1924 to 1930 (Kounadis, 2003b: 276).

The 'politakia' was a type of small mandolinata[15] with intense Spanish influence, in which only men participated, mainly with mandolins and guitars, while the singing is often lyrical, and occasionally polyphonic. The sound

---

[12] For example, Kalyviotis claims to have cooperated with Hugo Strötbaum (Kalyviotis, 2002: 11). See also Ordoulidis (2012: 66).

[13] The information comes from the research undertaken by Tony Klein, Nikos Politis and David Murray, who interviewed Spyros Peristeris's son Dimitris, in 2008.

[14] Additionally, it must be noted that Spyros's brother, Stelios, was himself a musician, a teacher of classical violin at the Athens Conservatory. Furthermore, according to information procured from Stelios's grandchild, George, who is himself a classical violinist at present, their cousin was the other Spyros Peristeris, son of Dimitrios Peristeris, physician and folklorist from Rododafni, Aigio. As we saw earlier, Spyros Dimitrios Peristeris was a teacher at the School of Byzantine music at the historical Athens Conservatory, the successor of the founder, Konstantinos Psachos, of the school in question from 1937 onwards, and First Cantor at the Metropolitan Cathedral of Athens.

[15] The Greek mandolinatas constitute another important case of syncretism, and, indeed, on a multitude of levels, their trips to America act as mediators. Repertoires and performance practices are structured in various locales, proposing interesting schools and styles (see, for example, mandolinata activity by Ierotheos Schizas and Michalis Syfnaios).

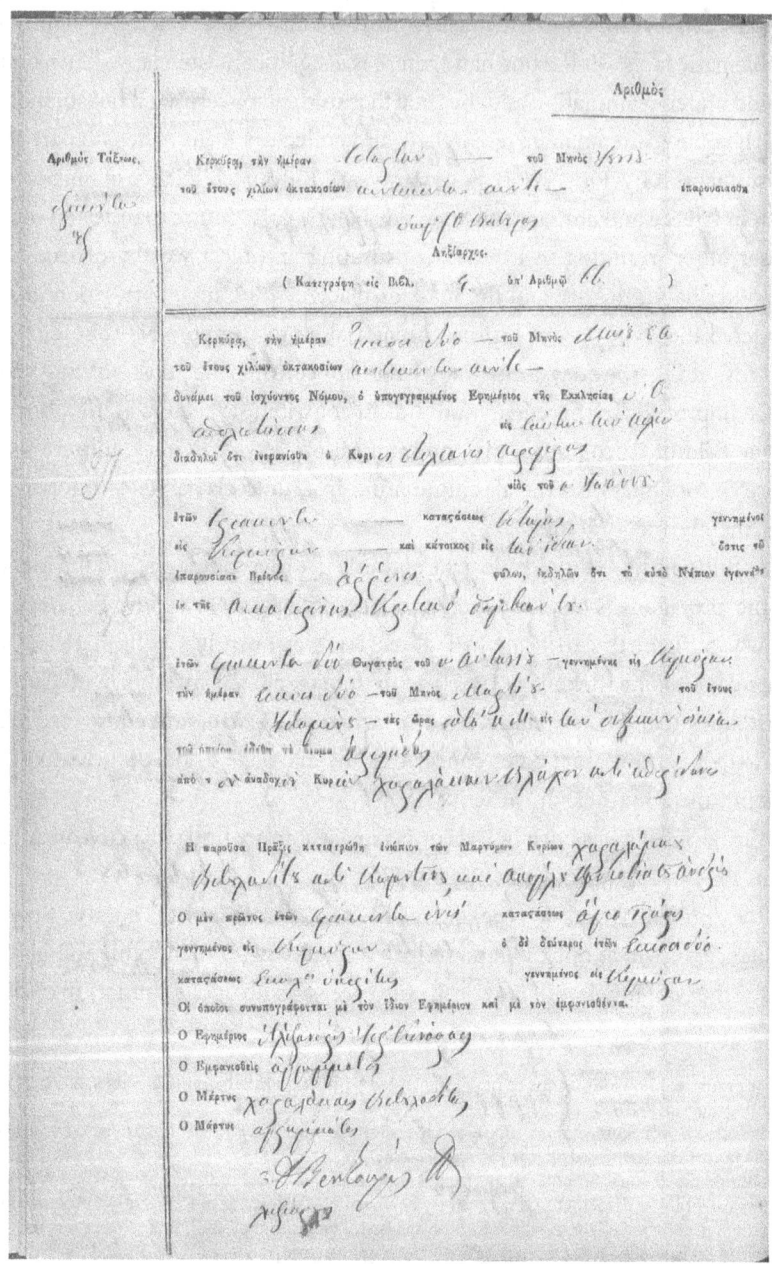

Figure 13.1 The birth certificate of Aristeidis Peristeris (22 March 1855), found in the General Archives of the State in Corfu.

salvaged by their discography is, to a great extent, the 'sound of Smyrna', whose environment could be considered the definition of cosmopolitanism of the period (see also Scott, 2015a and 2015b).[16] It should be stressed that the Greek collectors identify the 'politakia' with the 'Smyrnean estudiantina'. This claim needs further examination, because the available recording material does not always coincide with the reports which identify the 'Politakia' only with the European repertoire. In any case, the following names are encountered, revealed by discography, and they all refer to the 'Smyrnean estudiantina': 'Estudiantina from Smyrna', 'Estudiantina Vasilakis', 'Estudiantina Sideris'. Other estudiantinas active in this period not only in Smyrna but also in Constantinople and Athens, as revealed by discography, are, estudiantina Christodoulides, Constantinople estudiantina, the Panhellenic estudiantina, estudiantina Zounarakis and estudiantina of Athens. In some cases, we see alternative names for the same estudiantinas. However, we cannot be sure about this. For example, Giorgos Tsanakas is the singer of the estudiantina of Smyrna, but we also find record labels where we read estudiantina Tsanakas. It is possible that we are talking about the same estudiantina.

The descriptions of Angela Papazoglou, wife of Vangelis Papazoglou, hold special interest. Vangelis was an extraordinary music figure, prominent not only in Smyrna but also later in Athens. Angela's descriptions illustrate both the musical reality of Smyrna and that of the 'Politakia':

> Only during the carnival period did we play the music of Hamid with toubelekis and tabors. Listen up, Angela from Smyrna is telling you. In the bands of Smyrna and with the 'toys'[17] we would express our sorrow in Minore, with violoncellos, pianos, harps, dulcimers/santurs, mandolins, guitars and violins. No matter how many Minore we sang, we never got bored, ever. (Papazoglou, 1994: 9)

> There at the 'politakia' in the venue, two orchestras played. One on this side and one on that side. On this side was for folk music and Smyrna music. The 'politakia' were for European music. When one stopped on this side, the other started on the other side. (Papazoglou, 1994: 112)

What is particularly interesting is that apart from the live performances, the estudiantina is synonymous with erudition, the study which its etymology poses;

---

[16] For the 'politakia' and generally estudiantinas and the music life in Smyrna, see: Karakasis (1948); Solomonidis (1957); Papazoglou (1994); Kalyviotis (2002: 71); Kounadis (2003a: 294 and 2003b: 265); Jackson (2012); Ünlü (2016: 166–74); Fabbri (2016).

[17] In the Greek-speaking world of Smyrna and Constantinople, the word 'toys' means 'instruments'.

in other words, we have a musical education framework, which utilizes musical notation and reading. The whole management of the musical act is consequently distinguished by a scholarly process, which does not subtract from its popular, by nature, repertoire and its great popularity.

The photographic material proves the direct influence of the Spanish estudiantinas: a postcard of that period depicts the first 'politakia' in folklore attire (namely, in traditional Cretan costumes), mandolins and guitars, an image equivalent to traditional costume, which characterizes the theatrical aesthetic (which refers to auto-exoticism, a huge issue which this book will, however, not examine[18]) of the respective Spanish orchestra; however, their practices are not practices of mimicry.[19] As other musicians of Smyrna, having their ears open to the sounds surrounding them, they set a course of their own, shaping prototype aesthetics, style and repertoire.

It is important to understand certain basic characteristics of estudiantina activity, thus facilitating understanding also of the activities of the protagonists of the rebetiko during their subsequent stage, in Piraeus, since the condition of estudiantina was catalytic for the moulding of the artistic physiognomy. We should not forget that several protagonists of the Piraeus period originate from the world of the estudiantinas, such as, for example, Spyros Peristeris, Panagiotis Tountas and Vangelis Papazoglou (Papazoglou, 1994: 105–6). What is more, in understanding the physiognomy of the estudiantinas we will manage to decipher the term 'laiko' more. The term is granted diverse meaning, almost with every estudiantina recording.

Polystylism seems to dominate every urban popular musical form which develops within a condition that is characterized by two very important characteristics: the cosmopolitan aesthetic of everyday life and the direct connection of the musical act to discography, from the beginning of the twentieth century and onwards. Regarding the network constituted of the three urban centres which preoccupy us, that is, Constantinople, Smyrna and Athens, their cosmopolitanism is their characteristic trait. Should we also include in this network other large urban centres which communicate with the cities in question and, occasionally, participate indirectly in this common network, such as Bucharest, Cairo, Alexandria, Thessaloniki and Naples, then we shall ascertain

---

[18] See also Scott (2015b).
[19] This postcard can be found in Solomonidis (1957: 63), Kalyviotis (2002: 111), Kounadis (2003a: 295) and Ünlü (2016: 1710). See also www.akpool.co.uk/postcards/25532240-postcard-estudiantina-dorient-dirige-par-m-basile-sideris-musikgruppe-in-trachten-lauten.

that the cultural dialogues are multidimensional and extremely fecund.[20] In the communication amongst the points of this network, we must understand the catalytic role that discography plays, as music now travels faster and relays vaster amounts of information. In fact, it reaches the point of giving birth to not only new genres and idioms but also new specializations and occupations. Under these conditions, the estudiantinas constitute the 'radio' of the time, which, if nothing else, reproduces the hits – it deals in them, that is, its people subsist on this relationship but they also remodel them with every new performance, since laiki music is characterized by plasticity in performance. Thus, we have reached the point today to have access to a variety of performances of, supposedly, the same song, its performers, though, leaving evident signs of appropriation. We observe alterations in instrumentation, even in primary musical characteristics such as rhythmic accompaniment, melodic formulae and others.

In essence, the estudiantina sound is what has prevailed today as *fusion*. The sound products are dominated by certain characteristic traits:

1. The utilized instrumentation does not follow a particular 'traditional' prototype. Consequently, it is multi-selection and miscellaneous. Participation of instruments not only connected to laiko traditions, such as the mandolin, the folk clarinet, the lute and the santur, but also others with important tradition in high-status music, such as the horn, the violin and the violoncello.
2. Some of the protagonists are musically literate, able to read and write, while others function in the framework of orality.
3. Recordings take place with different guests every time (musicians and singers). Many of whom come from the opera house, while others from the 'stage' of a rural setting.
4. A motley amalgam of elements related to performance practices is observed, such as a congruous and incongruous coalescence of sound and/or instruments, voices and others. This fusion is confirmed by the record labels containing terms such as 'folk', 'folk-like', 'laiko', 'traditional', 'manes', 'rebetiko' and so on.
5. Composition form does not follow a certain prototype that could identify with some certain tradition of high-status music. It is, however, inextricably linked with the recording technology of the time.

---

[20] See also Fabbri (2016).

6. Freedom in performance practices is observed, which in essence is equal to non-existent musical notation, even though certain estudiantinas function as singular music schools.
7. Second recordings, often more than second, have been found of the same musical pieces which differentiate themselves on diverse levels.

The diverse musical languages which are involved in this composition freely share instrumentation, techniques, rhythmology, all types of modeness which characterize the various local ethno-cultural idioms, but also external influences, which disembark at its busy port; the Smyrna musical 'ecumene' functions in a spirit of perichoresis (co-inherence).[21]

Additionally, a statement by the santur player Kostas Tzovenos describes the fusion character of the repertoire vividly in another significant intersection of the cultural triangle which concerns us: in Athens. Based on the descriptions of Chatzipantazis (1986), after his exhaustive research, the migration of musicians from the East towards the Greek state is constant. In these groups of musicians, obviously, many from Smyrna are included. This deconstructs the claim of many years that the musical manifestations from the East reach the Greek state after the population exchange of 1923. Tzovenos explains:

> In 1925 at the Zefyros [a venue at Thision Square], we were a whole ensemble. We were better than the best mandolinata. Take Spyrakis Peristeris, Karipis, Ogdontas, myself, and Dalgas and you will know what I mean. We played everything there. Until ten o'clock, classical music including operettas. From ten until twelve, a mixed repertoire and after midnight, rebetika. (Schorelis, 1978, Vol. 3: 275-6)

In another part of her biography, Angela Papazoglou refers to the active repertoire of Smyrna:

> We played everything, ranging from the rebetiko to the European. All the operettas, Folk songs, Kleftika, Cretan, Kalamatiana, Fisounia, Thracian, from Ioannina, concertos with cavallerias, waltzes, dances by Brahms, serenades. We played everything. And certain parts from operas. ... We also played Jewish music, and Armenian, and Arabian. We are cosmopolitan. (Papazoglou, 1994: 58-9)

---

[21] The record label photographs taken in Smyrna and Constantinople and their ranking constitute perhaps the most vivid example of this syncretism (variety of languages, rhythm, genre, dromoi, makams, hymns, European, theatre, shadow theatre and others. See also Kalyviotis, 2002).

This spirit is, indeed, relayed thereafter to the Aegean, either in a natural way or via discography and the laterna (barrel piano), after the Asia Minor catastrophe. This, however, does not mean that the corresponding cultural reversal did not take place. In the Greek café amans of the nineteenth century, musician 'practiced their art in a cosmopolitan urban environment, wide open to a multitude of kaleidoscopic influences and new stimulations' (Chatzipantazis, 1986: 17). The way in which particular professional or/and ethno-cultural groups moved within the boundaries of Eastern Europe, the Balkans and the Mediterranean is definitely more complicated than what is happening at the port of Smyrna; certainly, a mutual musical enticement exists, musical 'wandering' in a dynamic network of exchange.[22]

Musicology which engages in folk-popular creations is already aware of the restrictions which come about from the examination of artistic creations, within the new reality of the nation states and their relevant ideologies. The Greek repertoires were 'locked' within a most specific geographical and cultural framework, that of the south-east Mediterranean, always subscribing to the now well-established lineage attitude. The relevant literature leaves two networks that seem to play an equally important role out of the equation: the musical 'ecumenes' of the Balkans and that of Eastern Europe, regions with a dynamic presence regarding Greek population. As seen from discography and historiography, both of these environs constitute basic discussants in a much larger, after all, network, than that of the south-east Mediterranean. If the counter-loans from Italy[23] and the Jewish world are added (Greeks and non-Greeks, Askenazis, Sephardis and Romaniots), and of course the world of America[24] and Egypt,[25] which present a great bulk of Greek discography, we can see that the network is even larger, more complex and much more interesting. In essence, there are parallel Greek discographies, of which only the Athenian one has been of any concern to us,[26] deemed always as a part of a closed group: that of the south-east Mediterranean. The last one is easily linked culturally to the Ottoman ecumene,[27] which in turn, in the relevant Greek literature, is also easily linked to the Byzantine.

---

[22] On the Greek diaspora, see indicatively Tziovas (2009).
[23] See Fabbri (2016).
[24] See Bucuvalas (2019).
[25] See Kalyviotis (1995).
[26] The two works of Aristomenis Kalyviotis are excluded, which, even though concern the most prevalent network, deal with the musical life and historical discography of Smyrna (Kalyviotis, 2002) and Thessaloniki (Kalyviotis, 2015).
[27] See Buchanan (2007).

Let us use the example of a song which discography credited to Giorgos Mitsakis titled 'In my own hut'[28] (popularly known as 'My own quilt'[29]). It seems that Mitsakis has used this particular musical melody in the song 'Clapping' too.[30] In Sephardic tradition, this melody is known as 'La Madre Comprensiva' and was recorded by David Saltiel,[31] renowned musician of the post-war period, who in fact chanted in the synagogue as a member of the Sephardic community of Thessaloniki. The older contributions to the melody must certainly be older than the recordings, since these refer to the Ottoman and Pontic (Black Sea region) repertoire ('Hamsi koydum tavaya').[32]

Can one, in the case mentioned earlier, detect point zero in history for the aforementioned song or try to credit it with a specific 'citizenship'? If so, it would mean, in the final analysis, isolating it from its constant evolution, that is, alienating it from its very nature. As Martin Stokes claims, such categorizations have an ideological function, which must be examined in relation to institutions and to the people that express it. But, above all, it matters little in relation to the music itself (Stokes, 1992: 4). Because music, and art in general, was never a self-powered field, isolated from a broader cultural reality. Quite the contrary, it interacts with other factors, such as society as a system, man as a personality, politics as power and so on.

The same musical melody is subject to aesthetical transformations, sketching the style of urban popular music, not as a superimposed trend with strict boundaries (rebetiko, klezmer, kanto, music of the lăutari), but as a purely intertextual field. On the one hand, specific aesthetic characteristics are recognized, whose nature, however, is purely fluid, since they are in perpetual transition. The plurality of implementation is obligatory, therefore, as a methodological starting point for their examination.

The examples of intertextuality from discography of urban popular musics of the twentieth century are numerous. The contemporary musicological toolbox examines them under the prism of inter-reference, borrowings/loans, collective composition, cultural co-inherence and syncretism. The concept of specific is

---

[28] Στην καλύβα τη δική μου, stin kalýva ti dikí mou: Odeon, DSOG 3173–7XGO 2650, 1965: https://youtu.be/7lmpVD0Z4sc.
[29] Το δικό μου πάπλωμα, to dikó mou páploma.
[30] Παλαμάκια, palamákia: Columbia, CG 2869–DG 6942, 1951: https://youtu.be/8NiEGh4cyBc.
[31] Album *Jewish-Spanish Songs of Thessaloniki*, Oriente Musik, LC 3592: https://youtu.be/JQ_l0InnbRM, 1998: track 5.
[32] See, for example, for the melody of 'Hamsi koydum tavaya': https://youtu.be/KTY7YcKFarE; https://youtu.be/LzTjMN0nmqc; https://youtu.be/TNYHEQ52_os; https://youtu.be/QQToReP-uF0; https://youtu.be/M0KFYvL9HNg.

redefined in these considerations. The reference of a popular work to some basic and distinctive musical characteristic of another work does not automatically constitute a conscious borrowing, at least as this is perceived in the strict context of the current copyright law. The reserves from which the protagonists draw on seem to be common property. The more the sound industry matures, the more substance does copyright and its protection acquire. In Greece, perhaps the most decisive instance for this was the renowned 'period of Indocracy', after 1958.[33] Before that, however, discography reveals that copying was not only not an act to be prosecuted, but also a basic tool of the protagonists.

Through discography examination, musical references, whose recognisability varies, have been ascertained. We detect pieces which clearly refer to earlier works but also others which cause a feeling of familiarity; what we usually refer to as 'it reminds me of something'. Even though 'copies', whether more or less, the intertexts are characterized by a sense of singularity.

What is interesting is the different categories of these references, as many times one perceives the clear intentions of the creators, while at others it seems the references have been made unconsciously.

Through reconsideration and the effort to redefine the text of the pieces, the words 'authentic' and 'original' become a focal point, words which undoubtedly constitute hotly debated topics in the negotiation of music. Can, however, a clear definition exist concerning the authentic and, at the same time, can it act as an indicative gauge of its meta-text?[34] To what degree is the material of a piece evident and specific? In the study of intertextuality in popular manifestations, the protagonists, having the musical act itself as a focal point, find themselves in a constant state of inter-reference, many times unconsciously and at others consciously.

Once familiar laiki music was identified with the marginalized rebetiko, it took on a new context in post-war Greece, with Vasilis Tsitsanis being the harbinger, who had already been revitalizing the atmosphere since the pre-war period.[35] However, its aesthetic self-efficiency was never recognized, and its

---

[33] 'This is the time when films from India started to be shown in Greece, from approximately 1954. These movies contained many popular and traditional songs from India. Many famous and not so famous songwriters of that period took some of these songs and applied Greek lyrics (done by either amateur or professional lyricists). Then, these people recorded the altered songs using Greek style popular orchestras, and by selling the records, great profits were made without people knowing the truth about their origins and the original songwriters being deprived of any credit' (Ordoulidis, 2014: 62). See also Tasoulas and Ambatzi (1998), and Pennanen (1999: 36, 69–75).

[34] See also Zoubouli and Ordoulidis (2018).

[35] For the work of Tsitsanis, see Ordoulidis (2014).

musical validity could not be emancipated: its acceptance is subject to certain conditions '"by the powers that be", or, in any case, "externally", in other words not by the socio-cultural world that created it' (Vlisidis, 2006: 13). Condemned by the old dipole East–West, the laiko becomes a synonym for simplistic, cheap and for the masses, subject to qualitative 'arbitration'.[36] As Vasilis Tsitsanis said just before his death:

> The custodians of 'this or that is forbidden', the pursuit of the police in order to isolate it [the rebetiko], rendered it, in that period, the song of a specific group of people. (Tsitsanis, 1983)

The rationale of 'defending' the laiko does not only concern the hegemony of the high-status. The community of the proponents of the rebetiko revival[37] developed reflexes, seeking authenticity and denouncing every supposed 'desecration'. What suffered a handicap in the all-round imminent interventions of the laiko culture is, naturally, our collective conscience.

---

[36] See Moschopoulos (1936), Euangelidis (1937), Papantoniou (1938), Kyr. (1946) and Kokkinos (1949).
[37] For the revival of the rebetiko, see Tragaki (2007). See also Karanikas (2011).

14

Reaffirming the laiko

Tsitsanis is from Trikala. His father is from Ioannina[1] and his mother from Zagori.[2] He comes into contact with diverse manifestations of urban repertoire: his father performs folk songs; in Trikala they operate a café aman and a café chantants; performance companies and shadow puppeteers pass through the region. Undoubtedly, Trikala is a key junction in a wide cultural network.[3]

At the time that Tsitsanis moves to Athens, Spyros Peristeris, artistic director of Odeon–Parlophone, has begun to capitalize on the bouzouki, proposing a discographical landscape based on it. According to the relevant literature, Peristeris, who is the fundamental 'orchestrator' of urban popular discography, attempts to grant the bouzouki commercial dimensions. It is then that recordings of Vamvakaris take place, approximately in 1933. With the recordings of Tsitsanis, beginning in 1936, in essence the first school of bouzouki is introduced, and the instrument now acquires a dominant role. It is a focal point and determines aesthetic evolution in the laiko song. The skill that has been cultivated and constantly developed by Tstitsanis is defining, as it contributes to the instrument acquiring autonomy, self-sufficiency and aesthetic identity.

Early repertoire based on the bouzouki was subsequently named 'rebetiko of Piraeus'.[4] In essence, fundamental protagonists are the plucked instruments,

---

[1] The location of Ioannina: https://goo.gl/maps/G92KLtXEKB8Snu2D6.
[2] The location of Zagori: https://goo.gl/maps/s8dLibySJe6vjphG6. For Tsitsanis's biography, see indicatively: Anastasiou (1995), Alexiou (2001 and 2003) and Barbatsis (2016).
[3] Regarding Trikala, see Kliafa (1996 and 2003) and Anastasiou (2014).
[4] In the event that we accept discography as a reference point, according to Stathis Gauntlett the term 'rebetiko' appears circa 1913 printed on gramophone record labels of England and America (Gauntlett, 2001). Additionally, Gauntlett justifiably assumes that 'the commercial use of the term requires at the very least its widespread recognition' (2001: 31-2). The rebetiko of Piraeus, which is based on the bouzouki, as proposed by Peter Manuel (1990) and Risto Pekka Pennanen (1999 and 2004), and in the event that the beginning of the discography of Vamvakaris is considered as a reference point, then this dates back to approximately 1933. If we take into account the recordings conducted in America beginning in 1926 (see Kourousis, 2013: 84) and the piece 'Τα δίστιχα του μάγκα' (ta dísticha tou mánga, the couplets of a toughie; Columbia, WG 233-DG 147), recorded in Athens in 1931 with Giorgos Manetas on the bouzouki, also notably the notorious recording of 'Μινόρε του τεκέ' (minóre tou teké; the minor of the opium den; Columbia, W 206584-CO

something which is connected to the world of the Greek estudiantinas and the mandolinatas of Smyrna and Constantinople, which had been recording from the early 1900s. This plucked sound is familiar to Tsitsanis. Apart from these soundscapes, even more Eastern sounds, which are perceived as Turkish, are old acquaintances of the Greek reality (see Chatzipantazis, 1986).

Due to ideological conflict and the general political situation in the Greek state, this type of urban repertoire is identified with marginalization. On the one hand, the lyrics which refer to 'inferior' issues, and on the other the alla turca sound constitute forbidden aesthetics. The repertoire, obviously, is regulated not only by these characteristics. The specific trends are extremely specific. They are enough, however, to dominate it completely. And let us not forget that the dipole battles between West and East and the search for an identity constitute issues of great controversy, for at least a century. The contemporary state attempts to respond to whether it desires a Western or an Eastern sound.

Tsitsanis's actions show that he perceives this polemic and marginalization of the urban repertoire. Perhaps, this is the reason that he prefers to use the term 'laiko' instead of the term 'rebetiko'. Despite this, we are not in a position to know which social classes use the term 'rebetiko' and how commonplace it is in their vernacular. In any case, Tsitsanis does not talk about his music in a dipole mentality, but rather poses issues of aesthetic. The prevalent literature considers Tsitsanis a protagonist in the transition in the world of the rebetiko to that of the more widespread laiko. Essentially, this concerns mostly the intellectual world, accepting of Tsitsanis, and through him the sounds of the urban popular song, with a fairly elitist attitude. Catalytic points are the renowned lecture by Hadjidakis (1949), as well as the change of attitude of the music critic Sophia Spanoudi, whose opinions defined the trends in the intellectual world. In reality, these issues are complex and Hadjidakis's lecture overestimated, as it refers to a very specific audience. Change comes from within, with the work of Tsitsanis as the main protagonist and its acceptance by the average person of different social levels. The Westernization of the rebetiko, with which he is credited, is unconvincing and is based on cultural borders. Both as geographical destinations and as cultural ones, the terms 'West' and 'East' seem restrictive

---

56294F) by Ioannis Chalikias in America, recorded in 1932 or perhaps even 1933, the appearance of the bouzouki in discography is dated earlier. Recently, in his bachelor thesis, Giorgos Gekas (2018) called attention to the recording of a song under the name of Panagiotis Tountas (the other 'orchestrator' of the urban sound, together with Peristeris), in which the bouzouki is the protagonist. The song is called 'Πειραιώτισσα γλυκιά' (peiraiótissa glykiá, sweet girl from Piraeus), and seems to have been recorded in 1931 (HMV OW 330–AO 2043, 1931: https://youtu.be/V8A-WC5zzKw).

where examination of such manifestations are concerned. Political borders rarely coincide with cultural ones, which are difficult to define.

With aesthetic criteria, Tsitsanis composes 'in the present' and indicates that he realizes fundamental points of musical creation. For the laiko, creation is a complex puzzle: the music stage, composition at home, rehearsal, recomposition during rehearsal and redefinition with every performance, collaborations with musicians and singers, discography as a process, the faring of the recording commercially and others (see Figure 14.1).[5]

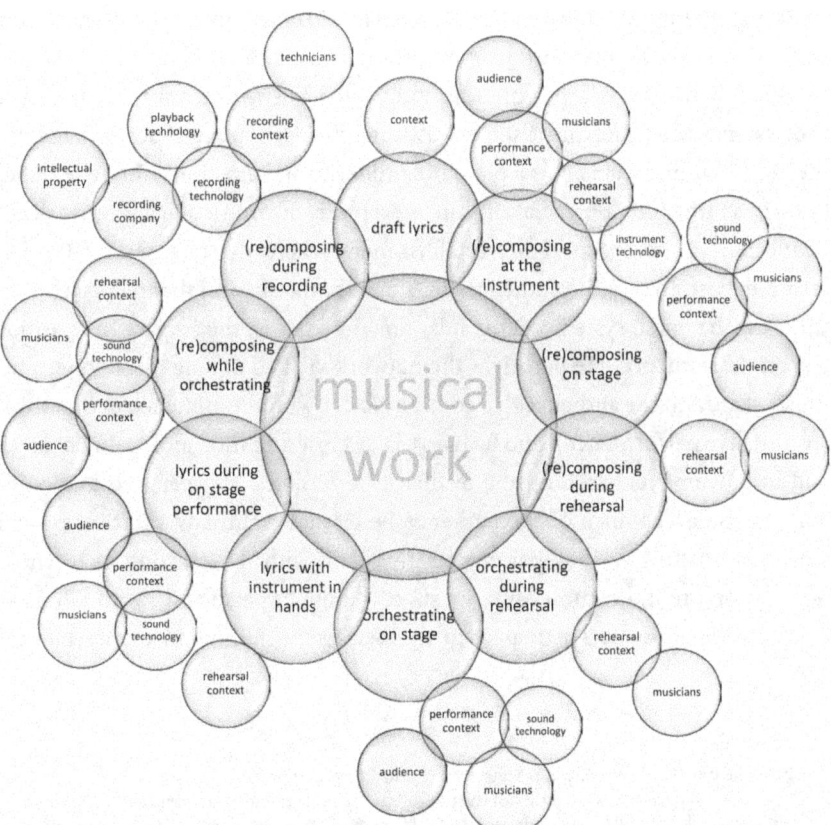

Figure 14.1 Thoughts on the creation puzzle of the work.

---

[5] In this discourse, the argument and rationale of Julian Johnson emerges who deems that 'the musical work is neither the score, the live performance, nor the recording; it exists somewhere between the idea of the work and its realization in performance' (Johnson, 2002: 55). Having excluded from this discourse the stereotypical dipole popular–high-status, we realize the gravity with which Tsitsanis works on the key part of actualizing the ideas, which he processes with persistence, seeking the 'high'

Tsitsanis is a workaholic and persistent, having constantly as a background the relationship of transmitter–receiver, that is, creator and audience. In a variety of features of all the above, he appears aware, concerning his choices: orchestration, utilized instrumentation, vocals, mainstream sound, the sound industry, lyrics and so on. He works on and revisits his original ideas again and again. He places much importance on what we would call a *hit*, having exonerated the mediation of the sound industry. He talks about the acceptance of the songs by the audience, something by which, according to him, even the tastes of the creator are defined. For him, a favourite song constitutes the favourite song of the audience.[6]

To all the aforementioned, we are obliged to add one more catalytic dimension: Tsitsanis ceaselessly plays on the music stage, since 1935 until his very last days. In other words, he is a person who knows the business from within; he is a professional artist. The music stage constitutes the per se place of performance for the laiko. For musicians, it is a place of familiarity and creation, with which they bond in a rather complex relationship.[7] As a place, the music stage is intrinsically connected to the space of the establishment where the receivers of the live creation exist, that is, the audience. Tsitsanis shows early on that he places great value on the value system of this relationship. That is, the impact his creation has on the audience. He perceives the network created among discography, the music stage and the audience. He communicates with the audience in every way (record, live performance), and he tries to pay close attention and makes changes and improvements based on the feedback he receives. He seems to know that without the acceptance of the audience he cannot claim any substance to his work. He realizes various parameters that deal with the creation as a whole: how to conjure it, how to ensure its success, how to perform it, with whom to cooperate in order to participate in the performance, how to orchestrate the

---

within the popular. Justifiably, it is Shusterman who assists comprehension of such issues, as, in this literature as well the aesthetic entity of the popular is highlighted (see Shusterman, 2000).

[6] He responds characteristically to the question of Giorgos Papastefanou regarding the number of his compositions 'songs do not matter, hits do'. Immediately after, Papastefanou asks him if he believes that 'Cloudy Sunday' is his most representative song. Tsitsanis answers, 'If the people think so, so do I' (Giorgos Papastefanou television programme: 'Music writes history'. Station of the Armed Forces (YENED), 1973 – https://youtu.be/imA1K9qlFgk [visited on 17/1/2016]).

[7] 'Palko ("stage") is actually a word that in Greek denotes the musical practice, too. "Being on the palko" is a phrase that literally means participation in musical performance. The performance of a rebetiko kompania from the elevated position of the palko places the musicians in a prominent location within the space of music-making. The stage clearly distinguishes the musicians from the patrons; it becomes a social barrier that symbolically manifests their identities in the performance context because it emphatically differentiates them as performers' (Tragaki, 2007: 200).

lyrics and so on. The artist improves and evolves constantly on stage.⁸ His skill is his tool in composition. The cultivation of his skill is not achieved through systematic study, but stems from his work, on stage, during rehearsal and during composition itself.

Even though Tsitsanis performs with a bouzouki, he usually processes musical ideas with a guitar in his hands.⁹ He seems to invest a lot in harmonic environs which he does not consider just chordal sequences, nor these instruments typical accompanying instruments. He perceives harmony as a fundamental crux of his creations, much like a framework on which he builds. In an overwhelming majority of his discographical corpus, he writes the lyrics as well. He is in complete control, that is, of the main axis in composition. In the laiko, many times these are worked on simultaneously, until a 'final' form is achieved.

The first discographical projects of the rebetiko of Piraeus at Columbia, as can be seen on the historical record labels, are orchestrated by Spyros Peristeris, who orchestrates Tsitsanis's first projects too. Soon after, however, the latter will take up the orchestrating baton, not only for himself, but also for other protagonists. It is logical that the sounds that exist in Tsitsanis's ears are the ones heard in Trikala. What is more, his brief study of European music, quite possibly granted him additional tools. Tsitsanis constitutes a key persona in discography, as up to then only cosmopolitan musicians who come from historical networks make decisions. Panagiotis Tountas, Spyros Peristeris and Kostas Skarvelis carry the experiences and the musical realities of the regions in which they lived with them: Constantinople, Smyrna, Alexandria and so on. Tsitsanis takes on the responsibility of artistic director at Columbia – His Master's Voice, signifying a turning point; the viewpoint of other junctions than those of the historical networks plays a leading role. It is the turn of the viewpoint of Trikala and Athens.

---

[8] At this point, the emblematic work of Simon Frith *Performing Rites – On the Value of Popular Music* comes to the forefront and the discourse initiated on the value code which regulates decisions made by musicians on different levels: 'Of everyone involved in the popular music world, musicians most routinely use value judgments, and use them to effect. Musicians have to make a series of decisions. … Such decisions are both individual, a reflection of one's own talent (musical talent describes, among other things, the ability to make the right decisions about what's good), and social – only other people, other musicians, can legitimate your decisions' (Frith, 1998: 52).

[9] This information was obtained during one of the many visits by the author to the artist's home. Specifically, his son Kostas talked about Tsitsanis and his obsession with the guitar (see also Ordoulidis, 2014: 121).

Part three

Factual highlights regarding ecclesiastical music

15

The reference text and the musical act

In ecclesiastical music, composers were often 'canonized', either literally or metaphorically; their work was considered to be inspired by the Divine and its performance was intrinsically connected to a life of worship. In laiki music, this ritualistic dimension is transferred to another context, where musicians are often idolized and their work is charged in a multitude of ways, ideologically and politically. The big difference here is when we factor in emotional reception. As Antonios Alygizakis claims, in a text from a publication of the recordings of Iakovos Naupliotis,[1] Byzantine music 'is not associated with the provocation of the senses, emotion, delight and enjoyment. ... It is not aesthetically based, but ontologically' (2008: 18). Chrysanthos in his *Great Theoretical Treatise* emphasizes: 'The perfect musician is the one who is able to chant while inducing; delight or sorrow, enthusiasm or indolence, cowardice or courage, or awe, or no emotion, one who is able to move the soul in any way (passion)' (1832: 4). On the other hand, laiko composers often spoke about such narratives concerning the passions of life, something which elicits an emotional response from the audience.[2]

The substance of a musical piece can be understood neither only from its notation nor from a particular performance, but through its multilevel actualization, which is described by the word 'performance', about which the fields of anthropology and musicology have already deliberated in a multitude of ways. However, the way with which we refer to a musical genre is defined substantially by its semiology, the 'starting point' being the 'text' of reference. In ecclesiastical music, this is detected in its notation, while in urban laiki music

---

[1] Naupliotis was a Lambadarios (left chanter) of the Patriarchate Church from 1905 to 1911 and First Cantor (right chanter) from 1911 to 1939. He was the first Patriarchate chanter who commercially recorded on seventy-eight rpm.
[2] See, for example, the autobiographies of Vamvakaris (Vellou-Kail, 1978) and Mitsakis (Oikonomou, 1995). See also Gauntlett's interview of Tsitsanis (2001: 176).

it seems to be found in the recording.[3] Evidently, this difference reflects, to a large extent, the variation in the degree of integration of each genre in the duo high-status–popular, which becomes even more noticeable when referring to the performance context. However, what must not be ignored here is that a convergence is, in fact, rendered: in both genres, the aural content may undergo important changes from one interpretation to another, reorganizing its basic 'text' in a way which permits it to be characteristically 'receptive' to additions and modifications; in this way, in fact, it often changes from one category to the next. And it is exactly here that imagination resides in the dipoles. From this perspective, there is no 'authentic' performance, creating a new 'text' each time, which may be documented notation, a live performance or a recording. Even though the 'text' of reference, a musical manuscript or a first performance is extremely important, dictating a form of 'obedience', it does, however, acquire new life and dynamic from subsequent renditions,[4] without being subjected to 'corruption'.

Consequently, the theoretical framework which describes both urban laiko idioms and Byzantine music does not precede the musical act, but follows it. Documentation, recordings or musical texts, no matter how detailed they may be, are not enough in order for their dynamic aesthetic to be understood. They correspond to a specific point in time and space, allowing the experience and the orally transmitted musical information to complete the performance (see also Plemmenos, 2015).

---

[3] About 'texts' in urban popular music idioms, see Moore (2001 and 2007).
[4] 'Oral tradition is animate because it does not care, primarily, about interpreting the vested stylistic prototype of some past composer's thought, but to creatively reproduce the meaning and the innuendo of the written musical text' (Giannelos, 2009: 10–11).

16

'Notes not noted in the text'

Constantinople as a reference point

The Patriarchate circular of 1880 constitutes a turning point in performance practices, as an order was issued, especially concerning inexperienced chanters, obliging them to use written music texts. Concerning experienced chanters, the need to memorize these music texts is emphasized. In addition, it was now prescribed what would be considered 'classical' and, consequently, accepted music documentation, as for example the *Brief Anastasimatario* by Petros of the Byzantine, the *Brief Doxastario*[1] by Petros of the Peloponnese, the *Hirmologion* by Petros of the Byzantine and so on. Issuing the order in question, on the one hand, the Patriarchate wanted to protect the 'authentic' yphos, but on the other it also perhaps wanted to grant it a special status. It is logical that through time a multitude of yphos among the chanters of Constantinople had developed. We should not forget that the ultimate level of the 'authentic' yphos was always bound to the Patriarchal Church of Saint George, at a time when a plethora of churches in the wider area of Constantinople functioned, some of which had eminent chanters.[2] Some chanters of other churches were key personas, because they not only participated actively in the teaching of ecclesiastical music and in the structure of its theoretical background, but also participated many times in the Patriarchate commissions, publishing texts (see, for example, the cases of Theodoros Phokaeas and Georgios Progakis). These chanters occasionally participated actively in the teaching of high-status secular music as well, which they often called 'external melodies': compositions by Greek-educated musicians of Constantinople based on the system of the makam. Nevertheless, it

---

[1] Αναστασηματάριο (ανάσταση), Resurrection Hymnal; δοξαστάριο (δόξα, praise), a set of hymns from several periods and feasts of the ecclesiastical year.

[2] 'In Istanbul, the leading cantors of the Patriarchate of Constantinople came to be viewed as the principal repositories of Byzantine chant. Their manner of singing was highly valorized by virtue of their belonging to the "school" of the Patriarchate' (Erol, 2015: 11).

is impossible for a musical idiom based to such an extent on orality to be placed in a 'mould', especially when it comes to its performance, something which Antonios Alygizakis notes:

> The Patriarchate style, however, does not constitute a rigid reality, as happens with the typical service of the West. In the East, with the Ecumenical Patriarchate as the epicentre, the Orthodox experience forges an intense cosmopolitan character through a multitude of local traditions. (Alygizakis, 2008: 24)

The systemization and regulation trends both in repertoire and in performance practice should be examined through the European Enlightenment prism too, which influenced music as well. Regarding the issue of tonality, we should mention the decision of the Music Committee of 1881 established by the Ecumenical Patriarchate, which determined the pitch of the note Ni. Initially, the proposal of the Committee, composed of Archimandrite Germanos Afthonidis, Andreas Spatharis, Georgios Violakis, Ioasaf Monk, Eustratios Papadopoulos and Nikolaos Ioannidis, was the respective of the European note C. As we are informed by the journal *Εκκλησιαστική Αλήθεια* (ekklisiastikí alítheia, ecclesiastic truth) (Α΄, 01/06/1881, issue Γ΄, pp. 47–8), the Committee sent a letter to the Patriarchate on 25 March 1881, proposing

> in order for a note with specific beats to be introduced into our music system as an initial foundation, with which the isons [the pitch] of every sound shall be related; we have accepted/determined Ni as such a note, corresponding to the European C (264 beats) according to the German tonary, and which is absolutely suitable for our established vocal system.

Finally, in the Theory of the Committee, printed in 1888, we are informed that 'we have introduced into teaching and into practice the tonal base with the determined height of 256 palms [cycles]' (Music Committee, 1888: 3). This important decision cast the die for the note C to facilitate the subsequent musicological comparative analysis of the two music worlds and should be viewed as a point of reference.[3] Misail Misailidis proceeds to draw a variety of parallels concerning ecclesiastical music of the Eastern Orthodox Church with that of European music, stressing that the West cultivated and evolved the music of ancient Greece (1902). All this denotes consistency towards the intense

---

[3] Concerning the specific analogy, see Chatzimichelakis (2013: 98).

modernistic attitude expressed by Chrysanthos in his theory, in the light of his evident confabulation with European trends and the spirit of Enlightenment.[4]

In the Theory of the Committee of 1881, published in 1888, there are two paragraphs which may be considered as the first official attempt at acknowledging yphos in a musicological prism:

> Recitation manner is expression or quality, which ornaments and graces the melody, without which it would be rendered graceless and somewhat lifeless. Consequently, in general, quality is reliant on the aesthetical elegance of the chanter, however, it is no less subject to certain rules, found at times either in a more powerful or milder tone of voice, and at others in the rapid connection of close notes, not noted in the text. (1888: 34–5)

Regarding the same issue, which is nothing but the negotiation of fluidity and pluralism in performance styles, we should mention the definition of the neume omalón ⎯⎯𝒇[5] in the same theory:

> The omalon requires a somewhat smooth vocal fluctuation towards the note above it, in order for a voice to connect very quickly with the next note, thus, this ⎯⎯ is approximately this ⎯⎯. (1888: 42)

What is explained in the aforementioned excerpt concerns the quality of the interpretation of the symbols in Byzantine notation. The interpretation manner adds or subtracts notes, modifying, that is, the musical text. In other words, were the aforementioned excerpt to be translated into staff notation, where we see ⎯⎯, we would roughly interpret ⎯⎯.

The conversion of notation, that is, the 'translation' of the visual prompt into sound, in a way constitutes the core of yphos. The latter varies, just like other 'translation' systems vary, for instance that of language, depending on the school, that is, the idiomatic manner of each executor. Thus, in this particular example, one school may interpret the neume omalón with a fast vibrato, while another in a much milder way, using an even higher note (a more intense sharp which would produce a bigger interval).[6]

---

[4] For the French sources of Chrysanthos, see the extremely interesting article by Haris Xanthoudakis 'The Great Theory of Chrysanthos and its French sources' (2007).
[5] Ομαλόν, neted.
[6] On the same issue, see the paper of Gerasimos Sofoklis Papadopoulos titled 'A "linguistic type" of approach to the contemporary chanting art', at the 2nd International Musicological and Interdisciplinary Conference of the Department of Psaltic Art and Musicology of the Volos Academy for Theological studies (2017).

For most of the chanting world, the point of reference, also used as a singular 'unit of measure' of yphos, is the performance practice which corresponds to the chanters who serve the Ecumenical Patriarchate of Constantinople.[7] The mindset behind the use of a point of reference falls within the framework of the 'authenticity' issue. Based on the sources and commonly accepted by music practitioners, the executive tradition of the Patriarchate performers indeed did not prescribe the use of music texts. To be exact, this lack of prescription was more a case of prohibition, as apprenticeship was completed after years beside an active chanter of the Patriarchate and resulted in off by heart experiential performance. What is written before the sheet music of *The Akathist Hymn* in Progakis's book, grants us an additional dimension to this particular discourse: 'το σύνηθες μέλος' (to sýnithes mélos, the common melody).

Music transcription 16.1 The 'common melody', as shown in Progakis (1909: 188).

'Common' implies not only fluidity and diversity in performance, but also approximation in the documentation of a melody, which bases its existence on the orality which governs its propagation. Furthermore, in the collection of Progakis, but also in that of Ioannis and Stefanos, there are a variety of references to previous composers; in documentation, that is, of performances by specific chanters of the Patriarchate (for example, 'another piece by Peter' and

---

[7] See also Angelinaras (1992), Alygizakis (2008: 18) and Khalil (2009).

'another piece by Raidestinos').[8] Konstantinos Psachos, in his renowned article on yphos (1908), condemned the Patriarchate chanters because they did not adhere precisely to the written melodic lines of the books. As we read earlier, Psachos was responsible for the establishment and function of the first school of Byzantine music in the Athens Conservatory, 'conveying' the Patriarchate yphos to the Greek state and systemizing the education of chanters. At this point, an important question arises and constitutes a bone of contention in the particular field. In an interview on the ERT (Greek National Radio and Television)[9] programme, *Night Visitor*,[10] Spyros Peristeris (1913–98), the First Cantor in the Metropolitan Cathedral of Athens since 1951, claims that he is the continuer of the first teacher of Byzantine music of the first school created at the Athens Conservatory by Konstantinos Psachos, who taught him the Patriarchate yphos. Peristeris states and describes the variation in the Thessaloniki yphos though, whose chanters also claim to be continuers of the Patriarchate yphos, due to the strong relations with Constantinople. During the interview, Peristeris gives a musical example, performing the same hymn initially in his own yphos and then in the yphos of the School of Thessaloniki, characterizing it as a 'misrepresentation' of the classical and 'correct' text and yphos, respectively.[11]

Undoubtedly, the issue of analysing the documented melodies of the so-called classical books is a focal point, with the most contentious point, even nowadays, being the manner with which the written melody is analysed during the performance. The way in which the different yphoses evolved through time constitutes an especially significant issue in the circles of musicians who practise the genre in question. A careful observation of live performance practices reveals

---

[8] Alexander Konrad Khalil's (2009) doctoral dissertation, having a musically centred axis, is wholly dedicated to the examination and analysis of the 'translation' of the visual (sheet music) to the audio (performance). Khalil, abiding with the trends of contemporary musicology, negotiates the case study of the chanting idiom of the Patriarchate Church. Doctoral dissertation title: 'Echoes of Constantinople: Oral and Written Tradition of the Psaltes of the Ecumenical Patriarchate of Constantinople' (Khalil, 2009). The issues regarding the contemporary scientific realities of musicology are analytically examined by Agamemnonas Tentes, in his introduction at the conference 'The Psaltic Art as an Autonomous Art', in 2014 in Volos, titled 'Proposals for an interdisciplinary approach to our musicology based on current trends in international research in humanities sciences' (2015).
[9] Based on the documentation of the ERT Archives, year of production is 1998 (http://archive.ert.gr/551 [visited on 29/8/2014]).
[10] Νυχτερινός Επισκέπτης, nychterinós episképtis.
[11] In an earlier broadcast, which seems to have been broadcast in 1989 by ERT 1, the scene with Peristeris sitting at the piano and talking about his research in folk music is impressive. Peristeris shows his skill on the piano by performing a kleftiko song titled 'Κατσαντώνης' (Katsantónis). He seems to have assimilated the idiomatic activity of the piece and, in a unique way, conveyed it to the instrument, transcending theoretical issues of well-temperedness. Unfortunately, it was impossible to find the whole interview, but only a specific excerpt on YouTube (https://youtu.be/VsbPgxJndxc).

a ceaseless creation of new and multiform yphoses, which oftentimes take on the significance of a whole school, whether identified with a specific persona or a local idiom (see, for example, the School of Peristeris, Karamanis, Chrysanthos, Taliadoros and Cephalonia, Zakynthos).

If anything, it is one of the many cases which concern music notation of diverse music idioms, where during the process of visualization of the audio phenomenon it is impossible to include the bulk of information relayed by sound and which differs from performance to performance. Perhaps this is also one of the main reasons for the evolution of music notation in different music genres and idioms, as new needs constantly come forth, dictating a more detailed documentation.[12] Many times these changes to documentation systems have even brought about the birth of new systems, such as, for example, spectrometers and charts, which are now considered music transcription in contemporary musicology. In this respect, a fluctuation in a human voice could be imprinted in greater detail and with much more information with this kind of practice, compared to the transcription of notes. On the other hand, there are arguments concerning the hegemony of sheet music, something which, in another context, is supported by Joanna Demers, mentioning that many composers, such as Beethoven, Wagner and Brahms, 'wrote pieces whose fundamental incarnations were the scores themselves. Performances were merely imperfect manifestations of the notated ideas' (Demers, 2006: 33–4). Something like this shifts the discussion to particulars concerning the basic content of an artistic piece, its basic 'material' and the modified messages of various performers.

---

[12] Kurt Stone's publication is indicative of the new ways of notating and imprinting audio phenomenon in contemporary 'classical' music: *Music Notation in the Twentieth Century. A Practical Guidebook* (1980).

17

Style, scores and the teacher

With regard to orthodox ecclesiastical chanting and its primary written text, the analysis reveals issues particularly complex and interesting. While theoretically sheet music constitutes an inviolable official document, which salvages the spiritual deposition of the creator unaltered, in many cases performance practices render it simply a type of 'guide'. There are those who are avid proponents of the stringent adherence to the interpretation of the music text (supporters of the rigid attitude of Konstantinos Psachos), while others argue that the text is descriptive and that it is without substance if we eliminate the performance practice.[1] Furthermore, another group supports the specific in analysis, that is, a standard performance-translation of the written music texts. For example, a specific way of performing the petastí neume, specific intonations in the vareía neume and so on.[2] Giannelos writes:

> With the continual transition from the descriptive to the specific, not only in graphic representation of music but also in its interpretation (and this occurs when interpretation is based more on text and less on memory), there is the danger that this notation will function as a series of symbols which will correspond to a reference system of predetermined and consciously reproduced actions, which shall transform it from a living oral tradition to an academically stylized tradition, as has, already, happened with other traditions. (Giannelos, 2009: 11)

The music texts which are performed already constitute, in many cases, extensions of the classical texts, that is, already-altered versions of the acceptable music books of the Ecumenical Patriarchate, according to classical tradition. The role of personal théseis[3] of each chanter, that is, the degree of diversification in performance compared to someone else in a common music text, reveals the

---

[1] See also Afthonidis (2003, originally published in 1876).
[2] Πεταστή, flutter; βαρεία, grave, heavy accent.
[3] Θέση (plural, θέσεις), thesi (theseis): locus.

important dimension of orality in the chanting art, which is found in the causal core of the evolutionary course of the genre.[4]

The focal point of this discussion is what is usually called 'yphos' by the circles of the chanting world, which constitutes an element acquired after years of practice beside a teacher, who imparts his yphos to his students. Yphos is intrinsically connected to the practice of performance and entails vocal timbre, articulation, pronunciation, breathing, vocal placement, rhythmic conduct, intervals, kinesiology of the performer, facial expressions, variegation, dynamics, intonations and much more. In essence, all the qualitative characteristics concerning the manner of interpretation, rendition and performance of an artistic creation, which will ultimately identify not only a whole school but also a unique performance.[5]

The term 'teacher' seems to take on different meanings from place to place and from time to time: teacher in a conservatory, teacher in a recognized school of Byzantine music in a diocese, teacher in an informal school in a village or town parish, practice-based performer in a village, a priest with an aptitude for chanting and others. Obviously, yphos is also formed according to the student, and the degree of similarity he bears to his teacher varies.

Chanters, just like other musicians, can be distinguished based on the level of their musical literacy: those who have theoretical knowledge of Byzantine music and those who are practice-based performers. It is impossible for the category of practice-based performers to perform, even approximately, the documented slow form of any hymn; thus, at this point we observe the phenomenon of improvisation. Depending on the kind of experience one has, an atmosphere is built, sometimes close to the documented music text and at others far from it. On the contrary, the category of literate performers concerns chanters who, in their overwhelming majority, have received formal education regarding Byzantine music either from a conservatory or from a school of Byzantine music.[6] In this category, we see various subcategories which refer to the school

---

[4] 'Théseis are melodic formulae of varying lengths. Théseis are specific to accent pattern, form, rhythmic genre, and mode. ... Although théseis can and frequently are written down, Stelios [chanter at the Patriarchate] maintains that théseis are beneath the surface of the melody, and that what we see on the page and call "thésis" is an expression of them' (Khalil, 2009: 144).

[5] Here, parallels could be drawn amongst other such phenomena concerning diverse music genres, as, for example, the Romanian, Turkish and Greek violin schools, the case of the alla greca laiko klarino and the clarinet (Epirus, Turkey, Klezmer), classic piano in Russia, Germany and Italy, jazz, latin and rock piano, the flamenco, the blues and the rebetiko guitar, eastern or modal piano in Algeria, Iran and Lebanon and others.

[6] Both are institutions recognized by the state with the same professional qualification rights.

of apprenticeship, that is, the teacher under which one apprenticed, which yphos was taught and to what extent the institution and the teacher follow either a severe or a mild policy concerning rigidity and the degree of difficulty for the acquisition of a degree. In other words, if one has attended a local conservatory in a rural area which follows a mild policy, it is quite likely that one has not been taught complex pieces (usually called μαθήματα, mathímata [singular: máthima], pieces/lessons), which are characterized by a high level of virtuosity. Thus, certain slow transcriptions of 'The Akathist Hymn,' in this particular case, require advanced skills, something which automatically means that such a graduate will never perform such a piece during the service of the Salutations.

The performance of the sheet music of a musical piece is dependent on the yphos of the performer, that is, how he 'evolved' the school he attended, and it is especially powerful. In many cases, extensive parts of the sheet music are difficult to recognize in the interpretation or many times they are not performed at all, giving up their place to instant improvisations, something which suggests a 'popular' aspect of chanting, as we shall see further on. The yphos of each teacher is enriched by each student in turn and is delivered to the next already processed, granting classical texts dimensions of 'recomposition' of their fundamental formulae (see also Zervas, 2007). Based on this, one observes the pluralism detected in local yphoses. For at least a century a certain practice has been ascertained: the publication of books by various performers which contain their personal theseis on the classical music texts, that is, all their implemented additions and modifications. This practice flourished even more round about the middle of the twentieth century. These performers were/are usually popular in their community and their school attracted and continues to attract a plethora of students. The practice of additions to a musical piece, in a background characterized by intense standardization and now mass production of this particular art, brings to the forefront an especially interesting aspect of the Byzantine culture, which are the ανθίβολα (anthívola, preparatory drawings), and their artistic evolution through time. The former First Cantor of the Patriarchal Church, Leonidas Asteris, in an interview on the television broadcast 'Archontaríki',[7] speaks about this particular practice by the chanters, who add their personal theseis to the classical texts and mentions that a new

---

[7] Αρχονταρίκι, guesthouse in a monastery; ERT, Sunday 16 June 2013; https://youtu.be/CNxoJJvVWa4 [visited on 25 June 2014].

element to this practice is the fact that now the name of the 'modifier' is added, which never occurred in the past, a phenomenon which he, himself, criticizes.[8]

Oftentimes, the choice of musical texts, alone, is enough for a chanter to subscribe to a particular school. For instance, one who has obtained the published musical texts of Athanasios Karamanis, without having apprenticed beside him, usually says that he 'chants Karamanis-like' or simply he 'chants Karamanis'. This phenomenon is based exclusively on the use of the specific mathimata with the possible assistance of some recording. It is evident that here a particularly interesting issue arises, which relates to the dissemination of information nowadays. What we mean to say is that the internet has opened up new opportunities for this singular long-distance study, as it offers the chance to someone who cannot attend a certain school of yphos, due to distance and time period, to apprentice 'beside' it by using the material found on the internet.[9] In essence, new extensive networks of apprenticeship are generated, where a student need not have the live and active presence of a teacher beside him, something which in the past was not only beneficial but also compulsory. In addition, as regards to the Mount Athos yphos, the utilization of mathimata is perhaps a more important factor for the identity of the yphos, rather than the performance practice itself; this is because the monasteries, most times, are the per se places of performance of antiquated, intricate and (especially) long-in-duration mathimata, something which poses a problem for the contemporary urban liturgies with their daily 'duration' and their social 'timeframe' per day. Furthermore, the 'place' of a monastery has undoubtedly less cosmic influences, something which defines the qualitative features of the performances.[10]

Regarding the choice of mathimata performed during not only the Salutations (the service pertinent to us due to 'The Akathist Hymn') but also generally in a church service, it must also be noted that it depends on the policy followed by the diocese to which it belongs as well as on the priests and mainly on the Rector of each church; it is additionally dependent on the time frame of the services. For example, there are Rectors who prefer brief services, a choice which is evidently a determining factor in mathimata selection. This practice severs the links that

---

[8] It should be noted that Spyros Peristeris is one of the few cases, and an exception to the above rule, concerning the practice of publishing books with personal theseis.

[9] The issue of technology and especially the internet and its intervention in art generally constitutes a crucial chapter in analysis. Obviously, the aforementioned regarding long-distance study is valid for most laiko idioms too. This crucial issue infers a key contemporary aspect of music education, which constantly evolves and seems to depend on the progress of technology more and more.

[10] Despite this, it must be noted that certain recordings that come from the Mount Athos choirs illustrate intense confabulations with external secular musical entities.

connect teaching to performance, since rehearsal of a slow Cherubic hymn in a conservatory lesson, mathimata, which demands advanced skills, could never be actualized in the actual place of performance, and which eventually renders such mathimata more or less museum and concert pieces, that is, performances removed from their actual 'place'. The case of the Cherubic hymn holds special interest. It is a slow mathima of long duration, whose duration gives the so-called 'time' to the priest to perform the required rites (prayers, etc.) inside the Holy Sanctuary. If the priest completes the necessary rites quickly, the flow of the mathima is interrupted in order for the Great Entrance to be performed (exiting the Holy Sanctuary and walking through the interior of the church). As a result the chanter recites a large part of the hymn, instead of chanting it. This has led to the implementation of a particular practice by the chanters. The part of the hymn where the text reaches the word 'Triadi' is the exact point where the chanter performs solo, often in free rhythm, even improvising, deviating from the musical text. In other words, it is a unique solo every Sunday, where the chanter has the chance to display his skill, his yphos, his performance flair. In fact, in the event of the priest signifying the Great Entrance, the chanter, in order to avoid reading the word 'Triadi' and thus losing the solo, reads the previous text, and specifically the phrase 'mystikós eikonízontes' (μυστικώς εικονίζοντες, mystically emulate).

18

Modernists and conservatives

Based on what we have learnt in the previous chapters, the popular yphoses, or the 'schools' as we have come to call them nowadays, have been composed as follows:

1. The patriarchal, with a focal subsidiary consisting of what was formed by three eminent chanters of Thessaloniki: Athanasios Karamanis (1911–2012), Chrysanthos Theodosopoulos (1920–88) and Charilaos Taliadoros (1926–).
2. The School of Spyros Peristeris (1913–98), which is often called the yphos of the Athens Metropolitan Church, or simply 'Athenian' in chanter circles.
3. A peculiar but extremely interesting yphos, which could be called polyphonic, without implying a wholly European approach. This yphos refers mainly to the islands of the Ionian and Crete. Despite this, the manifestations of this yphos render each local entity different to the other; consequently, their homogeneity is possibly atypical.[1]
4. The yphos of the Simon Karas School, with its main representative being Lykourgos Angelopoulos, developed after Karas established a new theoretical framework for Greek music (rural laiki, that is, folk songs, and Byzantine).
5. The yphos often referred to as 'Αγιορείτικο' (agioreítiko, Athonite), due to its development by the monks of Mount Athos,[2] mainly through the

---

[1] It should be noted that on the one hand there is literature concerning the existence of a polyphonic chanting idiom in Crete and on the other its conveyance to the Ionian Islands, after the conquest of Crete by the Ottomans in the middle of the seventeenth century and the migration of its inhabitants to the under Venetian rule Ionian Islands. Concerning the issue of Byzantine music in Crete, see Amargianakis (1988), Moschopoulos (1995), Giannopoulos (2004), Despotis (2006) and Makris (2009 and 2012).

[2] Mount Athos (Άγιο Όρος; Ágio Óros, sacred mountain) constitutes a self-governing part of the Greek state, and is located in the third 'leg', as it is called, of the region of Halkidiki, in the north of Greece. It is composed of autonomous monastic communities.

activity of two large brotherhoods: Thomades and Danielei (deriving from Thomas and Daniel). Perhaps a more apt term would be that of the 'monastic' yphos, because apart from Mount Athos other monasteries have developed idiomatic yphos during performance practice but also in the choice of utilized musical texts.
6. Lastly, the School of Ioannis Sakellaridis, which is connected to the polyphonic school and the renewed repertoire it created.

These schools are separated not only due to the choice of musical texts utilized but also due to the way they perform them. Despite this, it should be noted that the boundaries among these schools are not stable, and that constant interaction among them is observed. The result of these interactions is a singular and multilevel syncretism: somebody chants mathimata of Sakellaridis, using vocal placement that pertains to Karamanis from Thessaloniki, but the idioms observed in the theseis he uses pertain to Karas. The following paradox in the Patriarchate school is observed: none of the three (Karamanis, Theodosopoulos and Taliadoros) has anything to do with the Ecumenical Patriarchate of Constantinople, nor have any of them been chanted there. In this story, the following were the crucial factors: Thessaloniki, up to today, in the context of the relevant nationalistic ideologies bears the atypical title of 'συμβασιλεύουσα' (symvasileúousa, co-ruler city), a title which it seems to have within the Byzantine Empire as well. It is not by chance that often today the city is called the 'co-capital'. In modern history, Thessaloniki accepted refugees coming from Greek communities, one of which was Constantinople. These three personas associated with renowned chanters of the Ecumenical Patriarchate (for example, Konstantinos Pringos and Thrasyvoulos Stanitsas). Many times, they self-proclaim themselves as continuers of the Patriarchate style, even though they would print sheet music with their own theseis, which had discrepancies, some less and others more, from the theseis heard at the Patriarchate Church, which were never printed as sheet music, but were part of the oral tradition. In essence, however, they forged a syncretic personal style, which is obviously linked to the influences they had from the Patriarchate personalities, but it is clear that it is quite different from the Patriarchate style. Either way, the Patriarchate chanters themselves, in recordings available to us, seem to chant differently within the Patriarchate Church, while serving there, and differently in churches of the Greek state, after they moved there. The connection between the Patriarchate style and that of the Thessaloniki style is complex and cannot be analysed so briefly and easily. What we are interested in is that we should understand that today when someone says they support the Patriarchate style, usually they have not apprenticed directly at the Patriarchate Church or beside some Patriarchate chanter, but beside one of these three personas of Thessaloniki, who came into contact, at some specific point in their lives, with some Patriarchate chanter.

Competition amongst schools is tremendous, the central cause of which is the issue of 'authenticity' in chanting. This competition often turned into conflict, which took on civil war dimensions, as in the case of Psachos, who represented the Patriarchate School, and that of Sakellaridis, who was in charge of the Athenian Chanting School. A similar conflict wages today as well, on the one side we have the School of Karas and the renewed theory of Byzantine music, and on the other the Patriarchate School, which champions the classical yphos of performance and the classical musical texts.[3]

At this point, it is crucial that we mention a Patriarchate circular, issued in 1846 and concerning the harmonization practice of the utilized hymns and the forbidden use inside the church, an extremely common phenomenon (Patriarch Anthimos and Holy Synod, 1846). This particular topic is complex, as certain chanting schools are based and characterized by the three- and four-part harmonization, but also by counterpoint processes, characteristics which at first glance would classify them as Europeanized music. Such schools, Cephalonia, Zakynthos, Corfu and Sakellaridis, not only are characterized by the counterpoint presence of two or more voices, but also developed the specific idiom to such an extent, so that it may now be considered rather complex, virtuosic and particularly identifiable with the schools in question.[4] This

---

[3] See, generally, Papadimitriou (1939), Apostolopoulos (1999), Oikonomou (2002), Katsifis (2002), Akridas (2013), Anastasiou (2013) and Konstantinidis and Stogiannidis (2015).

[4] Even though this book does not concern itself with orthodox states beyond Greek borders, it must be noted that polyphony in Byzantine music did/does not constitute an issue exclusive to the Greek-speaking world, as other traditions, such as that of Romania, Bulgaria and Russia have always used a polyphonic yphos, something which still holds true in the present. After on-site research by the author in Romania and Bulgaria, inclinations towards change of the polyphonic reality to the 'traditional' Byzantine were observed. This results in the co-existence of various diversities, such as, for example, the case of Bucharest, where the Patriarchate Church now chants based on the Byzantine yphos (obviously with essential differences to the Greek and with referrals to other styles of singing), while other smaller but historical churches of the city continue the polyphonic tradition, even with small chorus groups (see also Gheorghita, 2010). In the last few decades, many people who engage in the chanting art have travelled to Greece in order to study Byzantine music. As we are informed by Marcel-Ionel Spinei, after the fall of the communist regime in 1989, 'In Romania the old churches opened again. ... There is, however, a lack of good chanters – and good chanting schools. On this level, the efforts of good teachers of chanting music that exist in Greece must continue. ... The first step was taken in 2006 when the professor Dr Achilleas Chaldaeakes, with myself ... proposed a collaboration concerning chanting music and musicology, to the dean of the Music University of Bucharest' (Spinei, 2011: 85).

discourse concerning the stereotypically polarized placement of West and East is in dire need of thorough research, as elements of intense and unmediated cross-cultural interchanges emerge. In other words, the resulting fusions were a product of the natural moulding of cultural elements found within a common context and which managed to converge. One of the most vital elements in this process lies in the fact that students were produced, that is, continuers of these mergers, and subsequently developed into schools.[5]

Concerning the same issue, should we consider the role of the contemporary 'polychronismos,' we will perceive that its occurrence is one of the most interesting points during the performance itself, in the 'place' of activity and before the Benediction and Dismissal, thus constituting (formally) a part of the ritual. A large part of the 'polychronismos' is rich in synthetic imagination and counterpoint vocal motion. The harmonization of the main melody, that is, the part of the ison, presents an uncommon diversity in motion, and phenomenally demonstrates intense confabulation and pertains to European polyphony.[6] A detached observation and analysis, however, proves that in essence, for the specific moments of time of the polychronismos, a 'place' within the main 'place' is created, which pinpoints to ground zero, as Theodorakis said in his famous quote (1986: 85-92) – the convergence of the two music worlds. This convergence is not dominated by the rationale of the prepared traveller heading towards a specific 'place' of which he has knowledge beforehand, but that of an inquiring and inquisitive mind, of one who meets his counterpart in a 'place' where they 'see eye to eye' conversing in their own Esperanto.[7]

The dynamic aesthetic of chanting not only concerns the aforementioned specific phenomena but also constitutes a condition within which chanting is constantly renewed. Regarding this condition, it is crucial to mention a singular urban syncretic style of interpretation. Characterized by the many 'external' influences which pertain to large categories of music genres and idioms, such as the Greek laiko (old and contemporary), the Turkish urban (high-status and

---

[5] We must mention that in the specific Patriarchate circular, what makes an impression is the use of the term 'γραικός' [graikós, Greco] instead of 'ελληνικός' [ellinikós, hellenic]: 'Ορθοδόξων Γραικών' [Orthodóxon Graikón, Orthodox Greco] and 'Ορθοδόξων Γραικικών Εκκλησιών' [Orthodóxon Graikikón Ekklisión, Orthodox Greco Churces].

[6] See, for example, polychronismoi: https://youtu.be/GcJ_8AP6Y74; https://youtu.be/1V_IebyQsLU; https://youtu.be/8qI_W51LmkO; https://youtu.be/QTBr0gx1rmY; https://youtu.be/CiSFPJLRXgk; https://youtu.be/D6h1mB1pGyc; https://youtu.be/HwC8AzoomRk [visited on 20/08/2016].

[7] 'Χαίρε Νύμφη' (haíre nýmphi, rejoice bride) constitutes a similar case in point, chanted after the Oikos during the service of Salutations.

popular), the Ottoman classical as well as other idioms of the Arabic world. Furthermore, it is characterized by its intense modernization attitude, which at times is in accordance with each regulatory framework, while at others it deviates. The anthropological and sociological grid concerning this style presents certain particularly interesting elements. One of the most defining elements refers to the musical experiences of the performer in supplementation to his spiritual readiness to serve a chanting idiom (spiritual readiness not only regarding the perception of orthodox theology, but also regarding an aesthetic of the musical performance generally). The regulator in balancing the two is vocal skill, which in the final analysis shall determine the level of transformation of the interpretation. For instance, someone with a cultivated voice and adroitness at intricate embellishments, and an attitude which serves him well in the participation of other music idioms as well, often manifests characteristics of modernization in his practice.[8] Indeed, many times these innovative theseis of chanters are transcribed and printed in hymn collections which are released.[9]

Regarding the musical act, a special syncretism is observed in chanters who cross over both aesthetically and as to their performance practice between the status of laiko singer and that of chanter, manifesting osmoses between the two styles and creating singular conditions of cross-reference. The two worlds do not interchange only style and performance practices, but also utilize common codes on a value-based, economic and commercial level. For example, a chanter agrees to chant as a guest of a town parish, which is celebrating a certain saint (in the relative festival), after a consensus regarding payment has been reached. Similarly, financial agreements and transactions are conducted in the world of the laiko musician. Furthermore, many a singer enjoys using a style pertaining to chanting idioms. This interchange and confabulation between the laiko and that of chanting is of special interest and proportion nowadays.[10]

---

[8] Remarkable and worth mentioning is the phenomenon of the choice of a high pitch by performers who have a relative skill and vocal ability. Many times the choice of this high pitch is made with a view to induce admiration from the congregation, the priesthood and the students (and, of course, smugness). Often in chanting discussions, the 'good' chanter or the 'good' voice is equal to the ability to perform on a high pitch. A popular chanter with many followers, who is at the same time also productive as far as discography is concerned, is in a position to demand a higher salary from the church in which he serves, a salary which is determined by the council of each church.

[9] For a different aspect on modernity in chanting, see Chaldaeakes (2005 and 2014).

[10] See, for example, the cases of Stamatis Gonidis, Zafiris Melas and Makis Christodoulopoulos regarding cases of confabulation between laiko and chanting practices and Sotiris Fotopoulos, Spyros Maidanoglou and Vangelis Daskaloudis regarding cases of chanter confabulation with the practices of laiko, respectively.

We should also take note of the open process of evolution which is detected even in the repertoire itself, in hymnology. We observe contemporary additions of hymns which are sometimes based on existing melodies of older hymns, for example hymns of new saints, and sometimes they are put to music from scratch, as in the case of a Cypriot song-hymn which has been established in the marriage service (Plemmenos, 2015: 429).

The aforementioned belong to the popular dimension of chanting, inextricably connected not only to the choice of mathimata but also to the way in which they will be performed. For example, certain performances (classical texts or transmissions) enjoy particular success, since a part of the congregation performs with the chanters, in this way manifesting their popularity but also the artistic-aesthetic power of particular melodies.

More aspects to this extremely interesting issue are added, concerning the process of consolidation of certain performances, as, for example, 'O Gladsome Light'[11] by Ioannis Sakellaridis.[12] The popularity and the laikoness of the specific piece has reached remarkable proportions, not allowing any other version to supersede it, even though Sakellaridis is not considered a classic, not even an 'authentic' chanter (according to the traditional Patriarchate yphos). The aforementioned 'laikoness' obviously does not mean the simplistic form of the well known 'of the people' or 'for the people' (laos = the people), but optimizes the aesthetic background of the laiko, that is, its code of validity which governs the relationship involving a fundamental triptych: creator-performer-audience or text-transmitter-receiver.[13]

A video-recorded excerpt where Archbishop of Greece Seraphim performs 'O Gladsome Light' by Ioannis Sakellaridis with the priesthood, the chanters and the congregation, inside the Metropolitan Cathedral of Athens is particularly

---

[11] Φως Ιλαρόν, fos ilarón.

[12] Worthy of notation is the interview of Archimandrite Father Irinaios Nakos conducted by Euangelos Katsinavakis, broadcast by the radio station of the Church of Greece on the programme 'Ministry of Orthodox Hymnology' concerning Ioannis Sakellaridis, on 22 January 2007: 'Many of his melodies, such as 'O Gladsome Light', were especially beloved and displaced every previous composition' (http://efkatsinavakis.blogspot.gr [visited on 05 March 2016]).

[13] The popularity in question also refers to the systemization and standardization, in good part, of education in Byzantine music, where the teacher resorts to various techniques, which obviously cannot be prescribed by the theory, in order to simplify or to render comprehensible what is taught (see also Konstantinidis and Stogiannidis, 2015). We should not forget that the spirit of modernization that dominated Chrysanthos during standardization of Byzantine music is dual: on the one hand, he 'confabulates' with Europe and introduces theoretical considerations and, on the other, he 'popularizes' a very complex system, reducing it to a 'schooling' method, in the sense of systemized education, something which was also his ultimate goal in this procedure (see also Xanthoudakis, 2007).

interesting.¹⁴ One can distinguish two very characteristic and extremely interesting acoustic elements: firstly, the holding of the ison, which logically comes from the chorus of the chanters or maybe from the priesthood as well, something common in the framework of service and in cases where musical pieces are performed by Priests or High Priests. While in theory the piece is structured within the framework of the second echos, the holding of the ison is heard on note Ni/C (instead of Vou/E and/or Di/G), structuring a remarkable sound, which refers to the Plagal of the Fourth echos. In addition, a constant parallel third part is heard above the basic melody, which is another common phenomenon in these kinds of popular hymns, as, for example, in the 'Eulogies' and the 'Beatitudes' (regarding the popularity of certain categories of hymns, see also Plemmenos, 2017).¹⁵ While watching the specific clip, we see Archbishop Seraphim indicating to the Right Chorus in the correct second voice in parallel third, which he himself subsequently performs.

It is remarkable that the same version of the piece was also performed by the Ecumenical Patriarch Bartholomew in the service of Vespers conducted at the Church of Saint Sophia in Kiev, Ukraine in 2008.¹⁶ In addition, one can see and hear the Ecumenical Patriarch Bartholomew performing Sakellaridis's version in the Patriarchal Church, in Constantinople, during the service of Vespers on Pentecost conducted in 2015.¹⁷ Note that there are also other classical recordings of the hymn, which in fact bear the label 'ancient melody' written in the slow type of melody (see, for example, Stefanos Lambadarios, 1863: 37), it is deemed necessary to note that even emblematic chanting personas, such as Athanasios Karamanis, the one who reformed many characteristics both in chanting composition and in performance, included in their publications Sakellaridis's version as well. In fact, in the case of Karamanis's publication *Vespers*, we read

---

¹⁴ 'O Gladsome Light'–Metropolitan Cathedral of Athens: https://youtu.be/YXKoJbHYXpk [visited on 01 May 2015].

¹⁵ Εγκώμια, egómia; μακαρισμοί, makarismoí. Remarkable is the fact that such pieces have been performed, video recorded, recorded and released commercially, by laiko singers and musicians of laiki music, such as Glykeria, Petros Gaitanos, Stamatis Gonidis, Nikos Xylouris, Manolis Mitsias, Vasilis Saleas and others. In addition, various composers experimented with and processed the pieces in question, for example Stamatis Spanoudakis. See, for example: Haris Alexiou: https://youtu.be/NGl1_Mc6VF8; Petros Gaitanos: https://youtu.be/56vFLIQSGds; Eleutheria Arvanitaki: https://youtu.be/xiUy7nJ2vQA; Mario: https://youtu.be/gejHXKEKFWA; Nikos Xylouris and Manolis Mitsias: https://youtu.be/2yW39rHxW2c; Glykeria: https://youtu.be/okOrdi5_Rno; Notis Sfakianakis: https://youtu.be/mC8X1g2-jT4.

¹⁶ 'O Gladsome Light'–Kiev: https://youtu.be/VZMfQgo2Zbs [visited on 12 June 2015].

¹⁷ 'O Gladsome Light'–Patriarchate: https://youtu.be/4fhJgJX3IjY [visited on 02 August 2016].

earlier the adaptation in question: 'Adapted for a more Byzantine yphos by Ath. Karamanis' (1982: 157).[18]

Radio and television played a defining role in the externalization of the chanting art but also in the en masse proliferation of particular practices. The sound of the Metropolitan Cathedral of Athens was the most common sound of the chanting act for many people, especially in the initial years of television broadcast, when there was no other way to listen en masse to any other church. The yphos of Spyros Peristeris became familiar and the music texts he used became 'classics' for many listeners (see also Plemmenos, 2015: 427–8). The Metropolitan Cathedral of Athens chorus often used counterpoint motions and additional vocals (for example, a second holding of the ison in cadences). This suggests more a condition of modernization rather than a condition of Europeanization, even though Peristeris was knowledgeable in European music too. This prism of modernization may assist in the observation of the evolution of performance practices, resulting in the redefinition of melodic compounds and the update of the whole music phenomenon. The role of certain prominent personas, as undoubtedly Peristeris was, became crucial for the externalization of the chanting art, as, managing to deal with the artistic spirit of his performances, without this being at the expense of his religious spirituality, accomplishing to highlight the role of chanting in the Greek music *ecumene*, amongst the rest of the present-day musical idioms.

The musical act of chanting is constantly evolving and syncretic towards performance practices. The interest generated by its present-day manifestations in the urban environment is huge as it highlights one of its aspects as an artistic phenomenon, revealing the timeless interdependence between orality and literacy. The multifariousness and syncretic core of performance practices in urban centres are clearly a point of reference and an identifying characteristic of the chanting art of today. Revealing the extent of musical reborrowing that refers to music genres in the Greek peninsula and not only accentuating a remarkable musical network which, excluding negligible exceptions, remains uninvestigated regarding research, especially when it comes to its autonomous observation, without being connected to a written musical text. Performance

---

[18] 'The reason why these variations have not been studied thoroughly until today is that they are often underestimated by the scholarly chanters of the church as products of ignorance, sciolism or inferior artistic value. However, their staying power (most oral melodies lasting a century) and their dissemination cannot be ignored by contemporary musicological science' (Plemmenos, 2017: 308).

today is essentially unexplored, constituting the ultimate contemporary tool in research of artistic compounds.[19]

The restless spirit found at the core of the nature of animate music constitutes a real tool in interchange. Especially when it comes to the protagonists of the musical act, who serve a diversity of repertoires, something stressed by Ioannis Plemmenos while observing the on-site research and recordings of Spyros Peristeris in rural areas: 'Occasionally, the status of performers as holy chanters or priests occurs almost effortlessly from performing folk songs' (Plemmenos, 2015: 428).[20] Musicological research has access to a characteristic artistic phenomenon where multifarious blooms nestle and converge: aesthetics, styles, forms, mentalities, practices. The examination of this phenomenon certainly contributes to the emergence of new evidence with regard to the negotiation of yphos and in general performance practice but also, in the final analysis, performance of Byzantine music.[21] The development of fluidity in performance annuls what we stereotypically call 'by the book' practices when comparing melodies. In essence, what we compare is a palimpsest, on which comparable melodies were etched, in such a simplistic way that they are alike.

---

[19] See also Lingas (1991 and 2003) and Khalil (2009: 7–8).
[20] Additionally, the notes of Spyros Peristeris in recordings conducted in Amfissa in 1964 'various ecclesiastical melodies are chanted by oral tradition', 'as heard from older chanters' and more (in Plemmenos, 2015: 429–32), indicate exactly the same 'open' character of chanting.
[21] Indicative sound examples of this syncretic urban psaltic yphos: https://youtu.be/V62H4RvPoMI; https://youtu.be/iDcnd3s3ANU; https://youtu.be/EtjLLPLIG9U; https://youtu.be/4JrJx486ThM; https://youtu.be/aGM3MSxrP9c; https://youtu.be/JHMkWJ-LxWU. Concerning the yphos of the Patriarchate chanters, see indicatively: https://youtu.be/1fCm6ljlFRc; https://youtu.be/_1yU9XrKSKE; https://youtu.be/gwdHnzWjFbM; https://youtu.be/2DWq4Z3CN98 [visited on 24 September 2016]. At this point an extremely interesting issue arises concerning the singular 'discography', which has emerged regarding Byzantine music in recent years. This is none other than the internet, which includes innumerable recordings not only in the per se places of performance (churches), but also in concert halls. These recordings come from private collectors, who either participated in the choruses of the lectern in the churches or observed the liturgies as an audience. A similar situation from the world of the laiko in the past is brought to the forefront, when during the rural festivals unofficial recordings took place via different means, which eventually landed up in make-shift places of sale (even in street stalls) in Athens and in other large urban centres, as well as in the country, which for years now constitutes a very dynamic commercial market (see also Kokkonis, 2017: 175–93).

Part four

Analyzing the two musical pieces

Starting with the sound

'Cloudy Sunday' was transcribed in the laikos dromos G Matzore (Ματζόρε). In all available issues (of the first recording), the piece is between F sharp and G, something common in historical recordings. The specific tonality is also appropriate for music transcriptions using the makam system, such as Rast, in its theoretical form, develops having as a base the European G.[1] With this in mind, 'The Akathist Hymn' was transcribed as well in the tonality of G, with the aim of facilitating the comparison of all musical transcription. Modally, the song functions in the context of the laikos dromos Matzore and the laiko rhythm of the old zeibekiko. The fact that it clearly belongs to the Matzore without wavering towards the relative laikos dromos Rast constitutes the first key observation which distinguishes it noticeably from the theoretical context of the Plagal of the Fourth echos of 'The Akathist Hymn'. Despite this, these modal music entities communicate constantly amongst themselves. In any event, one of the most crucial elements of the Matzore dromos relates to the use of the augmented seventh degree (F sharp) without it moving to the minor seventh (F natural). In other words, in the song only the F sharp note is performed and never the F note, even in descending movements from the high base (G'-F sharp-E-D and not G'-F [natural]-E-D). This observation is crucial as the repertoire of the rebetiko, early on, presents two different modeness categories. That is, songs which use the minor seventh in a Matzore/Rast context and others in which the seventh remains continually augmented, in the position of the leading tone, following the characteristic form of a Major scale. However, as mentioned before, these two modenesses communicate and many times their differentiation is found simply and only in the use of the seventh. We should, however, emphasize the 'personality'

---

[1] For the relationship between makam and echos see, indicatively, Chalatzoglou (1728) in Naupliotis (1900), Stefanos Lambadarios (1843), Kiltzanidis (1881), Mauroeidis (1999), Michailidis (2008), Chatzimichelakis (2013) and Samson (2013: chapter 6).

that the dromos Matzore (with the permanent VII sharp) developed, long before Tsitsanis's piece (see, for example, the recorded repertoire of the estudiantinas in Smyrna). Tsitsanis, with tonal harmony as his axis not only in the accompanying instruments, but also in solos (with counterpoint activity), evolved an alternative character of this dromos, something which perhaps, after all, excuses its use on his part, the term 'kantada' (serenade), when describing songs of his which belong to the modal music context in question. With regard to rhythm and the old zeibekiko, one can observe one of its ultimately 'classic' performance techniques, where the guitarist complements the beats with chords in eights on the upbeat, and he does not simply perform the basic backbone of the rhythm (see the following music transcription regarding the basic rhythmic pattern of the old zeibekiko). A transcription of 'Cloudy Sunday' in European and Byzantine notation follows.

Contrary to prevalent contemporary performances, the original recording only uses three chords: the first degree (G major), the second (A minor) and the fifth (D major). Generally, the sequence consists of a classic activity of chordal landscapes not only in the specific period but also generally in the Piraeus rebetiko based on the bouzouki.[2] In the first melodic phrase, a common gravitation is observed occurring in the third degree, which could be considered dominant in the laikos dromos Matzore.[3] According to Eastern modal theory, the note B (Vou), as a powerful centre of the III degree, attracts the note A (Pa) which is raised by a semitone. The interval of the semitone refers to the equal-tempered transcription of the staff notation, and this is because singer practice reveals the existence of diversity in the performance of such phrases, regarding the usage of the interval world. Consonance of the first and second degree holds

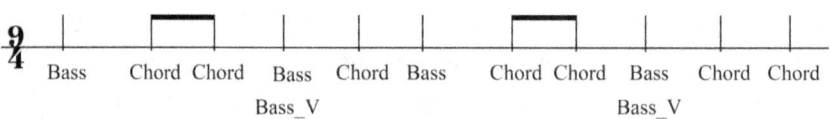

Music transcription 19.1 Old zeibekiko rhythmic pattern.[4]

---

[2] For chordal harmony, see also Pennanen (1997) and Ordoulidis (2014: chapters 4–5).
[3] Regarding Byzantine music terminology, which can be utilized in analysis of urban laiko repertoire, see Ordoulidis (2014: 118).
[4] This rhythmic pattern comes from the author's PhD thesis (Ordoulidis, 2012: 180). 'B' is for Bass, a single bass note, the first degree of the chord performed at the specific time. A 'Bass_V' is for the fifth degree of the chord.

Music transcription 19.2 Transcription of 'Cloudy Sunday' in staff notation.[5]

special interest, especially in the third metre where in the seventh beat an A minor chord is performed, while simultaneously the voice performs the note G. This occurs in all three verses of the piece and constitutes an excellent case in point for the observation of the management of the harmonic world and its use in the specific period.

The changes in 'orthodox harmony' are vast and dependent on many factors, such as instrument manufacture, cultural syncretism, the evolution of performance practice, the advancement of recording technology, sound practices and so on; in other words, the rationale of 'correct' in performance

---

[5] In the 'accompaniment' staff, the position of 'x' signals the bass beat of the guitar, while the headless notes are chord upbeats.

Ἠχος λ π ᾆ Νη

Συν	νε	φια	σμε	νη	Κυ	ρια	κη	μοια	ζεις	με
Syn	ne	fia	sme	ni	Ky	ria	ki	moia	zeis	me

την καρδια	μου	που	ε	χει	πα	ντα συν νε φια	συν
tin kardia	mou	pou	e	chei	pa	nta syn ne fia	sun

νε	φια	Χρι στε	και	Πα Χριστεκ'	Πα να για	μου
ne	fia	Chri ste	kai	Pa Christe k'	Pa na gia	mou

Music transcription 19.3 Transcription of 'Cloudy Sunday' in Byzantine notation.[6]

never applies to the real world of the act itself, as it evolves and alters constantly, redefining the term 'orthodox'. All the aforementioned interact with what could be simplistically called 'the ears of the audience', which, at the same time, they themselves evolve, an evolving 'aural logic' which concerns not only the listeners but also the creators (being simultaneously the audience themselves). That Chrysanthos describes something similar in his theory in another context as well is impressive:

> Composition is the ability to construct melodies. We construct melodies on the one hand, not only to chant various commonplace hymns, but also to devise and write singular new melodies, enjoyed by the audience. (Chrysanthos, 1832: 174)[7]

The second phrase of the piece (bar 2) is performed within the 'minore' landscape created by the A minor chord, something common in the Matzore

---

[6] Transcripts in Byzantine notation were actualized utilizing the transcription programme 'Music texts 4.4' by Dimitris Papadopoulos.

[7] Euangelos Katsinavakis on the connection concerning composer/performer with the audience expresses his opinion on Ioannis Sakellaridis and contemporary aesthetic criteria: 'This innovative composition of Sakellaridis ... satisfies the contemporary listener ... and renders his music truly aesthetically appealing, according to contemporary aesthetic criteria' (http://efkatsinavakis. blogspot.gr [visited on 05 March 2016]).

dromos (transition of the phraseology from the I major degree to the II minor). The consonance of the second chord (A/Pa) with the fourth note (C/Ga) which cultivates a sense of displacement of the minor modeness of the second degree is one of the most popular 'shifts' and acoustic displacements in a large part of the laiko repertoire. In the fifth beat of the same bar, the harmonic landscape returns to the initial tonality of G major, accompanied by the gradual descent of the vocal melody from the fifth degree (D/Di) to the first (G/Ni). At the beginning of the next phrase a gradual ascent takes place again from the second degree (A/Pa) and in a minor atmosphere. This gradual motion fortifies the tonal centre of the fifth degree, where a transcendental motion takes place from the last to the first of the next octave (D–G'/Di–Ni'). The biggest interval is performed in the next bar which is also the end of the vocal phrase, where from the first degree (G/Ni) of the basic region the note E/Ke (sixth degree) is performed, from whence a gradual descent towards the tonic begins once again, accompanied also by the change in the chordal landscape of D major (fifth degree/Di) which also strengthens the specific descent.

With regard to the modeness which dominates the melodic flow utilizing the theoretical background of ecclesiastical music, initially a switch is observed between the diatonic tetrachord of the Plagal of the Fourth echos based on Ni (Ni–Pa–Vou–Ga, intervals: 12–10–8) and the diatonic tetrachord of the First echos based on Pa (Pa–Vou–Ga–Di). Should we compare the second minor chord with the holding of the ison in chanting, then on the third beat of the second bar we observe the consonance of the base and the top of the tetrachord of the First echos (Pa–Vou–Ga–Di/A–B–C–D). From this note Di the descending phrase which heads towards the note Ni begins. Vou, as a dominant note in the Plagal of the Fourth, has only one cadence in the melody, which is found at the end of the first bar, at the end of the word 'Κυριακή' (Kyriakí, Sunday). Regulation of scale presents special interest, as Tsitsanis utilizes the tonality of G, in order to facilitate both the male and the female voice. The specific transcription refers to Prodromos Tsaousakis's vocals, and this is why after the second phrase ('καρδιά μου' [kardiá mou, my heart]) a descent of one octave occurs, beginning the next phrase from A below the tonic. At this point, the structuring of the melody in the environment of the Plagal of the First echos is observed, with the melody beginning from Pa and heading towards Ke, the dominant note in the Plagal of the First. The specific phrase ends on high Ni' (G') and in connection with the change of chords returns to the status of the Plagal of the Fourth. The word 'συννεφιά' (synnefiá, cloudy) pertains to the impact, again, of the First echos (Ni–Pa–Pa), revealing an especially popular phenomenon of the urban laiko idiom: the continual shifting of the tonal centre from the first to the second degree, alternating the environment of the major with that of the minor, as described earlier as well.

20

Starting with the sheet music

Four historical manuscripts of 'The Akathist Hymn' melody in its brief type follow: two in Byzantine music notation (Ioannis Lambadarios and Stefanos Domestichos and Georgios Progakis) and their transcription/translation in staff notation (see music transcriptions 20.1–20.8).

Initially the melody moves towards the first tetrachord (Ni–Pa–Vou–Ga/G–A–B–C) involving the harmonic environs of the first and second degree (pause on Pa/A) and concluding on Vou/B, which constitutes a dominant note of the Plagal of the Fourth echos. A determining point in the pause is the holding of the ison, which is reliant on the analytical approach of each performer to the guide-sheet music of the piece. This issue shall be further analysed, putting aside the theoretical substance of the discourse, the performance shall be examined, that is, the case of Iakovos Naupliotis and the rendition of the specific hymn.

During the whole course of the melody, perfect cadences on the note Vou/B are observed. In some case of performance practice, the holding of the ison is transferred from the note Ni/G to that of Vou/B, indicating the dynamic of the specific note in the Plagal of the Fourth echos. The note Pa/A, in incidents where the melody is established on or engages in the tonal centre of Vou/B, is attracted by the latter. In motions of ascension which begin at the base (Ni–Pa–Vou/G–A–B) again a gravitation is observed towards Vou/B, presenting, however, variations in the interval environment of each case. The note Pa/A almost touches the note Vou/B when the melody heads for a cadence in the last. A similar idiomatic behaviour is also observed in the note Ga/C, which is attracted by the powerful centre of Di/D, which constitutes the base of the second tetrachord of the Plagal of the Fourth echos, referring to the slow version called άγια (ágia) of the Fourth echos. The glissando of Ga/C to Di/D at the point of 'η πόλις' (i pólis, your city) constitutes a particularly popular practice. In cases of such a cadence, the note Di/D as the ultimately powerful centre attracts both Ga/C and Vou/B, giving the impression that the klitón shade has been placed on it.

Music transcription 20.1 Manuscript of 'The Akathist Hymn' by Ioannis Lambadarios and Stefanos Domestichos (1850: 392).

Translation from Byzantine notation was actualized in two ways. Initially, exact adaptation of the music text notation for the staff notation was actualized, utilizing the general applicability of the makam Rast. Makam transcription has its Turkish version as its theoretical base. With regard to Byzantine writing, precisely because it is a guide, all idiomatic usage is performed from memory and rarely is it noted in the transcription.[1] This usage was included in the

---

[1] Certain publications of contemporary chanters, which contain their modifications of classical texts (that is, their theseis), include certain additional points of intrusion which indicate idiomatic

Music transcription 20.2 Simple translation in staff notation of 'The Akathist Hymn' of Ioannis and Stefanos.

activity. It should be noted that Psachos was possibly the first to insist on the many written intrusions in the music texts. In an effort to establish certain gravitations and idiomatic behaviour in echoi (see, for example, Psachos, 1909). What is impressive is the fact that even though he was an avid proponent of modernization, he proposed the so-called 'line of consonance', which was one or even two additional lines, beneath the main melodic line, which contained versions of the holding of the ison, written in the form of melodic lines (ibid). In addition, he himself proposed the use of two new symbols, the fermata and the extender line (ibid).

Music transcription 20.3 Advanced translation in staff notation of 'The Akathist Hymn' of Ioannis and Stefanos.

subsequent, second transcription of notation to the staff notation. Once again general applicability of makam Rast was utilized and to the text, in general, idiomatic usage was added, which may present itself during the performance of the hymn. Indeed, it should be emphasized that the environment of the interval varies, depending on the performer and his yphos, as analysed earlier. In other

Music transcription 20.4 Manuscript of 'The Akathist Hymn' by Georgios Progakis (1909: 188).

words, a four comma sharp may apply instead of a five comma sharp and so on.[2] Additionally, the precise notes performed according to the analysis of each performer also vary: embellishments, ornamentation, pauses and so on, all depending on the school of attendance and the relative yphos.

In music transcription 20.3, we observe the most common interval motions (gravitations and generally idiomatic movements) which occur during performance. Gravitation in the third degree (B/Vou/Segâh) varies: a five comma

---

[2] For theoretical issues concerning Turkish makam, see indicatively Aydemir (2012).

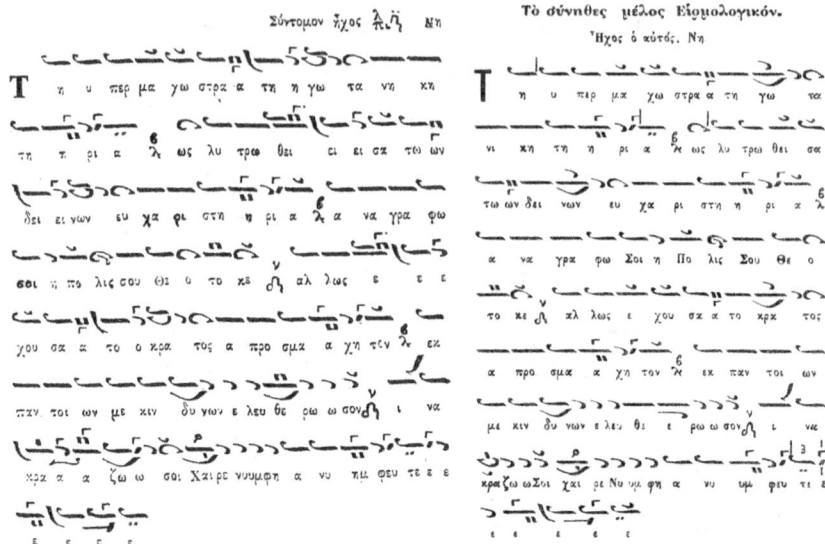

Music transcription 20.5 Comparison of manuscript by Ioannis and Stefanos with that of Progakis's.

sharp may possibly be applied to the second degree by certain performers or even a one comma sharp as well (see bar 9). The same occurs also to the gravitation of the fifth degree (D/Di/Neva). Raising and generally managing the fourth degree in similar theseis, varies, with the value of sharp or the quality or the non-existence of the glissando differing from performance to performance. It is also possible to observe other gravitations and glissandos too, as, for example, from the first to the second degree (Ni–Pa) in bars 2-3. Additionally, in notes whose duration is longer than eight, if the tempo is moderate or low, quite possibly idiomatic embellishments occur, depending on the skill and yphos of each performer.

Music transcription 20.4 refers to another manuscript, that of Georgios Progakis. In general, the basic text, the backbone, is the same as that of Ioannis's manuscript, especially if we take into account all the aforementioned concerning the use of music transcriptions as guides rather than inviolable music texts. We could note that Ioannis's manuscript is slightly more analytical; explanatory regarding specific points (bars 5, 12 and 14, which are repeated), even though it chronologically precedes from that of Progakis. The phrase of bars 28-31 is different in the two manuscripts. Ioannis's could also be considered as an 'explanation' of Progakis's simpler form. Bars 46 and 47 are especially

Music transcription 20.6 Simple translation in staff notation of 'The Akathist Hymn' of Georgios Progakis.

interesting, while also observing, a significant deviation in both manuscripts and a substantial difference between the two music contexts and, by extension, messages. The melodic line in Ioannis's manuscript is evidently more intricate and complex, structured on the lower value of the notes.

As in the case of the transcription-transliteration of Ioannis, the first manuscript of Progakis as well, is just a simple transfer to staff notation, utilizing

Music transcription 20.7 Advanced translation in staff notation of 'The Akathist Hymn' of Progakis.

the tools of Rast and subsequently with the inclusion of the most common idiomatic activity.

Keeping in mind the two aforementioned transcriptions referring to the two classical texts, the analysis moves on to its other dimension, that of the musical performance.

Music transcription 20.8 Comparison of the transcription of 'The Akathist Hymn' of Ioannis and Stefanos with that of Progakis's.

A historical recording of the hymn

Were the aural dimension our only concern, then the original 'text' of the hymn would be considered the recording, since even in the contemporary world, recordings of ecclesiastical hymns often take place, with the oldest conducted circa 1914 at Orfeon by the then First Cantor of the Ecumenical Patriarchate of Constantinople, Iakovos Naupliotis.[1] The second voice heard is that of Konstantinos Pringos, subsequent First Cantor in place of Iakovos. Oral testimonies, as well as the text published by Antonios Alygizakis, claim that the two chanters performed without the use of a music text. All of Naupliotis recordings were released in 2008 in an analytical edition accompanied by the texts. In the specific recording of the hymn, the two chanters perform in slow-brief time, utilizing a plethora of analyses of the basic text.[2] The 'opposite direction' of the following transcription, that is, the creation of a music transcription stemming from the performance, constitutes perhaps another prism in the examination of the basic 'text' and orality in the art of chanting (see Music transcription 21.1).

Angelos Voudouris, Naupliotis's assistant at the chanting lectern of the Patriarchate of Constantinople, in his book Triodion (1997), cites a transcription of the hymn, stressing that it is a performance by Naupliotis (different from that

---

[1] 'The Akathist Hymn' by Naupliotis: https://youtu.be/kwZygnLX7KY [visited on 14 September 2013]; album number 1, track 14–Orf 2032 11626 515 (Alygizakis, 2008). Naupliotis was born in 1864 and died in 1942. He was a Left Chanter (a Lambadarios, as is the title of the Left Chanter) in the Patriarchate Church from 1905 to 1911, and First Cantor from 1911 to 1939.

[2] At this point, we should mention one of the most powerful aesthetic norms of chanting art performance, which is the non-existence of a flat/invariable note. Vocal quality is perhaps one of the most dynamic differences between performances of the two pieces ('The Akathist Hymn' and 'Cloudy Sunday'); in the first period, both Prodromos Tsaousakis and Sotiria Bellou are characterized by their 'straight' voices on the longer notes. Generally, vocal technique in early post-war laiko, based on the bouzouki, is characterized by non-fluctuating voices, until the whole system concerning the music stage and discography changed; thus, we now see singers-celebrities in larger environs, directly linked to the now systemized music industry (discography, Media, etc.). From these singers onwards, melismas and more elaborated singing are rendered a basic issue (see, for example, the case of Stelios Kazantzidis, Stratos Dionysiou and Manolis Angelopoulos).

Ἦχος πλ. ἀ Νη

Τη υ περ μα α χω στρα α τη γω τα νι κη τη ρι ι α

ως λυ τρω θει ει σα των ων δει νων ευ χα ρι στη ρι ι α

α να γρα φω σοι η πο λι ις σου Θε ο το κε αλ

λως ε ε χου σα α το κρα τος α προ σμα χη η τον εκ

παν τοι ων με κιν δυ νων ε λευ θε ε ρω ω σον ι να

κρα ζω ω σοι χαι ρε νυ υμφη α νυ υμφε ευ τε

Music transcription 21.1 Transcription in Byzantine notation of 'The Akathist Hymn' from the performance of Iakovos Naupliotis.

on the album).[3] The differences constitute one more witness to the extent of fluidity in performance practice. The music pieces seem 'open' without being burdened not only by the validity but also by the grandeur of the term 'composer', who issues precise and inviolable instructions about how he wants his piece to be performed.

Further down follows a 'translation' of the performance by Naupliotis in the recording of Orfeon in the staff notation transcription system and utilizing the accidentals of makam. The transcription is a more accurate depiction of Naupliotis's performance than that of the text in Byzantine notation of the same performance. What is highlighted in this practice is the fact that, even though a chanter reads a certain form of sheet music, such as the one in Byzantine notation,

---

[3] This is a common practice where a transcriptionist transcribes the performance of a certain chanter, who is prestigious and enjoys popularity. Oftentimes, these transcriptions are incorporated in hymn collections which include transcriptions or simply copies of classical texts. This type of transcription may be akin to a recording, as a specific performance is imprinted. However, the performers perform the basic 'text' differently every time (diversity in analyses and melismas, different tempo, intonation and so on).

Music transcription 21.2 Transcription of a performance by Naupliotis by Angelos Voudouris (Voudouris, 1997: A: 257).

in the final analysis what he performs is something different, with regard to the sheet music text, of course always within the context of transferring it from a visual to an aural level. In other words, all the analyses of a performance of a text guide are transcribed and reflect a unique moment in time, that is, only one performance. This performance analysis of the text according to the performer, forces us to reconsider very basic elements of music theory and practice in its entirety. Terms such as 'note' take on a completely different dimension during a chanting performance, but also during the performances of popular idioms, as one note in written form corresponds to many notes in a performance; one note, in the final analysis, is so much more than just one note.[4]

---

[4] A typical case constitutes the analytical performance style of Thrasyvoulos Stanitsas.

This analytical consideration of hymn sheet music is one of the key points in comprehending the core of chanting performance through the ages, and generally orally transmitted music traditions. In essence, the aural transcription does not refer in an absolute way to the primary text. These two coincide mentally due to the different perspectives which govern the act. If we take into consideration the variation in each performance of the same performer (see the case of Naupliotis

Music transcription 21.3 Translation in staff notation of 'The Akathist Hymn' of Voudouris.

Music transcription 21.4 Analytical transcription in staff notation of Naupliotis's performance in the Orfeon recording.

with the two transcriptions-performances); hence, what constitutes yphos of a chanter may be considered the formulae, which he utilizes (melodic structure and compounds), as well as the qualitative characteristics which dominate his performance.[5]

---

[5] Regarding issues of authenticity of the 'Akathist hymn' and its melody, see also Khalil (2009: 180).

At this point, we must also mention the release of the hymn in an issue of *New Formiga*, transcribed by Konstantinos Psachos, who at this point runs the periodical and has implemented it as an instrument of his own conservatory, the Conservatory of National Music (Α΄, March 1st, 1921).

In this transcription, we observe four important elements, which illustrate the policy dictated by Psachos and which concern the systematization of teaching and the 'correct' performance of Byzantine music. Firstly, the consonance line of the holding of the ison constitutes an additional element in transcription, which is his own invention and a clear example of the European erudition which governs him, but also the canonical modernization which characterizes much of his activity. Furthermore, transcription into European music notation on the opposite page, an annotation concerning accurate tempo and the annotation found on the following page of the issue, immediately after the end of the transcription, constitutes some additional characteristics of the modernization in question.

Concerning the tempo, it should be noted that its value is more than twice that of the performance by Naupliotis. From the annotation at the end of the transcription, one can understand this while explaining that the equal-tempered system 'corrupts' the character of the Plagal of the Fourth echos and causes a 'very unpleasant and vexing' sound, however remaining 'committed', somehow, to the twenty-year-ago concealed agreement between the 'Byzantines' and that of Georgios Nazos (director of the Athens Conservatory), and concerned, in short, the standardization, rationalization (according to Nazos) and Europeanization of Byzantine music, as prerequisites for its integration into the schools of the Athens Conservatory. The agreement in question is described in the second part of this book.

Another two characteristics should also be noted: in the phrase 'η πόλις' (i polis, your city), while in the publication of 1921 Psachos places a sharp on Ga in order to indicate the specific gravitation, in the publication of 1909, which is included in *Leitourgia* (pages 42–4), this specific sharp is not present (bar 18 of Music transcription 21.7).[6]

In addition, in the phrase 'ἵνα κράζω σοι' (ína krázo soi, so that we may cry to thee), he presents an alternative version of the performance which begins on Vou and ends on Di, without the popular interval of the fourth (Di–Di–

---

[6] In the verse 'ευχαριστήρια' (eucharistíria, thanksgiving), there is an error in the notation, in the second consonance line, as the syllable 'χα' requires the character ison instead of the oligon which is used (bar 13 of Music transcription 21.7).

Music transcription 21.5a Transcription of 'The Akathist Hymn' in Byzantine and staff notation by Psachos (*New Formiga*, A', 1 March 1921 – Thanasis Trikoupis archive).

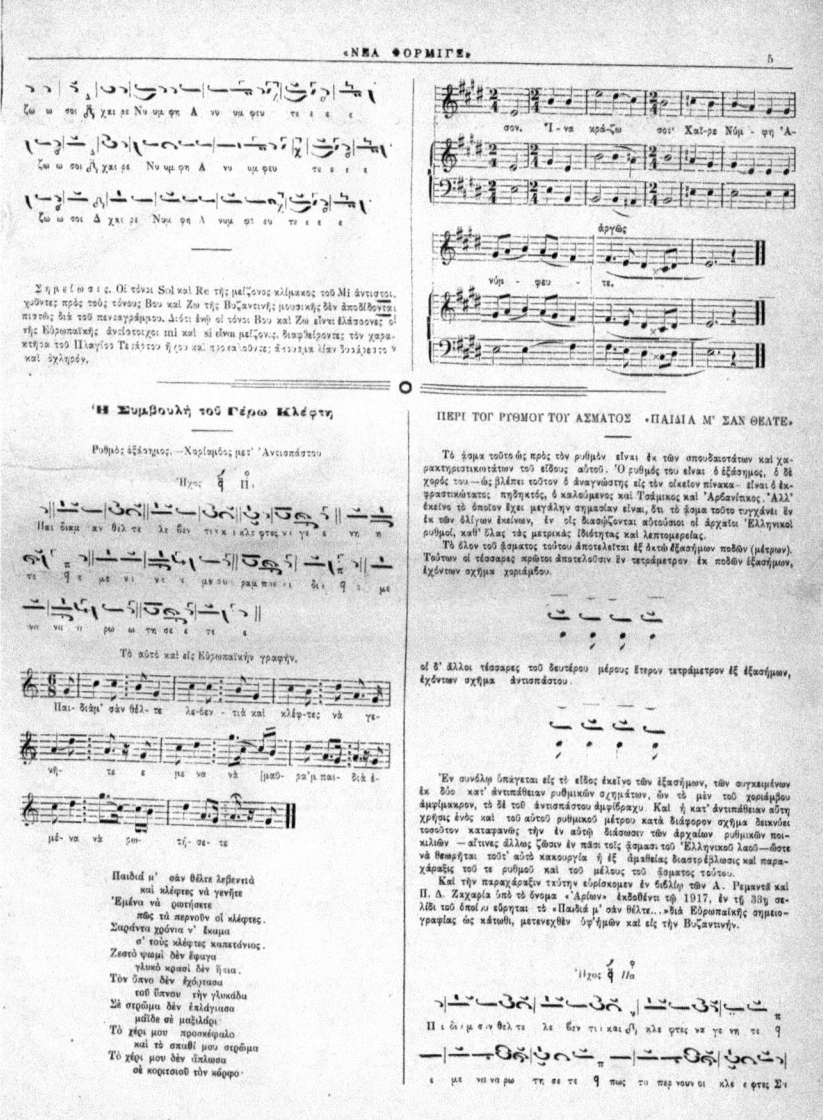

Music transcription 21.5b (Continued)

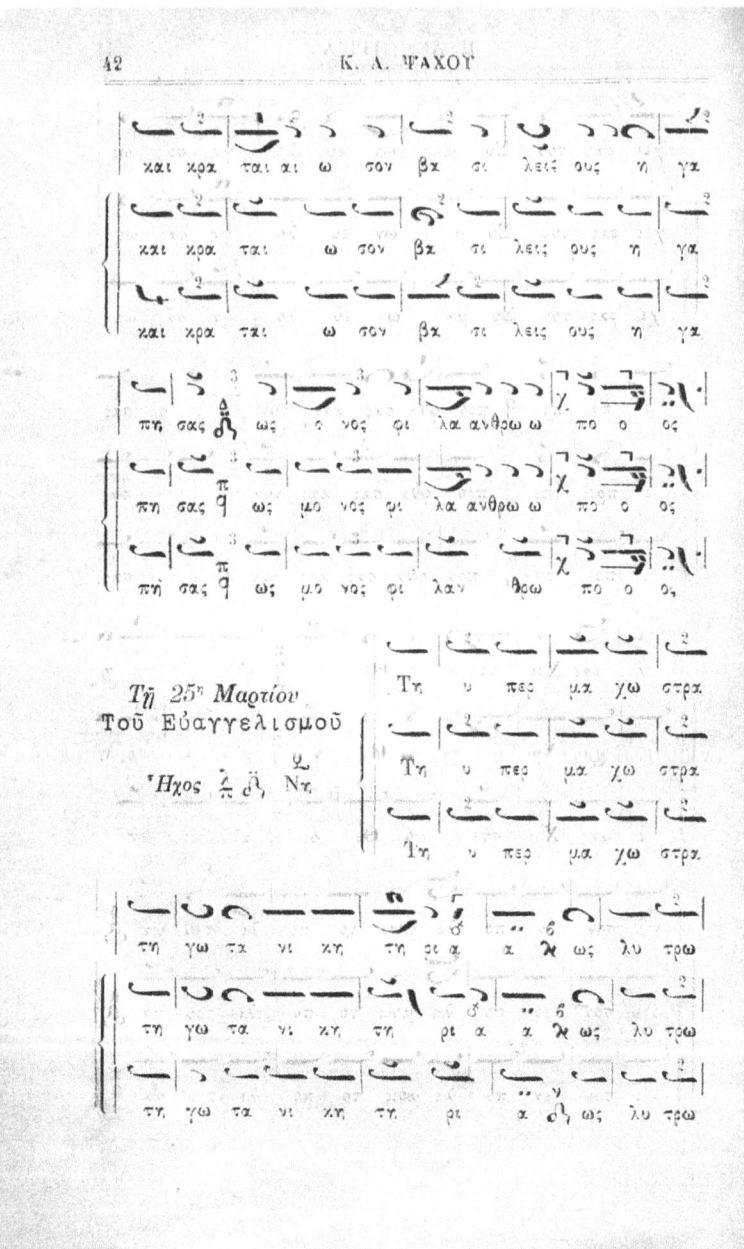

Music transcription 21.6a Transcription in Byzantine notation of 'The Akathist Hymn', by Psachos (1909: 42–4 – Aristotle University Library).

Music transcription 21.6b (Continued)

Music transcription 21.6c (Continued)

Music transcription 21.7 Translation of Music transcription 21.6 ('Akathist Hymn' by Psachos) in staff notation.

Ni'). Perplexing, also, is the fact that in *New Formiga* the hymn is transcribed in staff notation in the scale of E Major and not that of C, even though, as was mentioned earlier in the theory of the commission of 1881, the corresponding note to Ni was C.

Today, performance of the initial phrase of the hymn in the way with which it is transcribed in the book of Ioannis and Progakis, constitutes now a widespread practice, based on the dimension of popularity which was examined beforehand. On the other hand, a plethora of published texts and renditions are widely available, which perform the thesis which Naupliotis himself performs.

Father Nektarios, a monk, in one of the two brief transcriptions of the hymn in his book *Music Treasures of Vespers*[7] (1935) on pages 385–6 (which Nektarios attributes to Nikolaos First Cantor of Smyrna), not only notes that Naupliotis thesis is utilized, but also notes that the performance duration should be fifty-six seconds, which means that the hymn was performed in approximately twice the time than that of Naupliotis, albeit utilizing the same specific thesis. What is more, the phrase 'κινδύνων ελευθέρωσον' (kindýnon eleuthéroson, deliver us from all possible dangers) is presented in a rather contemporary mood, as the modulation token of note Di of the Plagal of the Second echos is placed on the syllable 'δύ', as a result it is performed in the chromatic genus, up to the syllable 'θε' where once again a diatonic modulation token is placed and the melody returns to the Plagal of the Fourth.

Concerning the tempo, the same is observed in the performances of the Fathers of Vatopaidi[8] and the choir of Simon Karas,[9] who also utilized Naupliotis's thesis, with the difference being that the Fathers of Vatopaidi completed the hymn in one minute and thirty-one seconds, while the choir of Karas did so in one minute and eighteen seconds. Worthy of note is the fact that even Sakellaridis utilized this thesis in the contentious phrase (1909: 127).

Moreover, also remarkable is the transcription of Georgios Pachtikos in four-part harmonization and in staff notation, which is found in the book titled *Apollo the music-leader*[10] (1910: 81–3). Pachtikos does not process the thesis with a gradual motion (I–I–I–II), but with that of Naupliotis (I–I–I–IV–III–II).

---

[7] Μουσικός θησαυρός του εσπερινού, mousikós thisaurós tou esperinoú.
[8] 'The Akathist Hymn' – Fathers of Vatopaidi: https://youtu.be/LPyCnTVPhSQ [visited on 5 October 2020].
[9] 'The Akathist Hymn' – Karas choir: https://youtu.be/uU92uQprqpY [visited on 20 April 2016].
[10] Απόλλων ο μουσηγέτης, Apóllon o mousigétis.

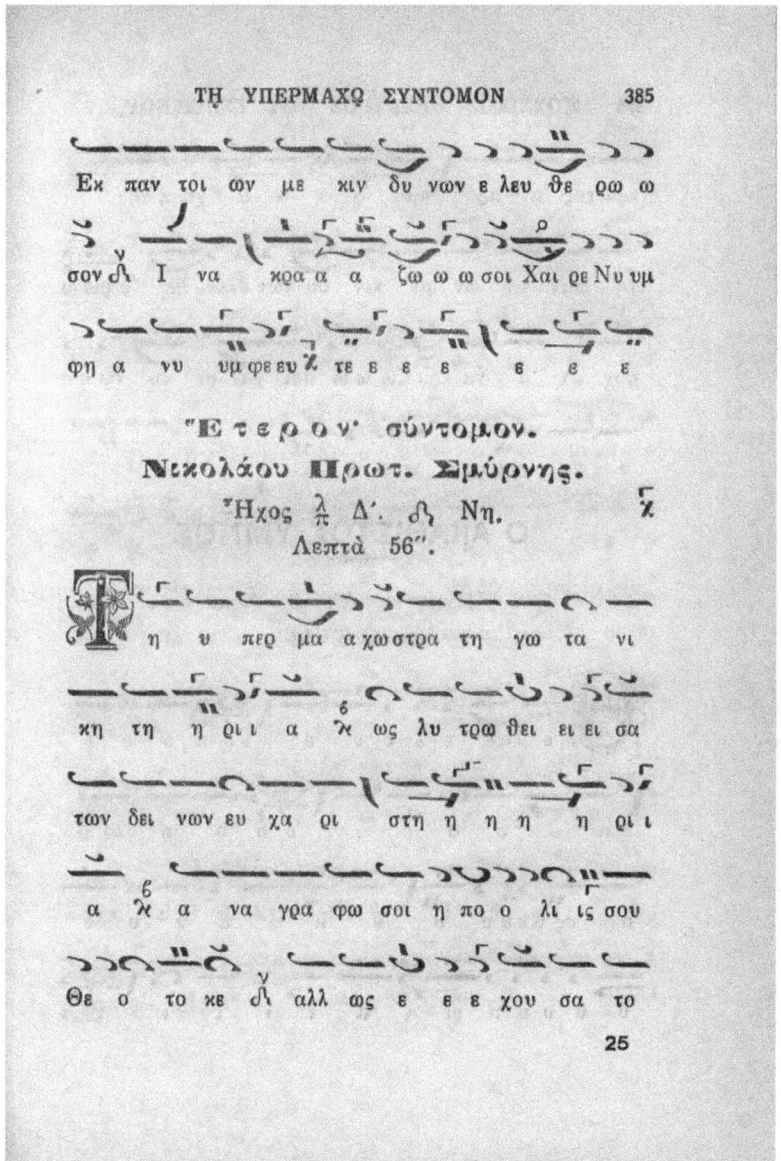

Music transcription 21.8a Transcription of 'The Akathist Hymn' by monk Nektarios, utilizing the formula of Naupliotis (1935: 385–6).

Music transcription 21.8b (Continued)

Music transcription 21.9 Translation in staff notation of Music transcription 21.8 ('Akathist Hymn' by monk Nektarios).

Finally, the case of the popular Greek film titled *Papaflessas*[11] presents extreme interest. The epicentre of the film is one of the most popular protagonists, a warlord of the Greek revolution for independence in 1821, the Archmandrite Grigorios Dikaios. The scene in which the armed struggle is declared, in the monastery of Agia Laura, the congregation chants 'The Akathist Hymn'. Even in this rendition, Naupliotis's thesis is used, with melodic motion from the I degree to the IV.[12]

In the following pages, three basic texts are depicted (Ioannis, Progakis, Naupliotis) in order for them to be compared visually (see music

---

[11] From the website of Finos Film: premiere, 1971 (that is, during the Colonels Junta, 1967–74); production, Finos Film, Paris James, EKK.

[12] 'The Akathist Hymn' as performed in the film 'Papaflessas': https://youtu.be/YABIqdKzpz8.

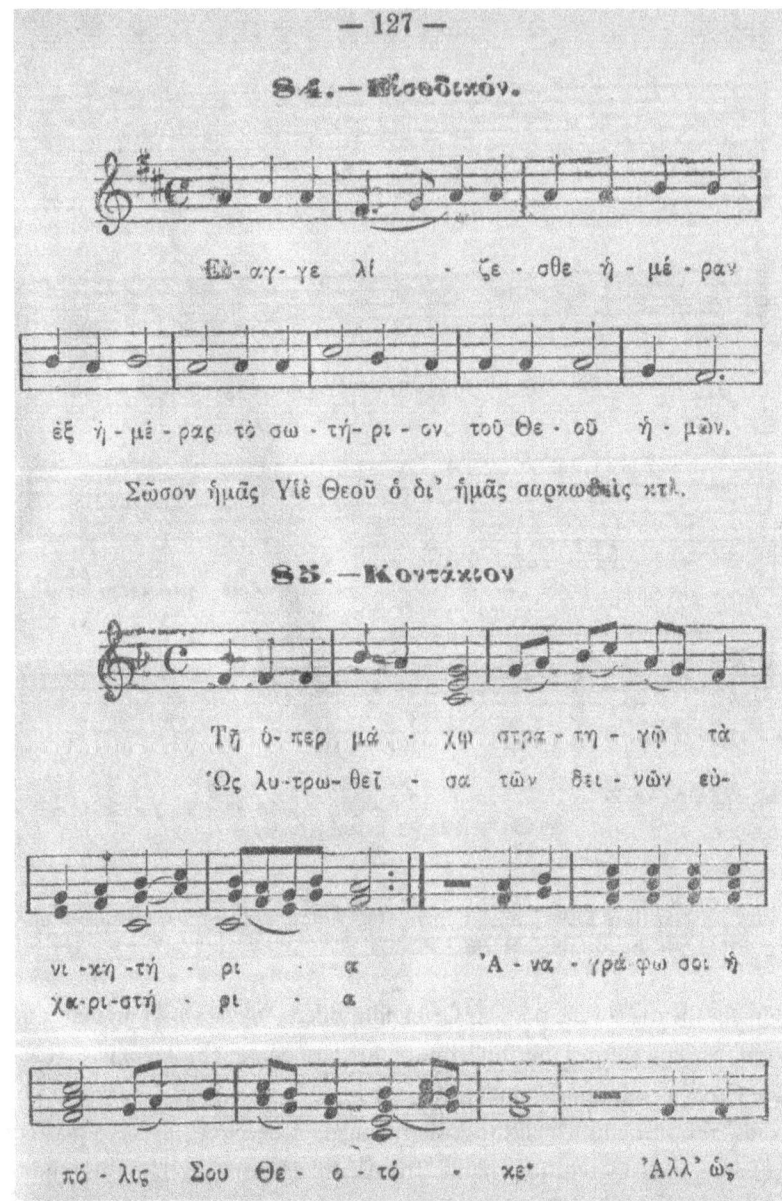

Music transcription 21.10 Transcription of 'The Akathist Hymn' in staff notation, by Sakellaridis, utilizing the formula of Naupliotis (Sakellaridis, 1909: 127).

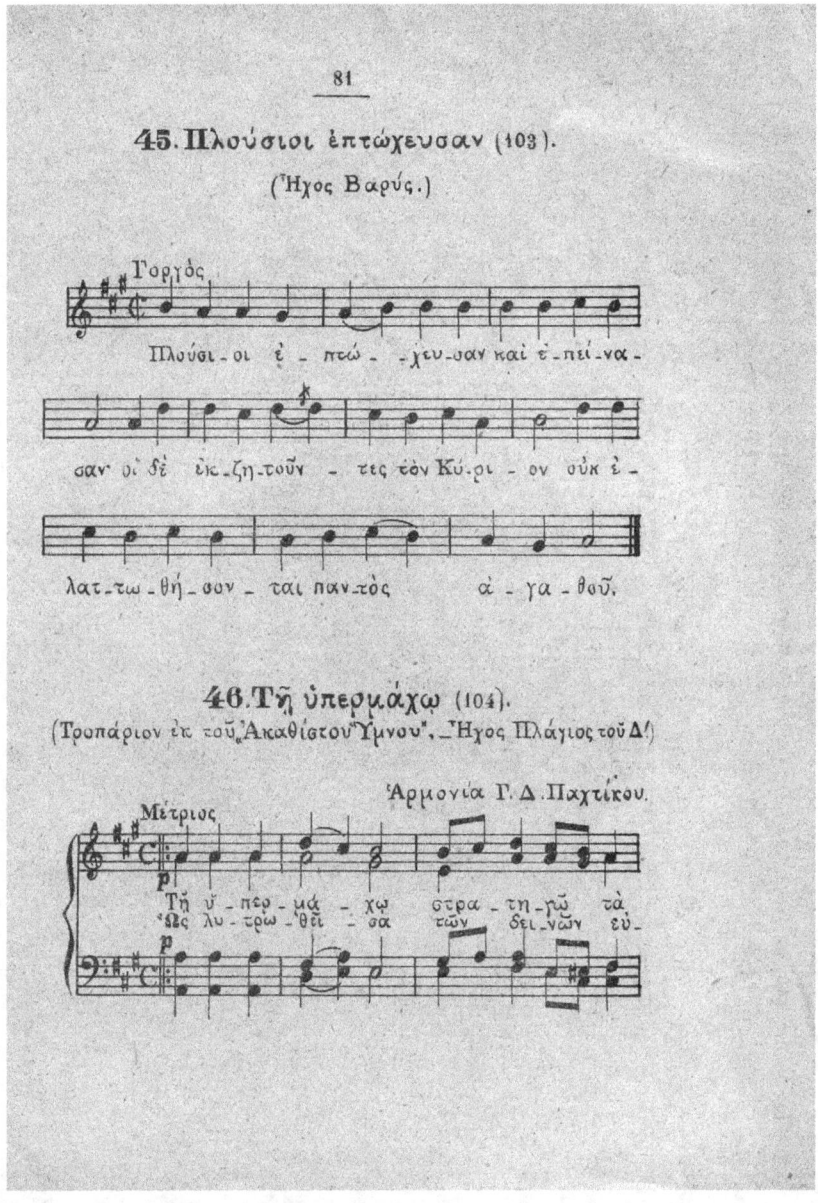

Music transcription 21.11a Transcription in staff notation by Pachtikos, utilizing the formula of Naupliotis (Pachtikos, 1910: 81–3 – Aristotle University Library).

transcription 21.12). The next sheet music, which also constitutes the conclusion to the present chapter, also contains excerpts of 'Cloudy Sunday' applied to the points where the relative literature claims similarity in the construction of the melody (see music transcription 21.13).

Music transcription 21.11b (Continued)

Music transcription 21.11c (Continued)

Music transcription 21.12 Citation of transcriptions by Ioannis and Stefanos, Progakis and Naupliotis.

A Historical Recording of the Hymn

Music transcription 21.13 Citation of the three texts and part of 'Cloudy Sunday'.

22

Postlude

Citation of the music transcriptions of the pieces proposes the conclusion of the comparative analysis as well. It is logical that theoretical analysis can play an explanatory role in practice, without this pertaining to a single origin, since in many cases a cultural 'confabulation' is evident. That is, the fact that a sequence of notes is similar or identical to that of another, and which may describe modal music styles based on one or more theoretical systems, does not also imply a conscious replication. Reborrowing in the arts constitutes a vast issue and the chanting art plays a vital role in it, not only as a 'lender' but as a 'borrower' as well, illustrating, if nothing else, the ultimate role of an animate art, which results from and is defined via a constant interaction with anything found in its environment, influencing it and Influenced by it. Clarification is rendered when this dipole is perceived more as a common 'ground' rather than two places with boundaries and sovereign traits, in order for erudition to become the prominent 'point' of reference for both, as a common dwelling with separate spaces shaped by the preferences of the denizens. A significant dimension in the issue examining the evolution of yphos constitutes, undoubtedly, cultural osmosis of a variety of heterogeneities from different places and periods.

Taking everything into consideration, while an aural common performance of 'The Akathist Hymn' is dominated by a 'symphonic' aesthetic, during which a 'major/Plagal of the Fourth echos' environment is established, utilizing the first and fifth degree in the holding of the ison with a gradual motion from the first to second in the melody, in the analytical performance the aesthetic differs (see music transcriptions 21.1-21.4, 21.8-21.11). In a case such as this, usually, the holding of the ison is transferred from the first to the second degree (Ni–Pa instead of Ni–Di) with the melody simultaneously sounding on the note Ga; thus a 'Minor/Plagal of the First echos' environment is established (Pa–Ga, intervals

10-8 instead of interval of the fifth Di–Ni, intervals 12-10-8). The two melodies convey a different message and form a different aural chromatic context, with definitions structuring 'another space' for each performance. In other words, the clarification of which performance of 'The Akathist Hymn' is catalytic, with which 'Cloudy Sunday' shall be compared, since, as examined earlier, the analytical performances are quite different from the aural atmosphere which structures the song. Based on this argument, the choice of the more 'symphonic' version by Kalomoiris for the fourth part of *Simfonia tis Leventias* (piece 21) seems rather logical.

Music transcription 22.1 Common holding of the ison in the transcription by Ioannis and Stefanos (Byzantine notation).

Music transcription 22.2 Common holding of the ison in the transcription by Ioannis and Stefanos (staff notation).

N			Π					N		

Τη υ περ μα α χω στρα α τη γω τα

N			Π					N		

Τη υ περ μα α χω στρα α τη γω τα

Music transcription 22.3 Common holding of the ison in the transcription by Iakovos Naupliotis (Byzantine notation).

Music transcription 22.4 Common holding of the ison in the transcription by Iakovos Naupliotis (staff notation).

In conclusion on a technical level as well, the performance by Naupliotis differs to a great extent from the melodic composition of 'Cloudy Sunday'; hence, any similarity between the two pieces is completely out of the question. Based on the discourse concerning fluidity in the specific music idioms, the most crucial question raised, when comparing two musical pieces which are defined by orality is (in the final analysis): Which performance? That is, which music 'text'?

23

Epilogue

The arguments developed constitute an initial approach to a multifaceted issue, which in no way concerns only the past, but is constantly pertinent to the present as well.

At the outset, we debated some of the most important rhetorics which were presented, regarding the connection of the two pieces in general. Two of these were accompanied by music analyses, which up to now seem to be the only ones available.[1] In short, the intellectual world was the one which first posed questions regarding descent and involved the relative literature and members-protagonists of the laiki music environment. The 'resistance' to the dictates of 'the powers that be' and the 'outsiders' were almost non-existent. On the contrary, quite a few laiko musicians embraced the Byzantine guise, indeed boasting of it in later life. However, with regard to the specific argument on descent, 'Cloudy Sunday' from 'The Akathist Hymn', the counterargument is presented by the composer himself, who consistently refused to accede to the Byzantine supposition. Additionally, while he, himself, remains from the start stoically steadfast in his beliefs, it is the intellectuals who change their minds, eventually integrating a part of the repertoire previously excluded.

This examination led to the search for answers concerning the causal factors which bore the rhetorics in question. These answers were sought out in the historiography of Byzantine music, which constitutes an issue especially complex, and certainly requires a much more thorough investigation. Despite this, by focusing on certain historical key facts, an effort to understand the causes which gave rise to what is known in the realm of chanting as 'the music issue' was made (see Filopoulos, 1990, 1993 and 1997). Not only does this issue remain

---

[1] An interesting paper by Thomas Apostolopoulos, which compares a plethora of similar cases of 'descent' of well-known laika songs from the Byzantine tradition, was published in the precedings of the eighth Interdepartmental Musicological Conference under the auspice of the Greek Musicological Society 'Effects and interactions' (25–27 November 2016). The paper is titled 'Modal music forms with the imprint of chanting in folk and laika songs' (Apostolopoulos, 2019).

unresolved to the present day, but it has also branched out into two levels. The first concerns the conflict which ensued with the dawn of the twentieth century, pitting two music 'leaders' against each other, Sakellaridis and Psachos, and the struggle of both for the prevalence of their own version concerning 'authentic' and 'Greek' ecclesiastical music. The second was the result of Simon Karas's activity and climaxed with the publication of his theory in 1982. Once again, the issue of 'Greekness' was at the epicentre, enlisting every tool and capability of the powerful link with regard to historical continuation of the nation and, inductively, its music too. Regarding laiki music, in the first two parts of the book we examined both selective exclusion in repertoire, and its intervention. The two big losers were, on the one hand, the urban laiko idioms, which were excluded due to failure to fulfil the prerequisite characteristics of Greekness, and on the other, the fluidity of performance practice. This fluidity was generally afflicted in laiko idioms (rural and urban), as the Byzantine theoretical substructure proposed required the standardization of the musical act and its teaching.

In the third and fourth part, a serious effort to focus on two fundamental axes was made: on the one hand, to comprehend, as much as possible, the world to which both pieces belong, but also the world they build, as autonomous entities, interacting both with each other and with other entities, with which they share common 'experiences'. Possibly, the last point constitutes the most crucial parameter, as the comparison and evaluation of differences in binary form, many times, unconsciously do not take into account the presence of other entities which co-exist with the directly compared ones. In other words, the common 'ground' of the two pieces does not constitute a cordoned and clearly demarcated area. Comparison of pairs poses a diversity of hazards as, having as its ultimate goal – perhaps even unconsciously – the 'discovery' of 'ground zero', that is, the birth, the process of continual evolution and plasticity of performance is marginalized, which as we saw, albeit the variations, constitutes a fundamental element of the entities in question. Such a rationale, would lead (sooner or later) to defining formalities of lineage.

Another axis concerned comparative analysis, utilizing a theoretical prism. Through this analysis certain technical musical characteristics were examined, in a negotiation of the extremely interesting and vast field of animate music idioms. These idioms evolved within an environment, which was distinguished by its cosmopolitism characteristics and was transposed into a new environment, that of the nation states. What must be stressed is the different mindset which governs the approach which is structured on a philosophy of conditions of *origin*, in comparison to that which perceives this as a condition of *reference*. The environment of reciprocal interpenetration and co-existence (alliloperichoresis) offers an alternative analysis toolkit, compared to that of the environment of retrenchment.

Justifiably, it is also crucial that the condition which is conducive to a *music ecumene* is emphasized, as described by Jim Samson (2013) and by the authors of *Balkan Popular Culture and the Ottoman Ecumene* (2007), as the mouldings which take place among its 'denizens' concern many and diverse levels, its two defining axes being space and time. Presently, the object of our discourse is a ceaseless confabulation between 'other' places and 'other' periods of time, a confabulation which spins the web of a multidimensional nexus. In other words, aural phenomena are examined through a syncretic (rather than through a comparative) prism; this search leads to greater depths, and to the palpation of diverse details and information which make up these phenomena. The need to manage this data through a variety of prisms is vital, in order to mutually encompass its multifaceted aspects through interdisciplinarity. In this way, one shall ascertain, for instance, that the 'bel canto' interpretation and the 'Europeanized' vocal placement of Mary Linda in *Epitáfios*[2] by Theodorakis, or the vocal placement on the mask of the face of Ioannis Miliaris in 'Lachanádes'[3] by Vangelis Papazoglou, are not elements which on their own could render the pieces in question 'Italian' or 'German'. According to the same methodology and based on the same rationale, activity on a theoretically minor pentachord (or Nihavend), as in 'Devil Pray'[4] by Madonna, cannot create a smyrnaic, laiko or Ottoman condition, even though the theoretical description and definition is feasible.

Music transcription 23.1 Melody activity in 'Devil Pray'.

In addition, the use of the Spanish guitar in the estudiantina, in the Piraeus rebetiko and the subsequent laiko, is not enough to render a song 'Spanish'; a

---

[2] Επιτάφιος: EMI 094637416624, 1963: https://youtu.be/P4584H54Ooc.
[3] 'Λαχανάδες': Orthophonic 89813–ORS 672, 7 May 1935: https://youtu.be/ERXBWhMvekw.
[4] Track 2, Album: *Rebel Heart*, Universal 4721168, 2014: https://youtu.be/0Yx-E-xG4kU.

bolero rhythm, on its own, is not able to render some other song 'Latin-American'; and the articulation manner and vocal placement of the chanter Spyros Peristeris (who, undoubtedly, presented chanting as an artistic phenomenon more than anybody else) cannot render a hymn an 'opera'.[5]

On the other hand, evolution in certain areas of chanting performance poses a new context and is deemed worthy of investigation, following the same detached and calm rationale when viewing the phenomena. For example, the use of sound equipment (in many cases, indeed, particularly cutting edge), such as the electronic audio console, the speakers, the microphones, the electronic holding of the ison, the electronic tuner application on smart phones, hand recorders and others, signifies a new age for chanting: not only an urban form of chanting but also a translocal one, animate and contemporary, always with an intense desire for modernization, interacting with the present, living in it, 'growing' with man. And let us not forget the interesting, complex ramifications of the – otherwise – uniform Byzantine music, for example, the Romanian and Russian idioms, which co-exist within the same communiqué.[6] All the aforementioned play a singular role in the configuration of the messages of the music pieces and, in general, the performances, whether they be sacraments of the church or a concert on a music stage. Clearly, the visual dimension, that is, how the one (the protagonist) who performs 'looks', determines the final product for the receiver.[7]

Theoretical models acquire power during their utilization as tools of comprehension of the act, which undoubtedly is the privilege of animate music. The demystification of the music theory toolkit, as a 'correctness referee' of a performance, contributed to the redefinition of the cultural factors of cosmopolitan societies, even those which developed in the new framework of nation states, exonerating the present-day musical performance. The examination of correctness in performance with the use of theoretical models, perhaps, inverts the physiology of human creation, which concerns not only art but all forms of conceptualization and thought. The redefinition of music products consists of a process of modernization, the transposition, that is, of the past into the present, not as a domineering dictator who demands the respect and awe of his 'subjects',

---

[5] For the phenomenon of similarity and the common condition observed in laiko pieces, see also Ordoulidis (2014: 151-3).
[6] See Gheorghita (2010).
[7] See also Georgios Maniatis's preface in Dahlhaus (2000: 9-11).

immured in his narcissistic fantasy,⁸ but as a new and contemporaneous creation mechanism which desires fulfilment. The creation governed by such a code shall reinstate the condition of reciprocal interpenetration and co-existence (alliloperichoresis), which, perhaps, is the sole designated 'guardian' of the road which leads to the 'celestial' and the 'super-celestial'.

---

⁸ Loudovikos, 2013: 270.

Works cited

Afthonidis, Germanos. 'Anekdoti pragmateia peri tou ellinikou ierou melous (epistoli pros ton Ilia Tantalidi, 1876)'. Edited by Markelos Pirar. *Mousikos Logos* 5 (2003): 86–117.

Akridas, Theodoros. *Elenchos mousikon dysplasion S. Kara*. Messolongi: Ekdoseis Gramma, 2013.

Alexandrou, Maria. *Exigiseis kai metagrafes tis vyzantinis mousikis – Syntomi eisagogi ston provlimatismo tous*. Thessaloniki: University Studio Press, 2010.

Alexiou, Sotos. *Vasilis Tsitsanis: I paidiki ilikia enos xechoristou dimiourgou*. Athens: Kastaniotis, 2001.

Alexiou, Sotos. *O xakoustos Tsitsanis*. Athens: Kochlias, 2003.

Alygizakis, Antonios. *Themata ekklisiastikis mousikis*. Thessaloniki: Ekdoseis Pournara, 1985.

Alygizakis, Antonios. 'I chrisi tis ekfonitikis psalmodias kai ton chyma anagnoseon'. In *Theoria kai praxi tis psaltikis technis (Proceedings of the 1st Panhellenic Conference of Psaltic Art, 3–5 November 2000)*, edited by Achilleas Chaldaeakes, 91–140. n.p., 2001.

Alygizakis, Antonios. 'Vyzantini mousiki ypo tou protopsaltou tis Megalis tou Christou Ekklisias Iakovou Naupliotou'. *Book and 5 CDs*. Istanbul: Kalan, 2008.

Amargianakis, Giorgos. 'Kritiki vyzantini kai paradosiaki mousiki'. In *Kriti: Istoria kai politismos*, edited by Nikolaos Panagiotakis, 319–32. Syndesmos Topikon Enoseon Dimon kai Koinotiton Kritis, 1988.

Anastasiou, Grigorios. 'I "trisynthetos glykofonia" tis psaltikis kata tripli ekdochi ton trion mousikodidaskalon; Ioannou Sakellaridou, Konstantinou Psachou, Simonos Kara'. In *Konstantinos Psachos: O mousikos, o logios (Conference proceedings, 30 November 2007)*, edited by Euangelos Karamanes, 29–48. Athens: Kentro Ereunis tis Ellinikis Laografias, 2013.

Anastasiou, Theofilos. *Paidaki me psychi kai zilemeno: 329 tragoudia tou Vasili Tsitsani*. Trikala: Ekdoseis Dimou Trikalon, 1995.

Anastasiou, Theofilos, and Foteini Anastasiou. *Sta Trikala sta dyo stena: Martyries gia tin laiki mousiki 1881–1935*. Trikala: Kentro Ereunas – Mouseio Tsitsani, 2014.

Anderson, Benedict. *Imagined Communities – Reflections on the Origin and Spread of Nationalism*. 2nd ed. (1983). London and New York: Verso, 1991.

Andrikos, Nikos. *Oi laikoi dromoi sto mesopolemiko astiko tragoudi – Schediasma laikis tropikis theorias*. Athens: Topos, 2018.

Angelinaras, Giorgos. 'I psaltiki paradosi tou Oikoumenikou Patriarchiou'. In *Antipelargisi: Timitikos tomos gia ton Nikolao A. Dimitriou*, 305–14. Athens: Pneumatiko Idryma Samou 'Nikolaos Dimitriou', 1992.

Apostolopoulos, Thomas. *I ekklisiastiki mousiki sto ekklisiastiko dikaio*. Thessaloniki: En Chordais, 1999.

Apostolopoulos, Thomas. 'Tropika schimata me to apotypoma tis psaltikis se dimotika kai laika tragoudia'. In *Effects and Interactions (Proceedings of the Annually Conference of the Hellenic Musicological Society, 25–27 November 2016)*, edited by Kostas Chardas, Kostas Vouvaris, Kostas Kardamis, Giorgos Sakallieros, and Ioannis Foulias, 581–5. Hellenic Musicological Society, 2019.

Argyropoulos, Athanasios. *I mousiki ton paidagogikon scholeion*. Athens: Typografeio Deligianni, 1915.

Artemidis, Klevoulos. *Orfiki lyra – Itoi asmata patriotika dimodi kai diafora alla*. Athens: Typografeio Kousoulinou, 1905.

Arvanitis, Ioannis. 'O rythmos ton ekklisiastikon melon mesa apo tin palaiografiki ereuna kai tin exigisi tis palaias simeiografias'. PhD thesis. Department of Music Studies, Ionian University, 2010.

Aydemir, Murat. *To tourkiko makam*. Translated by Sophia Kombotiati. Athens: Fagottobooks (original title: Turkish music makam guide, 2010), 2012.

Barbaki, Maria. *Opseis tis mousikis zois sta ellinika astika kentra to deutero miso tou 19ou aiona*. Athens: Ellinika Akadimaika Ilektronika Syngrammata kai Voithimata, 2015.

Barbatsis, Anestis. *To proimo ergo tou Vasili Tsitsani*. Athens: Fagottobooks, 2016.

Beaton, Roderick. 'Modes and Roads: Factors of Change and Continuity in Greek Musical Tradition'. *The Annual of the British School at Athens* 75 (1980): 1–11.

Bellonis, Giannis, and Gianna Papageorgakopoulou, ed. *Nikolaos Vergotis, Ta mousika mas idrymata: I istoria mias pentikontaetias [1871–1924]*. Athens: Ionian University, Department of Music Studies, Hellenic Music Research Lab and Edition Orpheus – P. Nikolaidou, 2016.

Buchanan, Donna, ed. *Balkan Popular Culture and the Ottoman Ecumene – Music, Image, and Regional Political Discourse*. Maryland: The Scarecrow Press, 2007.

Bucuvalas, Tina. *Greek Music in America*. Jackson: University Press of Mississippi, 2019.

Chaldaeakes, Achilleas. 'I psaltiki os techni kai os epistimi i paradosi kai neoterikotita sti vyzantini mousiki'. Paper presented at the 1st conference of Ieras Synodou Ekklisias tis Ellados (synodikis epitropis christianikis agogis tis neotitos - Epitropis kallitechnikon ekdiloseon): Elliniki mousiki meso paideias kai politismou *(17/12)*. Vyzantino kai Christianiko Mouseio Athinon, 2005.

Chaldaeakes, Achilleas. 'Musical Freedom and Ecclesiastical Rules at the Ecumenical Patriarchate of Constantinople during the 18th Century'. *Anatolis to Periichima* (2014): 87–129.

Chaldaeakes, Achilleas. 'Illustrating Melodies: Iconographical Instructions in Byzantine Music – Theory and Practice'. In *Church Music and Icons: Windows to Heaven*

(Proceedings of the Fifth International Conference on Orthodox Church Music, 3–9 June 2013), 138–52. University of Eastern Finland, Joensuu, Finland: The International Society for Orthodox Church Music, 2015.

Charkiolakis, Alexandros. 'To Odeio Athinon os kathoristikos foreas politismikis diamorfosis'. In *Continuities, Discontinuities, Ruptures in the Greek World (1204–2014): Economy, Society, History, Literature (Proceedings of the 5th European Congress of Modern Greek Studies of the European Society of Modern Greek Studies, 2–5 October 2014)*, edited by Konstantinos Dimadis, 572–9. European Society of Modern Greek Studies, 2015.

Chatzidoulis, Kostas. *Rebetiki istoria 1 (Perpiniadis – Genitsaris – Mathesis – Lekakis)*. Athens: Nefeli, 1979.

Chatzigiakoumis, Manolis. 'Autografo (1816) tou 'Megalou Theoritikou' tou Chrysanthou'. *O eranistis* 11 (1974): 311–22.

Chatzimichelakis, Georgios. 'I theoria kai i praxi exoterikou melous mesa apo ta entypa theoritika syngrammata tou 19ou ai'. PhD thesis. Department of Music Studies, Ionian University, 2013.

Chatzipantazis, Theodoros. *Tis asiatidos mousis erastai... I akmi tou athinaikou kafe aman sta chronia tis vasileias tou Georgiou I. Symvoli sti meleti tis proistorias tou rebetikou*. Athens: Stigmi, 1986.

Christoforidis, Michael. *Asturias – The Music of Spain – Guitar Trek, CD album*. Australia: ABC Classics, 2009.

Christoforidis, Michael. 'Serenading Spanish Students on the Streets of Paris: The International Projection of Estudiantinas in the 1870s'. *Nineteenth-Century Music Review* 15, no. 1 (2017): 23–36.

Chrysanthos of Madytos. *Theoritikon mega tis mousikis*. Trieste: Typografeio Weis, 1832.

Chrysostomos Bishop of Zakynthos. 'Eisigisis tou S. Mitropolitou Zakynthou kou Chrysostomou'. In *O ymnodos kai mousikodidaskalos Ioannis Sakellaridis (1853–1938) – Logoi ekfonithentes kata to filologikon tou mnimosynon en to Parnasso tis 12is Iouniou 1939*, edited by Chrysostomos Bishop of Zakynthos, 9–12. Athens: n.p., 1940.

Conejero, Alberto. *Carmina Urbana Orientalium Graecorum. Poéticas de la Identidad en la Canción Urbana Greco-Oriental*. Madrid: Consejo Superior de Investigaciones Científicas, 2008.

Dahlhaus, Carl. *Aisthitiki tis mousikis*. Edited by Giorgos Maniatis. Translated by Apostolos Oikonomou. Athens: Stachy (original title: Musikästhetik, 1986), 2000.

Demers, Joanna. *Steal This Music – How Intellectual Property Law Affects Musical Creativity*. Athens, GA: The University of Georgia Press, 2006.

Despotis, Sotiris. 'I paradosiaki kerkyraiki psaltiki techni'. *Grigorios Palamas* 812 (2006): 1029–44.

Drosinis, Giorgos. *O Georgios Nazos kai to Odeio Athinon*. Athens: Estia, 1938.

Emmerson, Simon. 'Where Next? New Music, New Musicology'. *'Languages' of Electronic Music: The Proceedings of the Electroacoustic Music Studies Network*. Leicester: De Montfort University, 2007.

Ennig, Ioulios. *Nea asmata paidagogika*. Athens: Typografeio Filadelfeos, 1883.

Erol, Merih. *Greek Orthodox Music in Ottoman Istanbul*. Bloomington: Indiana University Press, 2015.

Euangelidis, Dimitris. 'O makaritis amanes kai i aisthitiki (To Ethnos, 4/12)'. In *Spania keimena gia to rebetiko (1929-1959) (2006)*, edited by Kostas Vlisidis, 71–3. Athens: Ekdoseis tou Eikostou Protou, 1937.

Eutaxias, Athanasios. *I ethniki imon mousiki*. Athens: Typografeio Estia, 1907.

Euthymiadis, Avraam. *Mathimata vyzantinis ekklisiastikis mousikis*. Vol. B. n.p., 1972.

Fabbri, Franco. 'Mediterranean Triangle: Naples, Smyrna, Athens'. In *Neapolitan Postcards: The Canzone Napoletana as Transnational Subject*, edited by Goffredo Plastino, and Joseph Sciorra, 29–44. Lanham, Boulder, New York and London: Rowman & Littlefield Publishers, 2016.

Fallmerayer, Jakob Philipp. *Geschichte des Kaisertums von Trapezunt*. München: Weber, 1827.

Fallmerayer, Jakob Philipp. *Geschichte der Halbinsel Morea während des Mittelalters*. Stuttgart und Tübingen: Cotta, 1830.

Fallmerayer, Jakob Philipp. *Istoria tis chersonisou tou Moria kata to mesaiona*. Translated by Pantelis Softzoglou. 2 vols. Athens: Megali Poreia (original title: Geschichte der Halbinsel Morea während des Mittelalters, 1830), 2002 and 2014.

Fallmerayer, Jakob Philipp. *Peri tis katagogis ton simerinon Ellinon*. Translated by Konstantinos Romanos. Athens: Nefeli (original title: Welchen Einfluß hatte die Besetzung Griechenlands durch die Slawen auf das Schicksal der Stadt Athen und der Landschaft Attika, 1835), 1984.

Feldman, Walter. *Klezmer: Music, History, and Memory*. New York: Oxford University Press, 2016.

Filopoulos, Giannis. *Eisagogi stin elliniki polyfoniki ekklisiastiki mousiki*. Athens: Nefeli, 1990.

Filopoulos, Giannis. *Rosikes epidraseis stin elliniki polyfoniki ekklisiastiki mousiki*. Athens: Nefeli, 1993.

Filopoulos, Giannis. *I polyfoniki ekklisiastiki mousiki stin elliniki koinotita tou Londinou*. Athens: Parousia, 1997.

Frith, Simon. *Performing Rites. On the Value of Popular Music*. Cambridge, MA: Harvard University Press, 1998.

Gauntlett, Stathis. *Rebetiko tragoudi. Symvoli stin epistimoniki tou prosegisi*. Translated by Kostas Vlisidis. Athens: Ekdoseis tou Eikostou Protou (original title: Rebetiko Tragoudi as a Generic Term, 1982), 2001.

Gekas, Giorgos. 'To mousiko portraito tou Panagioti Tounta'. Bachelor thesis. Department of Popular and Traditional Music, TEI of Epirus, 2018.

Georgiadis, Triantafyllos. *Kipos chariton melistheis ypo Triantafyllou Georgiadou.* n.p., 1916.

Gheorghita, Nicolae. *Byzantine Chant – Between Constantinople and the Danubian Principalities – Studies in Byzantine Musicology.* Bucharest: Editura Sophia, 2010.

Giannakopoulos, Giorgos. 'O kosmos tis technis – O Vasilis Tsitsanis kai to laiko mas tragoudi'. *Ellinikos Vorras (24/6)*, 1960.

Giannelos, Dimitris. *Syntomo theoritiko vyzantinis mousikis.* Katerini: Ekdoseis Epektasi, 2009.

Giannopoulos, Emmanouil. *I anthisi tis psaltikis technis stin Kriti (1566–1669).* Athens: Idryma Vyzantinis Mousikologias, 2004.

Giorgos, Dertilis. *Istoria tou ellinikou kratous – 1830-1920.* 9th ed. (2004). Heraklion: Crete University Press, 2015.

Gracyk, Theodore. *Listening to Popular Music or, How I Learned to Stop Worrying and Love Led Zeppelin.* Ann Arbor: The University of Michigan Press, 2007.

Hadjidakis, Manos. 'Ermineia kai thesi tou synchronou laikou tragoudiou'. *Lecture (31/1).* Athens: Art Theatre (Aliki), 1949.

Hadjidakis, Manos. *O kathreftis kai to machairi.* Athens: Ikaros, 1988.

Herzfeld, Michael. *Pali dika mas: Laografia, ideologia kai i diamorfosi tis synchronis Elladas.* Translated by Marinos Sarigiannis. Athens: Alexandria (original title: Ours Once More: Folklore, Ideology and the Making of Modern Greece, 1986), 2002.

Hobsbawm, Eric, and Terence Ranger, ed. *The Invention of Tradition.* 2nd ed. (1983). Cambridge: Cambridge University Press, 2000.

Holst, Gail. *Road to Rembetika, Music of a Greek Sub-Culture. Songs of Love, Sorrow and Hashish.* 4th ed. (1975). Limni, Evia: Denise Harvey, 2006.

Ioannis Protopsaltis. *Anastasimatarion neon, argon kai syntomon.* Patriarchiko Typografeio, 1905.

Jackson, Maureen. '"Cosmopolitan" Smyrna: Illuminating or Obscuring Cultural Histories?' *The Geographical Review* 102, no. 3 (2012): 337–49.

Johnson, Julian. *Who Needs Classical Music?* New York: Oxford University Press, 2002.

Kallimopoulou, Eleni. *Paradosiaká: Music, Meaning and Identity in Modern Greece.* Bodmin, Cornwall: Ashgate, 2009.

Kalokyris, Konstantinos. *O mousourgos Ioannis Th. Sakellaridis kai i vyzantini mousiki: kritiki skiagrafia 50 chronia meta ton thanato tou.* Thessaloniki: n.p., 1988.

Kalomoiris, Manolis. *Armonia.* Vol. 2. Athens: Gaitanos, 1935.

Kalomoiris, Manolis. 'Oliga logia tou k. M. Kalomoiri'. In *O ymnodos kai mousikodidaskalos Ioannis Sakellaridis (1853-1938) – Logoi ekfonithentes kata to filologikon tou mnimosynon en to Parnasso tis 12is Iouniou 1939*, edited by Chrysostomos Bishop of Zakynthos, 37–8. Athens: n.p., 1940.

Kalomoiris, Manolis. 'O agnostos mousourgos tou dimotikou tragoudiou'. *Praktika tis Akadimias Athinon* 21 (1946): 274–90.

Kalomoiris, Manolis. 'Ta "rebetika" tragoudia kai ta "tango" (Ethnos, 8/1)'. In *Spania keimena gia to rebetiko (1929-1959) (2006)*, edited by Kostas Vlisidis, 126–7. Athens: Ekdoseis tou Eikostou Protou, 1947.

Kalomoiris, Manolis. 'Sophia K. Spanoudi'. *Nea Estia* NA', no. 597 (1952): 674.

Kalomoiris, Manolis. *Mousiki morfologia*. Vol. 2. Athens: Gaitanos, 1957.

Kalyviotis, Aristomenis. 'Oi ichografiseis ellinikon tragoudion stin Aigypto kai o tragoudistis Ioannis Moutsos'. *Sylloges* 137 (1995): 751–68.

Kalyviotis, Aristomenis. *Smyrni – I mousiki zoi 1900–1992. I diaskedasi, ta mousika katastimata, oi ichografiseis diskon*. Athens: Music Corner and Tinela, 2002.

Kalyviotis, Aristomenis. *Thessaloniki - I mousiki zoi prin to 1912*. Karditsa: Self-publication, 2015.

Kapsimalakou, Christina. 'Eleftheria kai anangaiotita kata ton Maximo ton Omologiti – Pros mia ontologia tou prosopou'. PhD thesis. Department of Philosophy, University of Patras, 2012.

Karakasis, Lailios. 'Laika tragoudia kai choroi tis Smyrnis'. *Mikrasiatika Chronika* 4 (1948): 301–16.

Karamanis, Athanasios. *Nea mousiki syllogi – Esperinos*. 4th pr. Vol. 3. Athens: n.p., 1982.

Karanikas, Charalambos. 'I anaviosi tou rebetikou tragoudiou kata tin periodo tis metapoliteusis (1974–1990). Theoritiki kai mousikologiki prosengisi'. Bachelor thesis. Department of Popular and Traditional Music, TEI of Epirus, 2011.

Karas, Simon. *Methodos tis ellinikis mousikis – Theoritikon*. 4 vols. Athens: Syllogos pros Diadosin tis Ethnikis Mousikis, 1982.

Katsifis, Vasileios. *Meleti – kritiki sto theoritiko tou Simonos Kara*. Katerini: Tertios, 2002.

Khalil, Alexander Konrad. 'Echoes of Constantinople: Oral and Written Tradition of the Psaltes of the Ecumenical Patriarchate of Constantinople'. PhD thesis. University of California San Diego, 2009.

Kiltzanidis, Panagiotis. *Methodiki didaskalia theoritiki te kai praktiki*. Constantinople: Typografeio Koromila kai Yiou, 1881.

Kliafa, Maroula. *Trikala: Apo ton Seifoulach ston Tsitsani*. 3 vols. Athens: Kedros, 1996, 1998 and 2000.

Kliafa, Maroula. *Mia serenata sto Lithaio: I mousiki kinisi sta Trikala (1881–1965)*. Athens: Kedros, 2003.

Kokkinos, Athanasios. 'Oi kindynoi tis mousikis (Ellas, 21/2)'. In *Spania keimena gia to rebetiko (1929-1959) (2006)*, edited by Kostas Vlisidis, 145–7. Athens: Ekdoseis tou Eikostou Protou, 1949.

Kokkonis, Georges. 'I kata Damianako chronologisi kai periodologisi tou rebetikou: mia nea anagnosi ypo to prisma tis mousikologias'. Paper presented at Agrotiki koinonia kai laikos politismos. *Epistimoniko synedrio sti mnimi tou Stathi Damianakou*. Athens, May 25–27, 2005.

Kokkonis, Georges. *La Question de la Grécité dans la Musique Néohellénique*. Paris: Association Pierre Belon – De Boccard, 2008.
Kokkonis, Georges. 'La création musicale savante et les collections des chants populaires en Grèce: découverte ou invention?' *Musique et globalisation: Une approche critique (Actes du colloque Musique et globalisation organisé par la revue Filigrane)*, 177–86. Paris: Delatour (Collection Filigrane), 2012.
Kokkonis, Georges. *Laikes mousikes paradoseis: Logies anagnoseis – Laikes pragmatoseis*. Athens: Fagottobooks, 2017.
Kokkonis, Georges. 'I mousiki logokrisia stin Ellada. Mia proti prosengisi'. In *Lexiko logokrisias stin Ellada. Kachektiki dimokratia, diktatoria, metapoliteusi*, edited by Pinelopi Petsini, and Dimitris Christopoulos, 134–45. Athens: Kastaniotis, 2018.
Kokkonis, Georges, Nikos Ordoulidis, Panagiota Anagnostou, Marika Rombou-Levidi, Maria Zoubouli, and Polina Tambakaki. 'Logia kai laika diakeimena stin neoelliniki mousiki. Meleti periptosis: oi exi laikes zografies tou Manou Hadjidaki (round table)'. In *Epidraseis kai allilepidraseis (Conference proceedings, 25–27 November 2016)*, edited by Kostas Chardas, Petros Vouvaris, Kostas Kardamis, Giorgos Sakallieros, and Ioannis Foulias, 654–733. Hellenic Musicological Society, 2019.
Konstantinidi, Maria. *Koinoniologiki istoria tou rebetikou*. Athens: Selas, 1994.
Konstantinidis, Antonios, and Athanasios Stogiannidis. 'Logiosyni kai paradosi, paidagogikes opseis kai didaktika provlimata tis psaltikis technis'. In *I psaltiki techni os autonomi epistimi (Conference proceedings 1ou diethnous diepistimonikou mousikologikou synedriou 29 June –3 July 2014)*, edited by Konstantinos Karagounis, and Georgios Kouroupetroglou, 280–7. Academy of Theology Studies, Section of Psaltic Art and Musicology, 2015.
Karamanes, Euagelos, ed. 'Konstantinos Psachos – O mousikos, o logios'. *Conference Proceedings (30 November 2007)*. Athens: Kentro Ereunis Ellinikis Laografias, 2013.
Kontaratos, Savvas. 'I mythopoiisi tis kath' imas Anatolis'. In *Mythoi kai ideologimata sti synchroni Ellada (Epistimoniko symposio, 23–24 November 2005)*, edited by Ourania Kaiafa, 135–51. Etaireia Spoudon Neoellinikou Politismou kai Genikis Paideias, 2007.
Korovinis, Thomas. *Oi zeibekoi tis Mikras Asias*. Athens: Agra, 2004.
Kosmas Madytinos. *Poimenikos aulos – Teuchos triton: Scholeiaka asmata*. Athens: Typografeio Kousoulinou, 1897.
Kounadis, Panagiotis. *Eis anamnysin stigmon elkystikon*. Vol. 2. Athens: Katarti, 2003.
Kounas, Spilios. 'To astiko laiko tragoudi tou elladikou chorou kata tin periodo ton proimon ichografiseon: yphologia, tropikotites, epitelesi'. PhD thesis. Department of Cultural Technology and Communication, University of the Aegean, 2019.
Kourousis, Stauros. *Apo ton taboura sto bouzouki: I istoria kai i exelixi tou bouzoukiou kai oi protes tou ichografiseis (1926–1932)*. Athens: Orpheumphonograph, 2013.

Kyr, M. 'N' apagoreuthoun ta mangika (Edo Athinai, v. 10, Nov.)'. In *Spania keimena gia to rebetiko (1929-1959) (2006)*, edited by Kostas Vlisidis, 113–15. Athens: Ekdoseis tou Eikostou Protou, 1946.

Lalioti, Vassiliki. '"Stay in Synch!": Performing Cosmopolitanism in an Athens Festival'. *Journal of Electronic Dance Music Culture* 5, no. 2 (2013): 131–51.

Lambadarios, Ioannis, and Stefanos Domestichos. *Pandekti tis ieras ekklisiastikis ymnodias tou olou eniautou*. Vol. A. Constantinople: Patriarchiko Typografeio, 1850.

Lambadarios, Stefanos. *Ermineia tis exoterikis mousikis kai efarmogi autis eis tin kath' imas mousikin*. Constantinople: Patriarchiko Typografeio, 1843.

Leotsakos, Giorgos. 'Gia to rebetiko'. *To Vima (6/4)*, 1974.

Leotsakos, Giorgos. 'Manolis Kalomoiris (1883–1962) – Spyros-Filiskos Samaras (1861–1917) – Mousikos dichasmos kai emfylios'. *Ta Nea (21/1)*, N14, 2000.

Liakos, Antonis. 'The Construction of National Time: The Making of the Modern Greek Historical Imagination'. *Mediterranean Historical Review* 16, no. 1 (2001): 27–42.

Liavas, Lambros. *To elliniko tragoudi apo to 1821 eos ti dekaetia tou 1950*. Athens: Emporiki Trapeza tis Ellados, 2009.

Lingas, Alexander. 'Byzantine Chant, Western Musicology and the Performer'. *Early Music News* (1991): 3–5.

Lingas, Alexander. 'Tradition and Renewal in Greek Psalmody'. In *Psalms in Community – Jewish and Christian Textual, Liturgical, and Artistic Traditions*, edited by Harold Attridge, and Margot Fassler, 341–56. Atlanta: Society of Biblical Literature, 2003.

Livingston, Tamara. 'Music Revivals: Towards a General Theory'. *Ethnomusicology* 43, no. 1 (1999): 66–85.

Loudovikos, Nikolaos. 'Possession or Wholeness? St. Maximus the Confessor and John Zizioulas on Person, Nature, and Will'. *Participatio – Journal of the Thomas F. Torrance Theological Fellowship* 4 (2013): 258–86.

Makris, Eustathios. 'I paradosiaki ekklisiastiki mousiki ton Eptanison. Synoliki istoriki prosengisi'. *Mousikos Logos* 8 (2009): 45–70.

Makris, Eustathios. 'Oktaichia kai polyfonia stin kritoeptanisiaki psaltiki paradosi. I periptosi tou "Christos Anesti"'. In *Epistimoniki Epetirida*, 595–602. Heraklion: Ecclesiastical Academy of Crete, 2012.

Maltos, Anastasios. *Terpsichori – Itoi syllogi chorikon asmaton pros chrisin ton scholeion*. Odessa: Typografeio Chrysogelou kai Sias, 1885.

Maniatis, Dionysis. *I ek peraton diskografia grammofonou – Erga laikon mas kallitechnon*. Athens: Ekdoseis tou Ypourgeiou Politismou, 2006.

Manuel, Peter. *Popular Musics of the Non-Western World*. New York: Oxford University Press, 1990.

Mauroeidis, Marios. *Oi mousikoi tropoi stin anatoliki Mesogeio*. Athens: Fagottobooks, 1999.

Merlier, Melpo. *I mousiki laografia stin Ellada*. Athens: Ekdoseis Mousikou Laografikou Archeiou, 1935.

Michael, Christina. 'I chrisi tis politismikis kai mousikis synecheias sti dialexi tou Manou Hadjidaki gia to rebetiko'. In *Continuities, Discontinuities, Ruptures in the Greek World (1204-2014): Economy, Society, History, Literature (5th European Congress of Modern Greek Studies of the European Society of Modern Greek Studies, 2-5 October 2014)*, edited by Konstantinos Dimadis, 523-32. European Society of Modern Greek Studies, 2015.

Michael, Despina. 'Tsitsánis and the Birth of the New "Laikó Tragoudi"'. *Modern Greek Studies (Australia and New Zealand)* iv (1996): 55-96.

Michailidis, Andreas. 'Oi syntheseis tou Ntente Efenti mesa apo tis romaiikes sylloges exoterikis mousikis – Metagrafi auton apo ti vyzantini simeiografia sto synchrono mousiko systima katagrafis tis Tourkias'. Bachelor thesis. Department of Popular and Traditional Music, TEI of Epirus, 2008.

Misailidis, Misail. *Neon theoritikon syntomotaton itoi peri tis kath' imas ekklisiastikis kai archaias ellinikis mousikis*. Athens: Analomasi tou Syngrafeos, 1902.

Moore, Allan F. *Rock: The Primary Text: Developing a Musicology of Rock*. Ashgate Popular and Folk Music Series, 2001.

Moore, Allan F, ed. *Critical Essays in Popular Musicology*. Hampshire: Ashgate, 2007.

Moschopoulos, Georgios, ed. 'Symvoli stin istoria tis eptanisiakis mousikis'. *Praktika Synedriou Istorias tis Eptanisiakis Mousikis (Argostoli – Lixouri, 14-18 October 1995)*. Etaireia Kefalliniakon Istorikon Ereunon, 2000.

Moschopoulos, N. 'Mi tragoudite tourkika–na pausi o amanes (Kathimerini, 17/9)'. In *Spania keimena gia to rebetiko (1929-1959) (2006)*, edited by Kostas Vlisidis, 51-2. Ekdoseis tou Eikostou Protou, 1936.

Mousiki Epitropi Oikoumenikou Patriarcheiou. *Stoicheiodis didaskalia tis ekklisiastikis mousikis*. Constantinople: Typografeio Patriarcheiou, 1888.

Murray, Kenneth James. 'Spanish Music and Its Representations in London (1878-1930): From the Exotic to the Modern'. PhD thesis. Melbourne Conservatorium of Music, University of Melbourne, 2013.

Myrsiades, Linda. 'The Karaghiozis Performance in Nineteenth-Century Greece'. *Byzantine and Modern Greek Studies* 2 (1976): 83-97.

Mystakidis, Dimitris. *Laiki kithara – Tropikotita kai enarmonisi*. Thessaloniki: Ekdoseis Pringipessa, 2013.

Naupliotis, Iakovos. 'Syngrisis aravopersikis mousikis pros tin imeteran ekklisiastikin ypo Panagiotou Chalatzoglou (apo cheirografo tou 1728)'. Parartima Ekklisiastikis Alitheias II, Patriarchiko Typografeio, 1900, 68-75.

Nektarios Monachos. *Mousikos thisauros tou esperinou*. Mount Athos: Kallitechniko Typografeio Ieras Koinotitos Agiou Orous-Athos, 1935.

O'Connel, John Morgan. 'The Legend of a Greek Singer in a Turkish Tavern'. In *Music of the Sirens*, edited by Linda Phyllis Austern, and Inna Naroditskaya, 273-93. Bloomington: Indiana University Press, 2006.

Oikonomou, Filippos. *To neo mousiko zitima stin orthodoxi ekklisia*. Athens: Koultoura, 2002.

Oikonomou, Leonidas. 'Rebetika, laika kai skyladika: oria kai metatopiseis stin proslipsi tis laikis mousikis tou 20ou aiona'. *Dokimes* 13–14 (2005): 361–98.

Oikonomou, Leonidas. *Stelios Kazantzidis – Trauma kai symvoliki therapeia sto laiko tragoudi*. Athens: Ekdoseis Pataki, 2015.

Oikonomou, Nikos. *Giorgos Mitsakis – Autoviografia*. Athens: Ekdoseis tou Eikostou Protou, 1995.

Ordoulidis, Nikos. 'The Greek Popular Modes'. *British Postgraduate Musicology* 11 (2011): http://britishpostgraduatemusicology.org/bpm11/ordoulidis_the_greek_popular_modes.pdf.

Ordoulidis, Nikos. 'The Recording Career of Vasílis Tsitsánis (1936–1983). An Analysis of His Music and the Problems of Research into Greek Popular Music'. PhD thesis. School of Music, University of Leeds, 2012.

Ordoulidis, Nikos. *I diskografiki kariera tou Vasili Tsitsani (1936–1983). Analysi tis mousikis tou kai ta provlimata tis ereunas stin elliniki laiki mousiki*. Athens: Ianos [PhD thesis translation in Greek], 2014.

Ordoulidis, Nikos. 'Tekmiriosi ton istorikon ichografiseon stin Ellada: I periptosi tou rebetikou'. *1st Annual Conference of Music Libraries and Archives (21–22/4)* – The Greek Branch of the International Association of Music Libraries, Archives and Documentation Centres. [pending publication], 2017.

Ordoulidis, Nikos. 'Cosmopolitan Music by Cosmopolitan Musicians: The Case of Spyros Peristeris, Leading Figure of the Rebetiko'. Paper presented at Creating Music Across Cultures in the 21st Century, The Centre for Advanced Studies in Music (25–27/5). Istanbul Technical University, 2017.

Ordoulidis, Nikos. 'Deconstructing Dipoles: The Term "Minor" in Smyrna'. Paper presented at the Fifth International Conference on Analytical Approaches to World Music (AAWM 2018) & Eighth Folk Music Analysis Workshop (FMA 2018). Thessaloniki, Greece (June 26–29), 2018.

Ordoulidis, Nikos. 'Apodoches kai aporipseis stis diaskeues ton rebetikon pou synkrotoun tis "exi laikes zografies"'. In *Effects and Interactions (Annually Conference of the Hellenic Musicological Society, 25–27 November 2016)*, edited by Kostas Chardas, Kostas Vouvaris, Kostas Kardamis, Giorgos Sakallieros, and Ioannis Foulias, 668–78. Hellenic Musicological Society, 2019.

Orlandi, Ugo. 'Circolo Mandolinistico Italiano'. *CD album*. CMI, 2010.

Pachtikos, Georgios. *260 dimodi ellinika asmata apo tou stomatos tou ellinikou laou*. Vol. 1. Athens: Typografeio Sakellariou, 1905.

Pachtikos, Georgios. *Apollon o mousigetis*. Constantinople: Typografeio Adelfon Gerardon, 1910.

Panagiotopoulos, Dimitrios. *Theoria kai praxis tis ekklisiastikis vyzantinis mousikis*. Vol. 4. Athens: Adelfotis Theologon 'O Sotir', 1986.

Papadimitriou, Konstantinos. *O Ioannis Th. Sakellaridis kai to par' imin mousikon zitima*. Athens: n.p., 1939.

Papadimitriou, Konstantinos. *O Ioannis Th. Sakellaridis os logios mousikos: symvouli eis tin istorian tis en Elladi ekklisiastikis kai scholikis mousikis*. Athens: n.p., 1940.

Papadopoulos, Gerasimos Sofoklis. 'Mia "glossologikou typou" prosengisi tis synchronis psaltikis technis'. In *'Apo chorou kai omothymadon,' exelixeis kai prooptikes tis diepistimonikis ereunas gia tin psaltiki (2o Diethnes Mousikologiko kai Diepistimoniko Synedrio, 9-11 June 2016)*, edited by Konstantinos Karagounis, and Kostis Drygianakis, 294–306. Ekdotiki Dimitriados, 2017.

Papaioannou, Giannis G. *Nikos Skalkotas*. 2 vols. Athens: Papagrigoriou – Nakas, 1997.

Papanikolaou, Dimitris. *Singing Poets – Literature and Popular Music in France and Greece*. Oxford: Legenda, 2007.

Papanikolaou, Dimitris. 'Omileite tin kaliarntin?" *The Books' Journal* 7 (2011): 58–64.

Papantoniou, Zacharias. 'O amanes en diogmo (Eleutheron Vima, 3/7)'. In *Spania keimena gia to rebetiko (1929-1959) (2006)*, edited by Kostas Vlisidis, 77–9. Athens: Ekdoseis tou Eikostou Protou, 1938.

Papazoglou, Giorgis. *Angela Papazoglou – Ta chairia mas edo*. Athens: Tameion Thrakis, 1994.

Patriarch Anthimos, and Holy Synod. 'Engyklios Patriarchi kai synodiki epistoli – Katargousa kai apagoreuousa tin kainotomon eisaxin kai chrisin tis kainofanous tetrafonou mousikis en tais ierais akolouthiais ton apantachou orthodoxon ekklision'. Constantinople: Patriarchiko Typografeio, 1846.

Pennanen, Pekka Risto. 'Review Essay: A Recent Reissue of Rebétika Recordings'. *Asian Music, Musical Narrative Traditions of Asia* 26, no. 2 (1995): 137–42.

Pennanen, Risto Pekka. 'The Development of Chordal Harmony in Greek Rebetika and Laika Music, 1930s to 1960s'. *British Journal of Ethnomusicology* 6 (1997): 65–116.

Pennanen, Risto Pekka. 'Westernisation and Modernisation in Greek Popular Music'. PhD thesis. University of Tampere, 1999.

Pennanen, Risto Pekka. 'The Nationalization of Ottoman Popular Music in Greece'. *Ethnomusicology* 48, no. 1 (2004): 1–25.

Pennanen, Risto Pekka. 'Commercial Recordings and Source Criticism in Music Research: Some Methodological Views'. *Svensk tidskrift för musikforskning*, no. 87 (2005): 81–98.

Petropoulos, Ilias. *Rebetika tragoudia*. 8th pr. (1968). Athens: Kedros, 1996.

Plemmenos, Giannis. 'Ekklisiastiki mousiki kai laografiki ereuna: Pros tin anathermansi mias palias schesis'. In *I psaltiki techni os autonomi epistimi (Praktika 1ou diethnous diepistimonikou mousikologikou synedriou, 29 June–3 July 2014)*, edited by Konstantinos Karagounis, and Georgios Kouroupetroglou, 425–38. Volos: Academy of Theology Studies, Section of Psaltic Art and Musicology, 2015.

Plemmenos, Ioannis. 'Proforikotita kai psaltiki techni: I genesi kai diamorfosi tis "koinis ekdochis"'. In *'Apo chorou kai omothymadon,' exelixeis kai prooptikes tis diepistimonikis ereunas gia tin psaltiki (2o Diethnes Mousikologiko kai Diepistimoniko*

Synedrio, 9–11 June 2016), edited by Konstantinos Karagounis, and Kostis Drygianakis, 307–39. Ekdotiki Dimitriados, 2017.

Polymerou-Kamilaki, Aikaterini. 'Stoicheia gia tis katagrafes dimotikon tragoudion apo ton Konstantino Psacho sto archeio tou Kentrou Ereunis tis Ellinikis Laografias'. In *Konstantinos Psachos: O mousikos, o logios (Conference proceedings, 30 November 2007)*, edited by Euangelos Karamanes, 11–26. Athens: Kentro Ereunis tis Ellinikis Laografias, 2013.

Prestige, Leonard. 'Περιχωρέω and περιχώρησις in the Fathers'. *The Journal of Theological Studies* 29, no. 115 (1928): 242–52.

Prograkis, Georgios. *Mousiki syllogi*. Vol. A. Constantinople: Patriarchiko Typografeio, 1909.

Psachos, Konstantinos. 'Peri yphous'. *Formiga [Period B΄, Year Γ΄ (E΄), 19–20, January]*, 1908.

Psachos, Konstantinos. *I leitourgia*. Athens: Typografeio Kousoulinou, 1909.

Psachos, Konstantinos. *I parasimantiki tis vyzantinis mousikis*. 2nd ed. (1917). Edited by Georgios Hatzitheodorou. Athens: Dionysos, 1978.

Remantas, Adamantios, and Zacharias Prokopios. *Arion – I mousiki ton Ellinon os diesothi apo ton archaiotaton chronon mechri tis simeron*. Athens: Koultoura, 1917.

Romanou, Kaiti. 'I metarrythmisi tou 1814'. *Mousikologia* 1 (1985): 7–22.

Romanou, Kaiti. *Ethnikis mousikis periigisis, 1901–1912 – Ellinika mousika periodika os pigi ereunas tis istorias tis neoellinikis mousikis*. Vol. 1. Athens: Koultoura, 1996.

Sakellaridis, Ioannis. *Agia kai megali evdomas*. Athens: Mousikos Ekdotikos Oikos Gaitanos, n.d.

Sakellaridis, Ioannis. *Christomatheia ekklisiastikis mousikis*. Athens: Typografeio Filadelfeos, 1880.

Sakellaridis, Ioannis. *Asmata ekklisiastika tonisthenta kata to archaion melos*. Athens: Typografeio Kousoulinou, 1893.

Sakellaridis, Ioannis. *Christomatheia ekklisiastikis mousikis*. Athens: Typografeio Kousoulinou, 1895.

Sakellaridis, Ioannis. *Ymnoi kai odai en armoniki, trifono, symfonia*. n.p., 1909.

Sakellaridis, Ioannis. *Ymnoi kai odai: en armoniki trifono symfonia*. Athens: Mousikos Ekdotikos Oikos Gaitanou, 1930.

Samson, Jim. *Music in the Balkans*. Leiden: Brill, 2013.

Schorelis, Tasos. *Rebetiki anthologia*. 4 vols. Athens: Plethron, 1977–81.

Scott, Derek. 'Cosmopolitan Musicology'. Paper presented at the 17th Nordic Musicological Congress, 2015.

Scott, Derek. '"I Changed My Olga for the Britney": Occidentalism, Auto-Orientalism and Global Fusion in Music'. In *Critical Music Historiography: Probing Canons, Ideologies and Institutions*, edited by Vesa Kurkela, and Markus Mantere, 141–58. Routledge, 2015.

Scott, Derek, ed. *The Ashgate Research Companion to Popular Musicology*. Ashgate, 2009.

Seiragakis, Manolis. 'Mia pio proimi chronologisi ton epidraseon tou rebetikou sto ergo tou Manou Hadjidaki'. *Nea Estia* 1845 (2011): 1-10.
Sentevska, Irena. 'Turbo-Folk as the Agent of Empire: On Discourses of Identity and Difference in Popular Culture'. *Journal of Narrative Theory* 44, no. 3 (2014): 413-41.
Shusterman, Richard. *Pragmatist Aesthetics. Living Beauty, Rethinking Art*. Rowman & Littlefield Publishers, Inc., 2000.
Sigalas, Antonios. *Syllogi ethnikon asmaton*. Athens: Typografeio Filadelfeos, 1880.
Sinopoulos, Sokratis. 'I chrisi tou makam stin katagrafi, ermineia kai didaskalia tis ellinikis paradosiakis mousikis'. In *Mousiki (kai) theoria – Tetradia 5*, 107-13. Department of Popular and Traditional Music – KEMO, TEI of Epirus, 2010.
Smith, Anthony. *National Identity*. London: Penguin Books, 1991.
Smith, Ole. 'Research on Rebétika: Some Methodological Problems and Issues'. *Journal of Modern Hellenism*, no. 6 (1989): 177-90.
Smith, Ole. 'The Chronology of Rebétiko – A Reconsideration of the Evidence'. *Byzantine and Modern Greek Studies*, no. 15 (1991): 318-24.
Solomonidis, Christos. *Tis Smyrnis*. Athens: Typografeio Mauridi, 1957.
Spanoudi, Sophia. 'Mousiki tou ellinikou laou (Eleutheron Vima, 7/10)'. In *Spania keimena gia to rebetiko (1929-1959) (2006)*, edited by Kostas Vlisidis, 80-3. Athens: Ekdoseis tou Eikostou Protou, 1938.
Spanoudi, Sophia. 'Katigoria stin yperaspisi (Ta Nea, 31/12)'. In *Spania keimena gia to rebetiko (1929-1959) (2006)*, edited by Kostas Vlisidis, 124-5. Athens: Ekdoseis tou Eikostou Protou, 1946.
Spanoudi, Sophia. 'Oi kosmoi tis laikis technis: o Tsitsanis'. *Ta Nea (1/2)* (1951): 205.
Sparks, Paul. *The Classical Mandolin*. USA: Oxford University Press, 2005.
Spinei, Marcel-Ionel. 'I vyzantini psaltiki paradosi sti Roumania: cheirografa kai roumanoi melopoioi'. PhD thesis. Department of Music Studies, National and Kapodistrian University of Athens, 2011.
Stathis, Grigorios. *I exigisis tis palaias vyzantinis simeiografias*. 4th pr. (1978). Athens: Koultoura, 1998.
Stokes, Martin. *The Arabesk Debate – Music and Musicians in Modern Turkey*. New York: Clarendon Press – Oxford, 1992.
Stone, Kurt. *Music Notation in the Twentieth Century. A Practical Guidebook*. New York, London: W. W. Norton & Company, 1980.
Synadinos, Theodoros. *I istoria tis neoellinikis mousikis –1824-1919*. Athens: Typografeio Typos, 1919.
Synadinos, Theodoros. *To elliniko tragoudi – Pente dialexeis-synaulies*. Athens: Akropoleos, 1922.
Tagg, Phillip. 'Why Are Popular Music Studies Excluded from Italian Universities?' *Electronic Article*, 2014: https://tagg.org/xpdfs/ItSystemBkgdV2.pdf
Tambakaki, Polina. 'Exetazontas ton mytho kai ti mythologia tis genias tou '30: i anakalypsi tou rebetikou apo ton Mano Hadjidaki kai o Giorgos Seferis'. In

Continuities, Discontinuities, Ruptures in the Greek World (1204–2014): Economy, Society, History, Literature (5th European Congress of Modern Greek Studies of the European Society of Modern Greek Studies, 2–5 October 2014), edited by Konstantinos Dimadis, 533–51. European Society of Modern Greek Studies, 2015.

Tasoulas, Manouil, and Eleni Ambatzi. *Indoprepon apokalypsi. Apo tin India tou exotismou sti laiki mousa ton Ellinon*. Athens: Perivolaki kai Atrapos, 1998.

Tentes, Agamemnon. 'Protaseis gia mia diepistimoniki prosengisi tis par' imin mousikologias vasei prosfaton taseon stin diethni ereuna ton epistimon peri ton anthropo'. In *I psaltiki techni os autonomi epistimi (Praktika 1ou diethnous diepistimonikou mousikologikou synedriou, 29 June – 3 July 2014)*, edited by Konstantinos Karagounis, and Georgios Kouroupetroglou, 525–41. Volos: Academy of Theology Studies, Section of Psaltic Art and Musicology, 2015.

Theodorakis, Mikis. 'To synchrono laiko tragoudi (Simerini Epochi, 23/10)'. In *Gia tin elliniki mousiki (1986); 2nd pr. (1961)*, edited by Mikis Theodorakis, 157–69. Athens: Kastanioti, 1949.

Theodorakis, Mikis. *Gia tin elliniki mousiki*. 2nd pr. (1961). Athens: Kastanioti, 1986.

Theodorakis, Mikis. *Mousiki gia tis mazes*. Athens: Olkos, 1972.

Theodorakis, Mikis. *To chreos – I dimiourgia 1967-1974*. 3 vols. Athens: Crete University Press, 2011.

Tombra-Lagopati, Hara. 'O rolos tou Konstantinou Psachou sto politistiko provlima tis Ellados ton archon tou 20ou aiona metaxy paradoseos kai exeuropaismou'. In *Konstantinos Psachos: O mousikos, o logios – Praktika Imeridas (30 November 2007)*, edited by Euangelos Karamanes, 177–84. Athens: Kentro Ereunis tis Ellinikis Laografias, 2013.

Tragaki, Dafni. *Rebetiko Worlds*. Newcastle: Cambridge Scholars Publishing, 2007.

Tsetsos, Markos. *Ethnikismos kai laikismos stin neoelliniki mousiki – Politikes opseis mias politismikis apoklisis*. Athens: Idryma Saki Karagiorga, 2011.

Tsitsanis, Vasilis. 'Vas. Tsitsanis – O magos tou bouzoukiou (Kyriakatikos Tachydromos, 15/4)'. In *Spania keimena gia to rebetiko (1929-1959) (2006)*, edited by Kostas Vlisidis, 168–72. Athens: Ekdoseis tou Eikostou Protou, 1951.

Tsitsanis, Vasilis. 'Ena provlima tis epochis mas. To laiko tragoudi – Ai apopseis enos ekprosopou tou (Interview with Nestoras P. Matsas)'. *Ethnikos Kiryx (11/5)* (1952): 2.

Tsitsanis, Vasilis. 'O vasilias tou rebetikou – Mia ora me ton Vasili Tsitsani (Interview with Dinos Christianopoulos)'. *Drasis (13/2)* (1961).

Tsitsanis, Vasilis. 'Vrisketai sti Thessaloniki – To megalo tou parapono (Interview with G. A. Dimopoulos)'. *Drasis (1/3)* (1965).

Tsitsanis, Vasilis. 'Saranta chronia adiafthoros (Interview with G. Lianis)'. *Epikaira*, (1972):10–13.

Tsitsanis, Vasilis. 'O Vasilis Tsitsanis giortazei ta mousika tou sarantachrona (Interview with N. Manolakis)'. *Eleutherotypia (23/11)* (1977): 5.

Tsitsanis, Vasilis. 'Stin pio synnefiasmeni Kyriaki tis zois tou o megalos laikos vardos anoigei diaplata tin kardia tou stin 'A' (Interview with Panos Geramanis)'. *Akropolis (30/11)* (1980): 6.

Tsitsanis, Vasilis. 'Tragoudia me to aima tis kardias mas (Interview with Ch. Ts.)'. *Rizospastis (10/4)* (1983): 14–15.

Tsitsanis, Vasilis. 'O Leuteris Papadopoulos synomilei me ton Vasili Tsitsani (Interview with Leuteris Papadopoulos)'. *Difono (28/1)* (1998):124–8.

Tziovas, Dimitris, ed. *Greek Diaspora and Migration Since 1700 – Society, Politics and Culture*. Farnham: Ashgate, 2009.

Ünlü, Cemal. *Git Zaman Gel Zaman, Fonograf-Gramofon-Taş Plak*. İstanbul: Pan Yayıncılık, 2016.

Velimirović, Miloš. *Study of Byzantine Music in the West*. Vol. 5, in *A biannual publication of the Institute for Balkan Studies*, 63–76. Thessaloniki: Balkan Studies, 1964.

Velimirović, Miloš. 'H. J. W. Tillyard, Patriarch of Byzantine Studies'. *The Musical Quarterly* 54, no. 3 (1968): 341–51.

Vellou-Kail, Angeliki. *Markos Vamvakaris – Autoviografia*. Athens: Papazisi, 1978.

Vlisidis, Kostas. *Opseis tou rebetikou*. Athens: Ekdoseis tou Eikostou Protou, 2004.

Vlisidis, Kostas, ed. *Spania keimena gia to rebetiko (1929–1959)*. Athens: Ekdoseis tou Eikostou Protou, 2006.

Voudouris, Angelos. *Triodion*. Athens: Europaiko Kentro Technis, 1997.

Wellesz, Egon. *A History of Byzantine Music and Hymnography*. Oxford: Clarendon Press, 1961.

Xanthoudakis, Haris. 'To mega theoritikon tou Chrysanthou kai oi gallikes piges tou'. *O eranistis* 26 (2007): 141–74.

Xanthoudakis, Haris. 'Composers, Trends and the Question of Nationality in Nineteenth-Century Musical Greece'. *Nineteenth-Century Music Review*, no. 8 (2011): 41–55.

Xanthoulis, Nikos. 'I antilipsi tis synecheias tis ellinikis mousikis sto ergo tou Konstantinou Psachou'. In *Konstantinos Psachos: O mousikos, o logios – Praktika Imeridas (30 November 2007)*, edited by Euaggelos Karamanes, 251–60. Athens: Kentro Ereunis tis Ellinikis Laografias, 2013.

Yano, Christine R. 'Covering Disclosures: Practices of Intimacy, Hierarchy, and Authenticity in a Japanese Popular Music Genre'. *Popular Music and Society* 28, no. 2 (2005): 193–205.

Zervas, Athanasios. 'Polyfonikes ekdoches monofonikou ymnologiou: Syngritiki analysi sti morfi kai anasynthesi'. Paper presented in I vyzantini mousiki ston 21o aiona: Provlimatismoi kai prooptikes. Thessaloniki: University of Macedonia, 2007.

Zoubouli, Maria, and Georges Kokkonis. 'I scholiki mousiki ekpaideusi, mia istoria diachronikis logokrisias'. In *I logokrisia stin Ellada*, edited by Pinelopi Petsini, and Dimitris Christopoulos, 185–93. Athens: Rosa Luxemborg Stiftung Office in Greece, 2016.

Zoubouli, Maria, and Nikos Ordoulidis. "Gia ton techniti kai to daneisma ein' en' apo ta organa tis prototypias tou' (K. Palamas)". In *I diki ton rebeton*, edited by Maria Zoubouli, and Pierrina Koriatopoulou-Angeli, 45–51. Department of Popular and Traditional Music and Law School of Athens, 2018.

Index

Byzantine music, generally
  ancient melody   74, 128
  Arab   67, 76, 79, 84, 96, 126
  Byzantine musicology   71, 84
  circular   12 n.11, 67, 75, 77, 111, 124
  eastern   36, 40, 66, 67, 76, 87, 102
    easternized   71
    eastern theory   134
  Formiga, newspaper   67, 72, 75,
    76 n.4, 78
    New Formiga   153, 160
  patriarchal music committee   11, 65,
    70, 85, 112–13, 160
  patriarchal yphos   32, 55,
    85, 122
  Persian   76, 79, 84
Byzantine music, persons
  Asteris, Leonidas   119
  Chrysanthos of Madytos   11, 65, 85,
    109, 113, 136
    ecumenical approach   80–1
    Karas reference   83
  Euthymiadis, Avraam   11
  Karas, Simon   74, 82–6, 122–4, 160
  Mantzouranis, Theodoros   75, 76
  Naupliotis, Iakovos   15, 32, 109, 139,
    148–53, 160-4
  Papadopoulos, Eustratios   75, 112
  Peristeris, Spyros   15, 75, 82 n.2,
    115–16, 122, 129–30
  Petros Peloponnese   111
    or Lambadarios   33
  Pringos, Konstantinos   123, 148
  Psachos, Konstantinos   71, 74–80, 85,
    115, 174
    akathist hymn   153–9
    conservatory of national
      music   76, 153
  Sakellaridis, Ioannis   66, 67, 76–80,
    123, 124, 174
    'The Akathist Hymn'   19, 160, 164
    'O Gladsome Light'   127–8

Stanitsas, Thrasyvoulos   20, 86, 123
Wellesz, Egon   71

co-existence   59, 89, 124 n.4, 175, 177
  and co-inherence   98
  and perichoresis   81, 96
  retrenchment (antonym)   175

folklore studies   26, 65, 76
  folkloristic, concept and
    methodology   14, 41, 82, 85, 94
  folk music   56, 78, 85, 87, 93
  Merlier, Melpo   5–8
  revival   37, 41 n.12, 87 n.11, 100

mass media
  radio   34, 47, 82, 95, 115, 129
  sound industry   99, 104
    Columbia   105
    discography   13, 35, 40, 54, 90
  television   13, 34, 36, 56, 115,
    119, 129

musical analysis
  alla turca   45, 48–50, 102
  appoggiatura   4, 33
  backbone   134, 144
  bassline   5
  consonance line   153
  dominant note   19, 32, 134, 137, 139
  embellishment   6, 13, 33, 87, 126,
    143, 144
  glissando   139, 144
  gravitation   16, 28, 134, 139, 143,
    144, 153
  idiomatic   28, 113, 123, 139–46
  klitón   52, 53, 139
  melismas   148 n.2
  melodic line   19, 28, 40, 50, 58,
    115, 145
    and musical line   53
    and vocal line   4
  modeness   53, 88, 96, 133, 137

196 Index

  modality 49, 50
    pentachord 175
    tetrachord 137, 139
  phrasing 5
    and phrase 5, 6, 33, 134, 137, 160
    and phraseology 137
  singing style 5, 20, 91
  slow-brief, melodic construction
      style 11, 33, 148,
    hirmologic 10, 11, 13, 33
  spectrometer 116
  vocalese 33
musical ecumene 96, 97, 129, 175
  borrowing 32, 36, 98, 99, 129, 170
  converse 58, 125
  cosmopolitan culture 38, 94, 97,
      112, 174
    people 96, 105, 176
    region 89
  cosmopolitism 24
    and cosmopolitanism 93, 94
  loan 67, 84, 89, 97, 98
  network, geographical and
      cultural 94, 95, 97, 101,
      105, 129
    apprenticeship 120
    music production 104
    performance 35
  reference 70, 98, 99, 126, 175
  syncretism, repertoire and
      culture 23, 88, 98, 123,
      126, 135
    hybrid (antonym) 70, 88
    and syncretic 59, 123, 125,
      129, 175
  translocal 176
music theory and act
  apprenticeship 68, 77, 114, 119,
      120, 124
  correctness 85, 176
  fluidity 5, 113, 114, 130, 149,
      172, 174
    and fluid 11, 98
  guide 76, 84, 117, 139, 140, 144, 150
  by heart 85, 114
  improvisation 35, 118, 119, 121
  innovation 4, 11, 21, 63, 126
  laiki aesthetic 4, 9, 20, 33, 40

  literacy 12, 85, 118, 129
  living art 58
    and animate art 130, 170,
      174, 176
  living tradition 117
    and living body 71
  mimicry 17, 31, 50, 58, 94
  modernism 78, 113, 126, 129,
      153, 176
  multifarious 63, 129, 130
  orality, chanting 74, 112, 114, 118,
      129, 148, 172,
    oral tradition 12, 74, 84, 85,
      117, 123
    popular 5, 95
  polymorphic 23
  polyphony, chanting 19, 24, 67, 78,
      79, 122–5
    popular 25, 91
  polystylism 88, 94
  preparatory drawings 119
  recomposition 103, 119
  redefinition 103, 129, 176
  thesi 117, 119, 123, 126, 144,
      160, 163
  transposition 176
  update 129

national music school 26, 31, 45, 65
  Athens conservatory 66, 72–6,
      115, 153
  Kalomoiris, Manolis 42, 65–6,
      76–7, 171
    amanés reference 45
    national conservatory 77
    Sakellaridis reference 80
    symphony of valour 31
  Lambelet, Georgios 66
  Nazos, Georgios 72–4, 76, 153

persons, general
  Christianopoulos, Ntinos 35
  Dertilis, Giorgos 64
  Ennig, Ioulios 77
  Fallmerayer, Jakob Philipp 64, 71
  Gauntlett, Stathis 36, 47
  Khalil, Alexander Konrad 71,
      115 n.8, 118 n.4

Index

Loudovikos, Nikolaos   58
Maximus the Confessor   59
Metaxas, Ioannis   42, 43
Moore, Allan   88
Mozart, Wolgang Amadeus   70
Otto, king   70
Pachtikos, Georgios   160, 165
Papadopoulos, Kostas   33
Scott, Derek   88, 93
Skalkottas, Nikos   23
Spanoudi, Sophia   34, 36, 42–6, 102
politics   63–5, 98
   adulterated   71
   aphoristic   22, 67
   authentic, chanting   24, 71–2, 76, 78, 111, 127, 174
      Greek music   26, 65, 68, 110
      laiko   34, 36, 99
      traditional   58
   authenticity   22, 23, 41, 84, 100, 114, 124
   descent, music   21, 35 n.3, 37–9, 53, 54, 173
      and origin   19, 24, 48, 59, 65, 170, 175
   dipole   100, 102, 110, 170
   erudition   80, 93, 153, 170
   Europeanization   30, 74, 124, 129, 153, 174
   exoneration   104, 176
   exoticism   22, 94
   genuine   35, 43, 67, 68
   hegemony   58, 100, 116
   orientalism   45
   paternalism   58
   political   25, 41, 56, 71, 102, 103
   westernization   21, 66, 71, 102
popular-like, music   41
   Hadjidakis, Manos   39–41, 55
      lecture   24, 43, 45, 102
      six popular pictures   41

Smyrna
   Asia Minor   21, 55, 63, 89, 97
   Peristeris, Spyros   4, 25, 90, 94, 96, 101, 105
   politakia   90–4
   Smyrna-style   48

sounding and aural
   atmosphere (chanting)   11, 13, 71, 118
   aural   171
   common   19, 20
   harmonious   21
   minor   58, 137
   musical   50
   sombre   44
   aural logic   19, 20, 136
   memory   55
   reality   48 n.8
   chordal harmony   21
   chordal sequence   9, 17, 105
   context   133, 134, 145, 171
   environment   48 n.8, 50, 90 n.11, 137, 138, 170
   and environ   105, 139
   harmonization   29, 31, 78, 85, 124, 125
      four-part   67, 81, 124, 160
   landscape   134, 136, 137
   musical reality   91, 93
   soundscape   102
state, Greek
   academy of Athens   76
   ancient Greek music   66, 67, 76, 81, 84
   citizenship   63, 91, 98
   civil war   27, 44
   education, European   45, 68, 74
      chanting   68, 71–5, 83, 115, 118
      music general   55–7, 70, 80, 87, 94
      public general   55, 64, 70
   Greekness   23–7, 36–43, 54, 64, 174
   Greek state conservatory of Thessaloniki   56, 57
   historical continuation, general   54, 65, 66, 174
      alla byzantina   45
   Karas   83
   Paparrigopoulos   64, 65
   Petropoulos   21
   Psachos   76, 78, 79
   Theodorakis   24, 27
   laikoness   25, 127

national music   35, 40, 55, 70, 74, 78, 83
  society for the propagation of national music   82
  protocol of independence of the Greek state   63
  romiosyni   26, 27
  systemization   23, 70, 73, 74, 87, 112

urban popular music
  amanés   45, 48, 50, 82, 88
  café aman   67, 97, 101
  café chantants   66, 101
  censorship   3, 42, 43, 47
  guitar   4, 57, 89–94, 105, 175
  hashish, songs subject   45
  and drugs   39, 47
  kantada   23, 90, 134
  and serenade   70, 90, 96, 134
  kanto   89, 98
  mandolinata   25, 91, 96, 102
  post-war   40, 98, 99, 148 n.2
urban popular music, persons
  Bellou, Sotiria   3–5, 15, 33
  Kazantzidis, Stelios   5, 15, 17, 20, 33
  Keromytis, Stelios   20, 47, 50–3
  Mitsakis, Giorgos   25, 98
  Perpiniadis, Stellakis   47–52
  Tsaousakis, Prodromos   3–5, 15, 21, 32, 33, 137
  Vamvakaris, Markos   25, 39, 47, 101

www.ingramcontent.com/pod-product-compliance
Lightning Source LLC
Chambersburg PA
CBHW072234290426
44111CB00012B/2090